Mind Gardening in the Creative Garden of Will (Your Mind) to Grow a Living Water Mentality!

CHILDREN OF THE MOST HIGH:
PRISTINE YOUTH AND FAMILY SOLUTIONS, LLC.
SONS AND DAUGHTERS OF THE MOST HIGH PUBLISHERS ®

*Oh, Gracious Most High Heavenly father, Holy is your name,
Your Will Be Done Now and Forever!*

By

**Woodie Hughes Jr.
CEO & Founder of the Children of the Most High:
Pristine Youth and Family Solutions LLC.
Sons and Daughters of the Most High Publishers®
Mr. Hughes is a Servant of the Most High, and a Teacher
of the Most High's Doctrine.**

I0154774

I

*Yashu'a (Jesus) said: "Thou shalt love the Most High
Heavenly Father, thy Sustainer with all thy heart, and
with all thy soul, and with all thy mind.
Thou shalt love thy neighbour as thyself."*

Mind Gardening in the Creative Garden of Will (Your Mind) to Grow a Living Water Mentality!

Editor: Sons and Daughters of the Most High Editors

ISBN: 978-1-948355-03-2
Library of Congress Control Number: 2020914406

FOR MORE INFORMATION CONTACT:

Woodie Hughes Jr., CEO & Founder of the Children of the Most High: Pristine Youth and Family Solutions, LLC.
Sons and Daughters of the Most High Publishers ®

Online ordering is available for all products at our Amazon Store Front on our website at: childrenofthemosthigh.com
Or, write to us at: Children of the Most High: Pristine Youth and Family Solutions, LLC. P.O. Box 6365, Warner Robins, Georgia 31095.

Yashu'a (Jesus) said: "Thou shalt love the Most High Heavenly Father, thy Sustainer with all thy heart, and with all thy soul, and with all thy mind. Thou shalt love thy neighbour as thyself."

Table of Contents

Yashu'a (Jesus) said: "*Thou shalt love the Most High Heavenly Father, thy Sustainer with all thy heart, and with all thy soul, and with all thy mind. Thou shalt love thy neighbour as thyself.*"

Table of Contents

Yashu'a (Jesus) said: "Thou shalt love the Most High Heavenly Father, thy Sustainer with all thy heart, and with all thy soul, and with all thy mind. Thou shalt love thy neighbour as thyself."

Table of Contents

V

Yashu'a (Jesus) said: "Thou shalt love the Most High Heavenly Father, thy Sustainer with all thy heart, and with all thy soul, and with all thy mind. Thou shalt love thy neighbour as thyself."

Table of Contents

*Yashu'a (Jesus) said: "Thou shalt love the Most High
Heavenly Father, thy Sustainer with all thy heart, and
with all thy soul, and with all thy mind.
Thou shalt love thy neighbour as thyself."*

Mind Gardening in the Creative Garden of Will (Your Mind) to Grow a Living Water Mentality!

CHILDREN OF THE MOST HIGH:
PRISTINE YOUTH AND FAMILY SOLUTIONS, LLC.
SONS AND DAUGHTERS OF THE MOST HIGH PUBLISHERS ®

Oh, Gracious Most High Heavenly father, Holy is your name,
Your Will Be Done Now and Forever!

Greetings:

We greet all members of humanity in peace! Nothing would exist if you Oh Gracious Most High Heavenly Father, The Creator didn't create it. You are alone in Your Greatness; you have no partners that share in your grace. To you all sovereignty is due and you are all powerful over everything. We seek refuge in you, the ever watchful Most High who hears and knows all things! Glory be to you as many times as the number of things you have created! All gratitude is due to you oh gracious Most High Heavenly Father, you are the Creator and Sustainer of all the boundless universes. You are the Yielder, and the most Merciful. The Ruler of the Day of Judgement. It's you whom we worship and it is you alone whom we beseech for help. Oh Guide, guide us to the narrow path **which reflects moral integrity and positive character traits in action** of the ones who stand straight, the narrow path of those who earned your grace not inclusive of those who brought an everlasting curse on themselves, those who conceal the facts of that which they know to be true in order to lead the **sincere-hearted seekers** of your truth astray. Amen

1

Yashu'a (Jesus) said: "Thou shalt love the Most High Heavenly Father, thy Sustainer with all thy heart, and with all thy soul, and with all thy mind. Thou shalt love thy neighbour as thyself."

Mind Gardening in the Creative Garden of Will (Your Mind) to Grow a Living Water Mentality!

CHILDREN OF THE MOST HIGH:
PRISTINE YOUTH AND FAMILY SOLUTIONS, LLC.
SONS AND DAUGHTERS OF THE MOST HIGH PUBLISHERS ®

Oh, Gracious Most High Heavenly father, Holy is your name,
Your Will Be Done Now and Forever!

What does the phrase: "those who earned your grace" mean as oppose to saying "those who receive your grace?" The word: "**grace**" in the King James Version (KJV) bible book of Genesis chapter 6 verse 8 is: חֵן **Khane** or **chen** pronounced as **khān (KJV bible Hebrew Strong's Concordance#2580)**. The word: "חֵן **Khane** or **chen**" means "**favor, kindness.**" The word: "**grace**" in the KJV bible book of John chapter 1 verse 17 is: χάρις **Kharece** or **charis** pronounced as **khä'-rēs (KJV bible Greek Strong's Concordance#5485)**. The word: "χάρις **Kharece** or **charis**" means "**joy, delight.**" So, the phrase: "those who earned your grace" is in reference **to those people who are no longer physically alive that have transitioned to a higher life** such as: **Yashu'a (Jesus)**, **John the Baptist**, **Yowkhanan Bar Zebedee (John Son of Zebedee who was Yashu'a (Jesus) beloved disciple)**, or **Ab-Ra-Kham (Abraham)**. The phrase: "**those who receive your grace**" is in reference **to any person or people** who the Most High Heavenly Father bestows **favor** on by allowing them to still be physically alive, and to have an opportunity to experience **joy** while still be physically alive.

Yashu'a (Jesus) said: "Thou shalt love the Most High Heavenly Father, thy Sustainer with all thy heart, and with all thy soul, and with all thy mind. Thou shalt love thy neighbour as thyself."

Mind Gardening in the Creative Garden of Will (Your Mind) to Grow a Living Water Mentality!

CHILDREN OF THE MOST HIGH:
PRISTINE YOUTH AND FAMILY SOLUTIONS, LLC.
SONS AND DAUGHTERS OF THE MOST HIGH PUBLISHERS ✣

*Oh, Gracious Most High Heavenly father, Holy is your name,
Your Will Be Done Now and Forever!*

Dedication

The "**Mind Gardening in the Creative Garden of Will (Your Mind) to Grow a Living Water Mentality**" book is dedicated to all youth and all adults who are children of the Most High that want to learn the doctrine of the **Most High (ELYOWN עֶלְיוֹן) God (EL אֵל)** in a way that reflects the original languages of the bible before being translated into the English language, and that reflects the original Most High Heavenly Father's doctrine that Yashu'a Ha Mashiakh (Jesus the Messiah) taught.

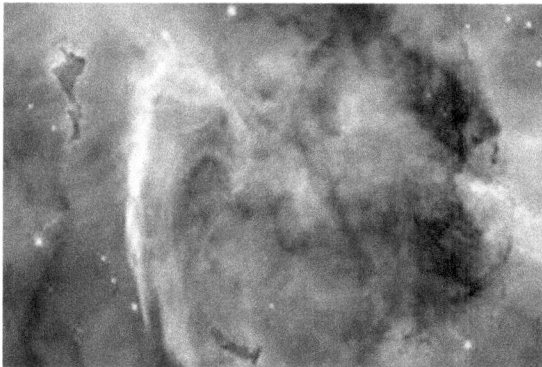

3

Yashu'a (Jesus) said: "Thou shalt love the Most High Heavenly Father, thy Sustainer with all thy heart, and with all thy soul, and with all thy mind. Thou shalt love thy neighbour as thyself."

Mind Gardening in the Creative Garden of Will (Your Mind) to Grow a Living Water Mentality!

CHILDREN OF THE MOST HIGH:
PRISTINE YOUTH AND FAMILY SOLUTIONS, LLC.
SONS AND DAUGHTERS OF THE MOST HIGH PUBLISHERS ®

Oh, Gracious Most High Heavenly father, Holy is your name,
Your Will Be Done Now and Forever!

In the KJV bible book of Genesis chapter 14 verse 18 states: "And Melchizedek king of Salem brought forth bread and wine: and he *was* the priest of the **Most High** God." The title: "**Most High**" is: the KJV bible Hebrew Strong's Concordance#5945 for the title: "**Most High**" (**ELYOWN עֶלְיוֹן EL אֵל**), **which means: "Highest, Most High, Name of God, as title, The Supreme: — (Most, on) high (-er, -est), upper(-most)."** The title: "**God**' **in this verse** is the KJV bible Hebrew Strong's Concordance#5945 for the title: "**God**" (**EL אֵל**), **which means: "God, god, power, mighty, goodly, great, idols, might, strong, god, god-like one, mighty one, mighty men, men of rank, mighty heroes, angels, god, false god, (demons, imaginations), and mighty things in nature."**

4

Yashu'a (Jesus) said: "Thou shalt love the Most High Heavenly Father, thy Sustainer with all thy heart, and with all thy soul, and with all thy mind. Thou shalt love thy neighbour as thyself."

Mind Gardening in the Creative Garden of Will (Your Mind) to Grow a Living Water Mentality!

CHILDREN OF THE MOST HIGH:
PRISTINE YOUTH AND FAMILY SOLUTIONS, LLC.
SONS AND DAUGHTERS OF THE MOST HIGH PUBLISHERS ®

Oh, Gracious Most High Heavenly father, Holy is your name,
Your Will Be Done Now and Forever!

Acknowledgements

We thank the Most High Heavenly Father who is: **The Most High Heavenly One, the Sustainer, the Nourisher, the Provider of Life**, and **the Creator of the boundless universes**, thank you for sending the Messiah Yashu'a (Jesus) who was a willing sacrifice, and for your angelic-beings that protect us, inspire us and guide us to obey you, inclusive of the **Sun of Righteousness** (the word for "**Sun**" is **Shemesh** צְדָקָה pronounced **Sheh'·mesh**, the word for "**Righteousness**" is **Tsĕdaqah** שֶׁמֶשׁ pronounced **T<u>sed</u>·ä·kä'**) who arises with healing in his wings as stated in the King James Version (KJV) bible book of **Malachi chapter 4 verse 2**, and we thank the Most High Heavenly One for life, for health and for everything else!

5

Yashu'a (Jesus) said: "Thou shalt love the Most High Heavenly Father, thy Sustainer with all thy heart, and with all thy soul, and with all thy mind. Thou shalt love thy neighbour as thyself."

Mind Gardening in the Creative Garden of Will (Your Mind) to Grow a Living Water Mentality!

CHILDREN OF THE MOST HIGH:
PRISTINE YOUTH AND FAMILY SOLUTIONS, LLC.
SONS AND DAUGHTERS OF THE MOST HIGH PUBLISHERS ®

Oh, Gracious Most High Heavenly father, Holy is your name,
Your Will Be Done Now and Forever!

A Special Thank You to: My Dad (**The Honorable**: Mr. Woodie Hughes Sr.), and Mom (**The Noble**: Mrs. Annette Hughes) for accepting the Messiah Yashu'a (Jesus) and raising me and my brothers in a Godly home filled with love as they like the Messiah Yashu'a (Jesus); willingly sacrificed their youth and many worldly possessions to ensure that my brothers and I had the greatest opportunity to achieve the maximum levels of success in all areas of our lives; **thank you Mom and Dad!**

6

Yashu'a (Jesus) said: "Thou shalt love the Most High Heavenly Father, thy Sustainer with all thy heart, and with all thy soul, and with all thy mind. Thou shalt love thy neighbour as thyself."

Mind Gardening in the Creative Garden of Will (Your Mind) to Grow a Living Water Mentality!

CHILDREN OF THE MOST HIGH:
PRISTINE YOUTH AND FAMILY SOLUTIONS, LLC.
SONS AND DAUGHTERS OF THE MOST HIGH PUBLISHERS ®

Oh, Gracious Most High Heavenly father, Holy is your name, Your Will Be Done Now and Forever!

A Special Thank You to: My Beloved Wife and best friend (Mrs. Tonya L. Hughes) who sacrificed her health and well-being to give birth to our children. Our children inspire me every day to keep working hard for our family and to continuously work hard to help uplift members of humanity so that we can work together to help people and the planet earth to maintain, and sustain positive health and balance for that great day, when: "Thy kingdom will come to earth as it is in heaven." We also thank the many other family members, friends, colleagues, mentors, and global spiritual family who are the children of the Most High and who are in the body of Christ.

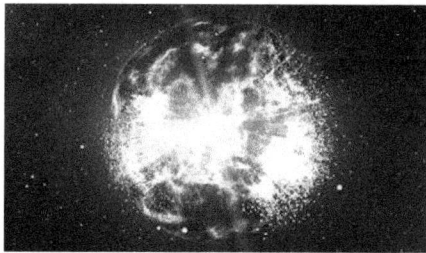

7

Yashu'a (Jesus) said: "Thou shalt love the Most High Heavenly Father, thy Sustainer with all thy heart, and with all thy soul, and with all thy mind. Thou shalt love thy neighbour as thyself."

Mind Gardening in the Creative Garden of Will (Your Mind) to Grow a Living Water Mentality!

CHILDREN OF THE MOST HIGH:
PRISTINE YOUTH AND FAMILY SOLUTIONS, LLC.
SONS AND DAUGHTERS OF THE MOST HIGH PUBLISHERS ®

*Oh, Gracious Most High Heavenly father, Holy is your name,
Your Will Be Done Now and Forever!*

Who are the Children of the Most High Pristine Youth and Family Solutions, LLC.?

We are teachers of the doctrine of the Most High; the doctrine that the real Messiah Yashu'a (Jesus) taught. In the KJV bible book of John chapter 7 verse 16; the Messiah Yashu'a (Jesus) stated: "My doctrine isn't mine, but his that sent me." The Children of the Most High, Pristine Youth and Family Solutions, LLC. purpose is to do the Most High Heavenly Father's will only! We exist and work under the authority of the Most High Heavenly Father, who is the Creator and the Ruler of all of the boundless universes! We acknowledge the Messiah Jesus as our Savior who **we refer to** in his original Judean/Galilean Aramic (Hebrew) language birth name **Yasu'a** or **Yashu'a** (ישוע) meaning "**Savior**" and **Jesus,** who is **the Son of God** in English.

8

Yashu'a (Jesus) said: "Thou shalt love the Most High Heavenly Father, thy Sustainer with all thy heart, and with all thy soul, and with all thy mind. Thou shalt love thy neighbour as thyself."

Mind Gardening in the Creative Garden of Will (Your Mind) to Grow a Living Water Mentality!

CHILDREN OF THE MOST HIGH:
PRISTINE YOUTH AND FAMILY SOLUTIONS, LLC.
SONS AND DAUGHTERS OF THE MOST HIGH PUBLISHERS ®

*Oh, Gracious Most High Heavenly father, Holy is your name,
Your Will Be Done Now and Forever!*

We have accepted the Lord Jesus Christ (Yashu'a Ha Mashiakh – Jesus the Messiah or Yehoshu'a, which means Yahayyu is Salvation or Yahayyu Saves) as our Savior and we are in the Body of Christ!

CHILDREN OF THE MOST HIGH:
PRISTINE YOUTH AND FAMILY SOLUTIONS, LLC.
SONS AND DAUGHTERS OF THE MOST HIGH PUBLISHERS ®

What is the Mission, Vision, and Motto of the Children of the Most High; Pristine Youth and Family Solutions, LLC?

The Mission is: To inspire and empower all children of the Most High to pristinely make the world a safe and healthy place for all members of humanity.

Yashu'a (Jesus) said: "Thou shalt love the Most High Heavenly Father, thy Sustainer with all thy heart, and with all thy soul, and with all thy mind. Thou shalt love thy neighbour as thyself."

Mind Gardening in the Creative Garden of Will (Your Mind) to Grow a Living Water Mentality!

CHILDREN OF THE MOST HIGH:
PRISTINE YOUTH AND FAMILY SOLUTIONS, LLC.
SONS AND DAUGHTERS OF THE MOST HIGH PUBLISHERS ®

Oh, Gracious Most High Heavenly father, Holy is your name,
Your Will Be Done Now and Forever!

The Vision is: To create a world that is ruled by Love and the "Will" of the Most High, void of negative emotions, greed, lusts and love of money. According to the KJV bible book of Matthew chapter 19 verse 26, the Messiah Yashu'a (Jesus) said unto them, "With men this is impossible; but with God all things are possible." According to the KJV bible book of Philippians chapter 4 verse 13; it states: "I can do all things through Christ which strengthened me." Therefore; with God and through Christ, the children of the Most High Pristine Youth and Family Solutions, LLC. Mission and Vision can become a reality for the children of the Most High!

Motto: There is no right way to do the wrong thing!

Yashu'a (Jesus) said: "Thou shalt love the Most High Heavenly Father, thy Sustainer with all thy heart, and with all thy soul, and with all thy mind. Thou shalt love thy neighbour as thyself."

Mind Gardening in the Creative Garden of Will (Your Mind) to Grow a Living Water Mentality!

CHILDREN OF THE MOST HIGH:
PRISTINE YOUTH AND FAMILY SOLUTIONS, LLC.
SONS AND DAUGHTERS OF THE MOST HIGH PUBLISHERS ®

*Oh, Gracious Most High Heavenly father, Holy is your name,
Your Will Be Done Now and Forever!*

Who is the Most High to the Children of the Most High Pristine Youth and Family Solutions, LLC.?

The Most High Heavenly Father is Love, the Sustainer, the Nourisher, the Provider of all Life, and the Omnipotent and the Omnipresent Creator of the boundless universes. The Most High Heavenly Father encompasses and interpenetrates all existence inclusive of every part of nature both visible as well as invisible. Oh, Most High Heavenly Father, you are all, and there is nothing nearer to us than you; for you encompass all things! Glory be to you alone! In the KJV bible book of John chapter 4 verse 23, the Messiah Yashu'a (Jesus) said: "God is a Spirit: and they that worship him must worship him in spirit and in truth."

Yashu'a (Jesus) said: "Thou shalt love the Most High Heavenly Father, thy Sustainer with all thy heart, and with all thy soul, and with all thy mind. Thou shalt love thy neighbour as thyself."

Mind Gardening in the Creative Garden of Will (Your Mind) to Grow a Living Water Mentality!

CHILDREN OF THE MOST HIGH:
PRISTINE YOUTH AND FAMILY SOLUTIONS, LLC.
SONS AND DAUGHTERS OF THE MOST HIGH PUBLISHERS ®

Oh, Gracious Most High Heavenly father, Holy is your name,
Your Will Be Done Now and Forever!

In the KJV bible book of Genesis, chapter 14 verse 18 states: "And Melchizedek (**Malkiy-Tsedeq, מַלְכִּי־צֶדֶק**) king of Salem brought forth bread and wine: and he was the priest of the **Most High** (ELYOWN עֶלְיוֹן) **God** (**EL אֵל**)."

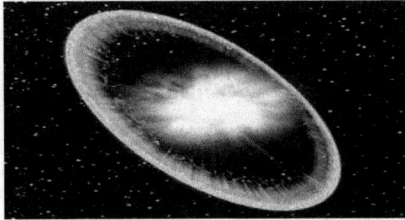

Who is the Real Messiah Jesus to the Children of the Most High Pristine Youth and Family Solutions, LLC.?

The Children of the Most High, Pristine Youth and Family Solutions, LLC., acknowledges the Real Messiah Jesus as our Savior who **we refer to** in his original Galilean/Judean Aramic (Hebrew) language, original birth name **Yasu'a (يسوع)** or **Yashu'a (יֵשׁוּעַ)** meaning "**Savior**" also spelled Yeshua or

Yashu'a (Jesus) said: "Thou shalt love the Most High Heavenly Father, thy Sustainer with all thy heart, and with all thy soul, and with all thy mind. Thou shalt love thy neighbour as thyself."

Mind Gardening in the Creative Garden of Will (Your Mind) to Grow a Living Water Mentality!

CHILDREN OF THE MOST HIGH:
PRISTINE YOUTH AND FAMILY SOLUTIONS, LLC.
SONS AND DAUGHTERS OF THE MOST HIGH PUBLISHERS ®

Oh, Gracious Most High Heavenly father, Holy is your name,
Your Will Be Done Now and Forever!

Yehoshu'a, **Iesous** (Ἰησοῦς) in the Greek translation and as **Kurios** (Greek word for Lord), and **Issa** or **Isa** in Ashuric Syriac (Arabic). Now when **Yehoshu'a** is translated in the Hebrew language it translates as **Yahayyu Saves** or simply **Joshua**, and in the Galilean language as Yashu'a or **Yasu'a** Inar **Rab** (which translates as **Jesus Son of the Sustainer**), **Yashu'a Bar Yahayyu** (يـبار حـ, **Existing One**). In Modern Hebrew translates as **Savior Son of the Everliving** or **Savior Son of the Existing One** or **Living One**, **Yasu'** and **Haru** as **Karast** "**Christ**" to the **Ancient** original indigenous Egyptian people of what is called: "Egypt" today, not to be confused with the Egyptians who are the nonindigenous people who migrated to what is now known as Egypt. Yashu'a called **Jesus, is the Son of God** in English. Yashu'a (Jesus), **the Son of the Most High God** is the way back to the Most High.

13

Yashu'a (Jesus) said: "Thou shalt love the Most High Heavenly Father, thy Sustainer with all thy heart, and with all thy soul, and with all thy mind. Thou shalt love thy neighbour as thyself."

Mind Gardening in the Creative Garden of Will (Your Mind) to Grow a Living Water Mentality!

CHILDREN OF THE MOST HIGH:
PRISTINE YOUTH AND FAMILY SOLUTIONS, LLC.
SONS AND DAUGHTERS OF THE MOST HIGH PUBLISHERS ®

Oh, Gracious Most High Heavenly father, Holy is your name,
Your Will Be Done Now and Forever!

In the KJV bible book of John chapter 14 verse 6; the Messiah Yashu'a (Jesus) said: "I am the way, the truth, and the life: no man (the words: "no man" is not in the original language that this verse was revealed in. The original word for "no man" in the Greek KJV bible translation is: "**Oudeis**" (οὐδείς, Oudeis (is the KJV bible Greek Strong's Concordance#**3762**) means: *not one; no one, nothing*. So, this phrase is inclusive of males and females, not just males) cometh unto the Father, but by me." However, according to the Messiah Yashu'a (Jesus), no one can come to him unless the Most High Heavenly Father sends them to him. Yashu'a (Jesus) said in the KJV bible book of John chapter 6 verse 44: "No man (**οὐδείς oudeis**) can (**δύναμαι** *dynamai*) come (**ἔρχομαι** *erchomai*) to (**πρός** *pros*) me (**μέ** *mé, meh*), except (**ἐὰν μή** *ean mē*;"

14

Yashu'a (Jesus) said: "Thou shalt love the Most High Heavenly Father, thy Sustainer with all thy heart, and with all thy soul, and with all thy mind. Thou shalt love thy neighbour as thyself."

Mind Gardening in the Creative Garden of Will (Your Mind) to Grow a Living Water Mentality!

Oh, Gracious Most High Heavenly father, Holy is your name, Your Will Be Done Now and Forever!

"KJV bible Greek Strong's Concordance#**3362** meaning: **if not, unless, whoever... not**) the Father which hath sent me draw (ἕλκω *helkō*; KJV bible Greek Strong's Concordance#**1670** meaning: **to draw by inward power, lead, impel; to drag (literally or figuratively)** him: and I will raise him up at the last day." Again, in the aforementioned verse, the words: "no man" is not in the original language that this verse was revealed in. The original word for "no man" is: "**Oudeis**" (οὐδείς, Oudeis (KJV bible Greek Strong's Concordance#**3762**) means: *not one; no one, nothing*.

What does the Children of the Most High Pristine Youth and Family Solutions, LLC. do?

The Children of the Most High; Pristine Youth and Family Solutions LLC. does the will of the Most High Heavenly Father.

15

Yashu'a (Jesus) said: "Thou shalt love the Most High Heavenly Father, thy Sustainer with all thy heart, and with all thy soul, and with all thy mind. Thou shalt love thy neighbour as thyself."

Mind Gardening in the Creative Garden of Will (Your Mind) to Grow a Living Water Mentality!

CHILDREN OF THE MOST HIGH:
PRISTINE YOUTH AND FAMILY SOLUTIONS, LLC.
SONS AND DAUGHTERS OF THE MOST HIGH PUBLISHERS ®

Oh, Gracious Most High Heavenly father, Holy is your name,
Your Will Be Done Now and Forever!

We are **Teachers** and **Administrators** of the Most High Doctrine and work diligently to teach youth and adults how to solve problems, and how to successfully work through difficult problems or issues or situations by utilizing the **Children of the Most High Pristine Youth and Family Solutions, LLC. 9X9 True Vine "Yashu'a" (Jesus) B.A. (Soul) K.A. (Spirit) R.E. (Sun) ("RE" is pronounced as "RAY") Sequential Order of Learning. More information about the True Vine "Yashu'a" (Jesus) B.A.-K.A.-R.E. Sequential Order of Learning will be expounded on in chapter 9.** Our targeted audiences are youth (who are between the 5th and 12th grades) and adults who are children of the Most High. So, we teach in an effort to make the doctrine of the Most High clear in the minds of people who want to learn the original message or messages of the scriptures before they were translated into other languages, and we teach in an effort to create an opportunity for them to learn how to apply the doctrine of the Most High in all that they aspire to do!

16

Yashu'a (Jesus) said: "Thou shalt love the Most High Heavenly Father, thy Sustainer with all thy heart, and with all thy soul, and with all thy mind. Thou shalt love thy neighbour as thyself."

Mind Gardening in the Creative Garden of Will (Your Mind) to Grow a Living Water Mentality!

CHILDREN OF THE MOST HIGH:
PRISTINE YOUTH AND FAMILY SOLUTIONS, LLC.
SONS AND DAUGHTERS OF THE MOST HIGH PUBLISHERS ®

*Oh, Gracious Most High Heavenly father, Holy is your name,
Your Will Be Done Now and Forever!*

Why does the Children of the Most High Pristine Youth and Family Solutions, LLC. refer to themselves as <u>T</u>eachers / <u>A</u>dministers of the Most High Heavenly Father's Doctrine instead of <u>P</u>reachers?

The Children of the Most High Pristine Youth and Family Solutions, LLC. refer to themselves as <u>T</u>eachers and **<u>A</u>dministers of the Most High Heavenly Father's Doctrine** that Yashu'a (Jesus) taught instead of <u>P</u>reachers because the Most High inspired and endowed them with the knowledge and with the ability to teach with the True-Vine (Yashu'a, Jesus) Spirit of the Word of Knowledge in the KJV bible book of 1st Corinthians chapter 12 verse 8 to teach the Most High's Doctrine as mentioned in the KJV bible book of John chapter 7 verse 16.

Yashu'a (Jesus) said: "Thou shalt love the Most High Heavenly Father, thy Sustainer with all thy heart, and with all thy soul, and with all thy mind. Thou shalt love thy neighbour as thyself."

Mind Gardening in the Creative Garden of Will (Your Mind) to Grow a Living Water Mentality!

CHILDREN OF THE MOST HIGH:
PRISTINE YOUTH AND FAMILY SOLUTIONS, LLC.
SONS AND DAUGHTERS OF THE MOST HIGH PUBLISHERS ®

*Oh, Gracious Most High Heavenly father, Holy is your name,
Your Will Be Done Now and Forever!*

In the KJV bible book of Matthews chapter 28 verses 19-20, the Messiah Yashu'a (Jesus) said: "Go ye therefore, and <u>teach</u> all nations, baptizing them in the name of the Father, and of the Son, and of the Holy Ghost. <u>Teaching</u> them to observe all things whatsoever I have commanded you: and, lo, I am with you always, even unto the end of the world. Amen." The word in the aforementioned KJV bible book of Matthews chapter 28 verse 19 for *teach* is: the **KJV bible Greek Strong's Concordance#3100 mathēteuō (μαθητεύω) which means: teach, instruct, be disciple**.

18

Yashu'a (Jesus) said: "Thou shalt love the Most High Heavenly Father, thy Sustainer with all thy heart, and with all thy soul, and with all thy mind. Thou shalt love thy neighbour as thyself."

Mind Gardening in the Creative Garden of Will (Your Mind) to Grow a Living Water Mentality!

CHILDREN OF THE MOST HIGH:
PRISTINE YOUTH AND FAMILY SOLUTIONS, LLC.
SONS AND DAUGHTERS OF THE MOST HIGH PUBLISHERS ®

*Oh, Gracious Most High Heavenly father, Holy is your name,
Your Will Be Done Now and Forever!*

The word in the book of Matthews chapter 28 verse 20 for *Teaching* is: the **KJV bible Greek Strong's Concordance#1321 didaskō (διδάσκω) which means: to teach, to hold discourse with others in order to instruct them, deliver didactic discourses, <u>to be a teacher,</u> to discharge the office of a teacher, <u>conduct one's self as a teacher,</u> to teach one, to impart instruction, <u>instill doctrine into one,</u> the thing taught or enjoined, to explain or expound a thing, to teach one something.**

The word for **"Preach" in the KJV bible book of Matthew chapter 11 verse 1** is: the **KJV bible Greek Strong's Concordance#2784 kēryssō (κηρύσσω) which means to: preach, publish, and proclaim.**

19

Yashu'a (Jesus) said: "Thou shalt love the Most High Heavenly Father, thy Sustainer with all thy heart, and with all thy soul, and with all thy mind. Thou shalt love thy neighbour as thyself."

Mind Gardening in the Creative Garden of Will (Your Mind) to Grow a Living Water Mentality!

CHILDREN OF THE MOST HIGH:
PRISTINE YOUTH AND FAMILY SOLUTIONS, LLC.
SONS AND DAUGHTERS OF THE MOST HIGH PUBLISHERS ®

Oh, Gracious Most High Heavenly father, Holy is your name, Your Will Be Done Now and Forever!

In the KJV bible book of Matthew chapter 11 verse 1; it states: "And it came to pass, when Jesus had made an end of commanding his twelve disciples, he departed thence to **teach** and to **preach** in their cities. The plural noun of "**teach**" is "Teachers": the **KJV bible Greek Strong's Concordance#1320 didaskalos (διδάσκαλος,** meaning one who teaches or teachers) and has the same root foundation as the word for "**Teach**" (the **KJV bible Greek Strong's Concordance#1321 didaskō (διδάσκω)** in the book of Acts chapter 13 verse 1; and states: "Now there were in the church that was at Antioch certain prophets and **teachers**; as Barnabas, and Simeon that was called **Niger**, and Lucius of Cyrene, and Manaen, which had been brought up with Herod the tetrarch, and Saul."

20

Yashu'a (Jesus) said: "Thou shalt love the Most High Heavenly Father, thy Sustainer with all thy heart, and with all thy soul, and with all thy mind. Thou shalt love thy neighbour as thyself."

Mind Gardening in the Creative Garden of Will (Your Mind) to Grow a Living Water Mentality!

CHILDREN OF THE MOST HIGH:
PRISTINE YOUTH AND FAMILY SOLUTIONS, LLC.
SONS AND DAUGHTERS OF THE MOST HIGH PUBLISHERS ®

*Oh, Gracious Most High Heavenly father, Holy is your name,
Your Will Be Done Now and Forever!*

In the aforementioned verse, the word: "**Niger**" is the **KJV Bible Greek Strong's Concordance#3526 Νίγερ (Niger)** which means: **Νίγερ Níger, neeg'-er**; **of Latin origin**; **black**; **Niger, a Christian**: **Niger**. According to the African American Registry (2019): "The history of the word **nigger is often traced to the Latin word Niger**, **meaning Black**. This word became the noun, Negro (Black person) in English." The KJV bible book of Hosea, chapter 4 verse 6; states: "My people are destroyed for lack of knowledge: because thou hast rejected knowledge, I will also reject thee, that thou shalt be no priest to me: seeing thou hast forgotten the law of thy God, I will also forget thy children." The KJV bible book of Isaiah, chapter 5 verse 13; states: "Therefore my people are gone into captivity, because they have no knowledge: and their honorable men are famished, and their multitude dried up with thirst."

21

Yashu'a (Jesus) said: "Thou shalt love the Most High Heavenly Father, thy Sustainer with all thy heart, and with all thy soul, and with all thy mind. Thou shalt love thy neighbour as thyself."

Mind Gardening in the Creative Garden of Will (Your Mind) to Grow a Living Water Mentality!

CHILDREN OF THE MOST HIGH:
PRISTINE YOUTH AND FAMILY SOLUTIONS, LLC.
SONS AND DAUGHTERS OF THE MOST HIGH PUBLISHERS ®

*Oh, Gracious Most High Heavenly father, Holy is your name,
Your Will Be Done Now and Forever!*

So, the Children of the Most High Pristine Youth and Family Solutions, LLC. refer to themselves as **Teachers** instead of **Preachers** because after over 25 years of teaching and studying the scriptures in the languages that they were originally revealed in, the children of the Most High don't find themselves **preaching**, they found themselves **teaching**. According to the Online American Heritage Dictionary, **teaching means; instructing, explaining, and elaborating**. So, we **teach** in an effort to ensure that the children of the Most High do their best to make the doctrine of the Most High clear in the minds of people who want to learn the original message or messages of the scriptures before they were translated into other languages.

22

Yashu'a (Jesus) said: "Thou shalt love the Most High Heavenly Father, thy Sustainer with all thy heart, and with all thy soul, and with all thy mind. Thou shalt love thy neighbour as thyself."

Mind Gardening in the Creative Garden of Will (Your Mind) to Grow a Living Water Mentality!

CHILDREN OF THE MOST HIGH:
PRISTINE YOUTH AND FAMILY SOLUTIONS, LLC.
SONS AND DAUGHTERS OF THE MOST HIGH PUBLISHERS ®

*Oh, Gracious Most High Heavenly father, Holy is your name,
Your Will Be Done Now and Forever!*

According to the Online American Heritage Dictionary (2020), **Administer** is defined as:

ad·min·is·ter (ăd-mĭn⬚ĭ-stər)

v. **ad·min·is·tered, ad·min·is·ter·ing, ad·min·is·ters**

v.tr.

1. To have charge of; manage.

2.a. To apply as a remedy: *administer a sedative*. **1.** To manage as an administrator. **2.** To minister: *administering to their every whim*. [Middle English *administren*, from Old French *administrer*, from Latin *administrāre* : *ad*, ad- + *ministrāre*, to manage (from *minister, ministr-*, servant; see MINISTER).]

23

Yashu'a (Jesus) said: "Thou shalt love the Most High Heavenly Father, thy Sustainer with all thy heart, and with all thy soul, and with all thy mind. Thou shalt love thy neighbour as thyself."

Mind Gardening in the Creative Garden of Will (Your Mind) to Grow a Living Water Mentality!

CHILDREN OF THE MOST HIGH:
PRISTINE YOUTH AND FAMILY SOLUTIONS, LLC.
SONS AND DAUGHTERS OF THE MOST HIGH PUBLISHERS ®

Oh, Gracious Most High Heavenly father, Holy is your name,
Your Will Be Done Now and Forever!

So, we are "**Administers of the Most High's Doctrine**" by way of the Most High Heavenly Father giving the Children of the Most High: Pristine Youth and Family Solutions, LLC. **charge of managing the administering** of his Doctrine to inspire and empower all children of the Most High to pristinely make the world a safe and healthy place for all members of humanity. Which occurs by <u>**applying the Doctrine of the Most High as a remedy to create a world that is ruled by Love and the "Will" of the Most High, void of negative emotions, greed, lusts and love of money**</u>.

24

Yashu'a (Jesus) said: "Thou shalt love the Most High Heavenly Father, thy Sustainer with all thy heart, and with all thy soul, and with all thy mind. Thou shalt love thy neighbour as thyself."

Mind Gardening in the Creative Garden of Will (Your Mind) to Grow a Living Water Mentality!

CHILDREN OF THE MOST HIGH:
PRISTINE YOUTH AND FAMILY SOLUTIONS, LLC.
SONS AND DAUGHTERS OF THE MOST HIGH PUBLISHERS ®

*Oh, Gracious Most High Heavenly father, Holy is your name,
Your Will Be Done Now and Forever!*

Why does the work that the Children of the Most High Pristine Youth and Family Solutions, LLC. do Matter?

In order for the Children of the Most High; Pristine Youth and Family Solutions LLC. to be obedient to the Most High Heavenly Father, we seek to be positive difference makers who helps and teach youth and adults how to apply the doctrine of the Most High through the **True Vine "Yashu'a" (Jesus) B.A.-K.A.-R.E. Sequential Order of Learning** to teach them how to create positive predetermined goals, how to achieve positive success according to what positive success means to them, how to achieve positive happiness according to what positive happiness means to them, and how to learn to work together with members of humanity to create a world where all youth and all adults are happy, healthy, and balanced mentally, spiritually, physically, emotionally, financially, personally, professionally, and socially.

25

Yashu'a (Jesus) said: "Thou shalt love the Most High Heavenly Father, thy Sustainer with all thy heart, and with all thy soul, and with all thy mind. Thou shalt love thy neighbour as thyself."

Mind Gardening in the Creative Garden of Will (Your Mind) to Grow a Living Water Mentality!

CHILDREN OF THE MOST HIGH:
PRISTINE YOUTH AND FAMILY SOLUTIONS, LLC.
SONS AND DAUGHTERS OF THE MOST HIGH PUBLISHERS ®

Oh, Gracious Most High Heavenly father, Holy is your name,
Your Will Be Done Now and Forever!

"Happiness is associated with and precedes numerous successful outcomes, as well as behaviors paralleling success, Lyubomirsky, King, & Diener, (2005). Furthermore, the evidence suggests that positive affect is the hallmark of well-being and may be the cause of many of the desirable characteristics, resources, and successes correlated with happiness, (Lyubomirsky, King, & Diener, (2005)." It also matters for our youth to receive the protection from the Most High Heavenly Father from all harm during the pre-adult years and beyond, in order to have an opportunity to become adults that can continue to create a world where all youth and all adults are happy, healthy, and balanced mentally, spiritually, physically, emotionally, financially, personally, professionally, and socially.

Yashu'a (Jesus) said: "Thou shalt love the Most High Heavenly Father, thy Sustainer with all thy heart, and with all thy soul, and with all thy mind. Thou shalt love thy neighbour as thyself."

Mind Gardening in the Creative Garden of Will (Your Mind) to Grow a Living Water Mentality!

CHILDREN OF THE MOST HIGH:
PRISTINE YOUTH AND FAMILY SOLUTIONS, LLC.
SONS AND DAUGHTERS OF THE MOST HIGH PUBLISHERS ®

Oh, Gracious Most High Heavenly father, Holy is your name,
Your Will Be Done Now and Forever!

According the bible, this can only occur if our youth learn God's knowledge and obey God's laws. In the KJV bible book of Hosea chapter 4 verse 6, the LORD states: "**My people are destroyed for lack of knowledge**: because thou hast rejected knowledge, I will also reject thee, that thou shalt be no priest to me: <u>**seeing thou hast forgotten the law of thy God, I will also forget thy children**</u>." So, according to the aforementioned verse, in order to best prepare today's youth to survive and thrive until adulthood and beyond, they need to learn **God's (אלהים Elôhîym) knowledge (Elôhîym, אלהים is the original word for "God" before being translated as the word: "God" in the KJV bible book of Genesis chapter 1 verse 1**), and **God's (אלהים Elôhîym)** laws to be eligible to receive **God's (אלהים Elôhîym)** protection from all harm.

27

Mind Gardening in the Creative Garden of Will (Your Mind) to Grow a Living Water Mentality!

CHILDREN OF THE MOST HIGH:
PRISTINE YOUTH AND FAMILY SOLUTIONS, LLC.
SONS AND DAUGHTERS OF THE MOST HIGH PUBLISHERS ®

Oh, Gracious Most High Heavenly father, Holy is your name,
Your Will Be Done Now and Forever!

Therefore, today's youth must be informed with **God's (אלהים Elôhîym) All, Wise, Abundant, Right, Exact (A.W.A.R.E.) Knowledge**. How do you know? Because God's **A.W.A.R.E.** knowledge is **best**, **accurate**, **correct** (**right, healthy**) and **exact** and best to guide and protect all of the global children of the Most High from all harm. For this reason, **God's (אלהים Elôhîym) A.W.A.R.E. Knowledge** gives the children of the Most High the ability to develop the habit of **positive thinking** or correct (**right, healthy) thinking** as oppose to **negative thinking** or **wrong thinking**.

28

Yashu'a (Jesus) said: "Thou shalt love the Most High Heavenly Father, thy Sustainer with all thy heart, and with all thy soul, and with all thy mind. Thou shalt love thy neighbour as thyself."

Mind Gardening in the Creative Garden of Will (Your Mind) to Grow a Living Water Mentality!

CHILDREN OF THE MOST HIGH:
PRISTINE YOUTH AND FAMILY SOLUTIONS, LLC.
SONS AND DAUGHTERS OF THE MOST HIGH PUBLISHERS ®

Oh, Gracious Most High Heavenly father, Holy is your name,
Your Will Be Done Now and Forever!

A person with **wrong knowledge** thinks negatively by having **wrong I. D. E. A. S.** (**I**mpure **D**esires **E**motionally **A**ctivated **S**equentially) or negative thoughts continuously, which leads to negative thinking, negative speaking, negative actions, and negative character. <u>**Learning, applying and obeying the laws of Elohiym (God), activates the will of the Most High Heavenly Father in the mind which initiates all thoughts, and a person acts and speaks, as he or she thinks!**</u> This is why in the KJV bible book of Hebrews chapter 8 verse 10; it states: "For this is the covenant that I will make with the house of Israel after those days, saith the Lord; <u>**I will put my laws into their mind, and write them in their hearts**</u>: and I will be to them a God, and they shall be to me a people."

29

Yashu'a (Jesus) said: "Thou shalt love the Most High Heavenly Father, thy Sustainer with all thy heart, and with all thy soul, and with all thy mind. Thou shalt love thy neighbour as thyself."

Mind Gardening in the Creative Garden of Will (Your Mind) to Grow a Living Water Mentality!

CHILDREN OF THE MOST HIGH:
PRISTINE YOUTH AND FAMILY SOLUTIONS, LLC.
SONS AND DAUGHTERS OF THE MOST HIGH PUBLISHERS ®

Oh, Gracious Most High Heavenly father, Holy is your name,
Your Will Be Done Now and Forever!

In the KJV bible book of Revelation chapter 22 verses 12-16; Yashu'a (Jesus) stated: "And, behold, I come quickly; and my reward is with me, to give every man according as his work shall be. I am Alpha and Omega, the beginning and the end, the first and the last. Blessed are they that do his [the Most High, Heavenly Father's, **ELYOWN** עֶלְיוֹן **EL** אֵל] commandments, that they may have right to the tree of life, and may enter in through the gates into the city. For without are dogs, and sorcerers, and whoremongers, and murderers, and idolaters, and whosoever loveth and maketh a lie. "I Jesus [Yashu'a] have sent mine angel to testify unto you these things in the churches. I am the root and the offspring of David, and the bright and morning star."

30

Yashu'a (Jesus) said: "Thou shalt love the Most High
Heavenly Father, thy Sustainer with all thy heart, and
with all thy soul, and with all thy mind. Thou shalt love
thy neighbour as thyself."

Mind Gardening in the Creative Garden of Will (Your Mind) to Grow a Living Water Mentality!

CHILDREN OF THE MOST HIGH:
PRISTINE YOUTH AND FAMILY SOLUTIONS, LLC.
SONS AND DAUGHTERS OF THE MOST HIGH PUBLISHERS ®

*Oh, Gracious Most High Heavenly father, Holy is your name,
Your Will Be Done Now and Forever!*

Hence, **God's (אלהים Elôhîym) A.W.A.R.E. Knowledge** is the **best knowledge** for our youth to be taught in order for them to have the best opportunity to be recipients of **Elohiym** (God's) protection, and to help ensure that our youth will become the future positive leaders of tomorrow, today!

The Children of the Most High: Pristine Youth and Family Solutions, LLC. is putting forth this book entitled: "**Mind Gardening in the Creative Garden of Will (Your Mind) to Grow a Living Water Mentality**!" By the will of the Most High Heavenly Father to <u>inspire **ALL youth and ALL adults who are children of the Most High**</u> to obey the Most High Commandments now and forever, and to become empowered, inspired, and guided by the "**WILL**" **of the Most High ONLY!!!**

31

Yashu'a (Jesus) said: "Thou shalt love the Most High Heavenly Father, thy Sustainer with all thy heart, and with all thy soul, and with all thy mind. Thou shalt love thy neighbour as thyself."

Mind Gardening in the Creative Garden of Will (Your Mind) to Grow a Living Water Mentality!

CHILDREN OF THE MOST HIGH:
PRISTINE YOUTH AND FAMILY SOLUTIONS, LLC.
SONS AND DAUGHTERS OF THE MOST HIGH PUBLISHERS ®

Oh, Gracious Most High Heavenly father, Holy is your name,
Your Will Be Done Now and Forever!

Introduction:

Do you think like Jesus? If there was a way to **transform your thinking, to transfigure your mentality to grow into the "Jesus Mind", would you want to learn how to do so?** What would your life be like if you thought like Jesus? **Imagine the blessings and benefits** of **the dynamic opportunity to experience the process of becoming** a **True Vine (Jesus) <u>active</u> Mind Gardening Farmer in the Creative Garden of Will (Your Mind)! "For who hath known <u>the mind</u> of the Lord, that he may instruct him? But we have <u>the mind of Christ</u>, 1st Corinthians 2:16 KJV Bible."**

32

Yashu'a (Jesus) said: "Thou shalt love the Most High Heavenly Father, thy Sustainer with all thy heart, and with all thy soul, and with all thy mind. Thou shalt love thy neighbour as thyself."

Mind Gardening in the Creative Garden of Will (Your Mind) to Grow a Living Water Mentality!

CHILDREN OF THE MOST HIGH:
PRISTINE YOUTH AND FAMILY SOLUTIONS, LLC.
SONS AND DAUGHTERS OF THE MOST HIGH PUBLISHERS ®

Oh, Gracious Most High Heavenly father, Holy is your name,
Your Will Be Done Now and Forever!

This book entitled: "**Mind Gardening in the Creative Garden of Will (<u>Your Mind</u>) to Grow a Living Water Mentality!**" is being put forth by the "**WILL**" of the **Most High Heavenly Father** in an effort to teach youth and adults who are children of the Most High about the **True Vine (Jesus) Mind Consciousness and Conscientiousness! How**? By learning the **God (אלהים Elôhîym) <u>A</u>ll <u>W</u>ise <u>A</u>bundant <u>R</u>ight <u>E</u>xact (A.W.A.R.E.) Knowledge that <u>ACTIVATES</u> the True Vine (Jesus) Mind Master Gardner – children of the Most High (God) Mind! Thereby, UNLOCKING YOUR POTENTIAL** inside <u>**YOUR Creative Garden of Will (Your Mind)**</u>, which **ENABLES the** children of the Most High **to successfully create, be innovative, solve personal and professional issues, accomplish all of their positive predetermined goals, and the POWER to make all of <u>YOUR</u> dreams come true!**

33

Yashu'a (Jesus) said: "Thou shalt love the Most High Heavenly Father, thy Sustainer with all thy heart, and with all thy soul, and with all thy mind. Thou shalt love thy neighbour as thyself."

Mind Gardening in the Creative Garden of Will (Your Mind) to Grow a Living Water Mentality!

CHILDREN OF THE MOST HIGH:
PRISTINE YOUTH AND FAMILY SOLUTIONS, LLC.
SONS AND DAUGHTERS OF THE MOST HIGH PUBLISHERS ®

Oh, Gracious Most High Heavenly father, Holy is your name,
Your Will Be Done Now and Forever!

Why does this matter? It matters because in the KJV bible book of Matthew chapter 22 verses 37-38; **The Messiah Yashu'a (Jesus)** said: unto him, "Thou shalt love the Lord thy God with all thy heart, and with all thy soul, and with all thy mind. This is the first and great commandment." A person acts and speaks as a reflection of how they think. Therefore, in order for the children of the Most High to obey this first and great commandment, we must experience a **True Vine Yashu'a (Jesus) renewal (mental resurrection) of the mind** from a mentally unconscious state due to lacking God's (אלהים **Elôhîym**) **A**ll, **W**ise, **A**bundant, **R**ight, **E**xact (**A.W.A.R.E.**) **Knowledge**.

34

Yashu'a (Jesus) said: "Thou shalt love the Most High Heavenly Father, thy Sustainer with all thy heart, and with all thy soul, and with all thy mind. Thou shalt love thy neighbour as thyself."

Mind Gardening in the Creative Garden of Will (Your Mind) to Grow a Living Water Mentality!

CHILDREN OF THE MOST HIGH:
PRISTINE YOUTH AND FAMILY SOLUTIONS, LLC.
SONS AND DAUGHTERS OF THE MOST HIGH PUBLISHERS ®

*Oh, Gracious Most High Heavenly father, Holy is your name,
Your Will Be Done Now and Forever!*

According to the KJV bible book of Romans chapter 12 verse 2; it states: "And be not conformed to this world: **but be ye transformed by the renewing of your mind**, that ye may prove what [is] that good, and acceptable, and perfect, will of God." The KJV bible Greek Strong's Concordance word for the words "**by the renewing**" in this verse is **#342 ἀνακαίνωσις Anakainōsis. Anakainōsis** means: "**a renewal, renovation, complete change for the better**." What is the difference between **unconscious** and **conscious** as it relates to the renewal of the mind? **Unconscious** is the opposite of conscious. According to the Online American Heritage Dictionary (2020), **unconscious** is defined as: "1. Lacking awareness and the capacity for sensory perception; not conscious. 2. Occurring in the absence of conscious awareness or thought: unconscious resentment; unconscious fears."

35

Yashu'a (Jesus) said: "Thou shalt love the Most High Heavenly Father, thy Sustainer with all thy heart, and with all thy soul, and with all thy mind. Thou shalt love thy neighbour as thyself."

Mind Gardening in the Creative Garden of Will (Your Mind) to Grow a Living Water Mentality!

CHILDREN OF THE MOST HIGH:
PRISTINE YOUTH AND FAMILY SOLUTIONS, LLC.
SONS AND DAUGHTERS OF THE MOST HIGH PUBLISHERS ®

Oh, Gracious Most High Heavenly father, Holy is your name, Your Will Be Done Now and Forever!

"**Conscious** is defined as: "1. a. Characterized by or having an awareness of one's environment and one's own existence, sensations, and thoughts. See Synonyms at aware. b. Mentally perceptive or alert; awake: 2. Capable of thought, will, or perception: the development of conscious life on the planet. 3. Intentionally conceived or done; made a conscious effort to speak more clearly. 4. Inwardly attentive or sensitive to something; 5. Showing awareness of or preoccupation with something." **The Messiah Yashu'a (Jesus) is also is in charge of the Resurrection at the end of the world.** In the KJV bible book of John chapter 11 verses 25-26; **The Messiah Yashu'a (Jesus)** said: "I am the resurrection, and the life: he that believeth in me, though he were dead, yet shall he live. And whosoever liveth and believeth in me shall never die. Believest thou this?"

36

Yashu'a (Jesus) said: "Thou shalt love the Most High Heavenly Father, thy Sustainer with all thy heart, and with all thy soul, and with all thy mind. Thou shalt love thy neighbour as thyself."

Mind Gardening in the Creative Garden of Will (Your Mind) to Grow a Living Water Mentality!

CHILDREN OF THE MOST HIGH:
PRISTINE YOUTH AND FAMILY SOLUTIONS, LLC.
SONS AND DAUGHTERS OF THE MOST HIGH PUBLISHERS ®

*Oh, Gracious Most High Heavenly father, Holy is your name,
Your Will Be Done Now and Forever!*

In order for this to occur, today's youth and adults must have the necessary knowledge needed to achieve positive success in all of their endeavors. **What is success**? According to the Children of the Most High Pristine Youth and Family Solutions, LLC., **"Success is doing the "Will" of the Most High, success is being obedient to the Most High, and success is the progressive realization of a worthy idea; which works in conjunction with the <u>virtues of seriousness and sincerity</u>."** <u>**To possess these virtues, is to have tranquility, which is the mental, emotional and spiritual foundation for clarity, patience, and perseverance**</u>. The attributes of **clarity**, **patience**, and **perseverance**; helps' a person to **<u>create and work</u>** towards achieving their **positive predetermined goals** that are required for them to **succeed in life**. <u>**Goals inform people of the directions to where they want to go in life**</u>.

37

Yashu'a (Jesus) said: "Thou shalt love the Most High Heavenly Father, thy Sustainer with all thy heart, and with all thy soul, and with all thy mind. Thou shalt love thy neighbour as thyself."

Mind Gardening in the Creative Garden of Will (Your Mind) to Grow a Living Water Mentality!

CHILDREN OF THE MOST HIGH:
PRISTINE YOUTH AND FAMILY SOLUTIONS, LLC.
SONS AND DAUGHTERS OF THE MOST HIGH PUBLISHERS ®

*Oh, Gracious Most High Heavenly father, Holy is your name,
Your Will Be Done Now and Forever!*

Goals also help people to **create** the necessary **plans or strategic steps in their minds that they must take, and know** in order to make all of their dreams come true. <u>**Thought initiates all actions**</u>. **The key to success and failure is that people become a reflection of their most dominant and frequent thoughts.** The choices that people make will determine what their actions will be. Consequences are the result of positive or negative actions. Consequences follow as a natural effect or a result of a previous action. Successful completion of short-term or long-term goals, especially long-termed goals; requires patience. **Patience is a virtue; of what? Patience is a virtue of success!**

38

Yashu'a (Jesus) said: "Thou shalt love the Most High Heavenly Father, thy Sustainer with all thy heart, and with all thy soul, and with all thy mind. Thou shalt love thy neighbour as thyself."

Mind Gardening in the Creative Garden of Will (Your Mind) to Grow a Living Water Mentality!

CHILDREN OF THE MOST HIGH:
PRISTINE YOUTH AND FAMILY SOLUTIONS, LLC.
SONS AND DAUGHTERS OF THE MOST HIGH PUBLISHERS ®

Oh, Gracious Most High Heavenly father, Holy is your name,
Your Will Be Done Now and Forever!

So, it is important that we, as true followers of the **Real Messiah Yashu'a (Jesus Son of God**) utilize this book as a 9X9 True Vine "Yashu'a" (Jesus) **B.A.-K.A.-R.E. (pronounced as RAY). Sequential Order of Learning Habits of Success self-help tool that** can **help all youth and all adults who are children of the Most High to learn how to work together to create a world that is ruled by love and not ruled by negative emotions, greed, lusts and love of money**; a world where all youth and all adults are happy, healthy, and balanced mentally, spiritually, physically, emotionally, financially, socially, personally, and professionally. If you place soil or water under a high-powered microscope, you will see "**life**" in the form of living organisms. "For the life of the flesh is in the blood, KJV Leviticus 17:11." Where there is life, there is growth. Any person, thing, agency, organization, business, or **mind** that is not growing in some capacity **is dying or is dead!**

Yashu'a (Jesus) said: "Thou shalt love the Most High Heavenly Father, thy Sustainer with all thy heart, and with all thy soul, and with all thy mind. Thou shalt love thy neighbour as thyself."

Mind Gardening in the Creative Garden of Will (Your Mind) to Grow a Living Water Mentality!

CHILDREN OF THE MOST HIGH:
PRISTINE YOUTH AND FAMILY SOLUTIONS, LLC.
SONS AND DAUGHTERS OF THE MOST HIGH PUBLISHERS ®

Oh, Gracious Most High Heavenly father, Holy is your name,
Your Will Be Done Now and Forever!

Chapter 1: Is the Creative Garden of Will (Your Mind) Like a Magic Garden?

CHILDREN OF THE MOST HIGH:
PRISTINE YOUTH AND FAMILY SOLUTIONS, LLC.
9X9 TRUE VINE "YASHU'A" (JESUS) B.A.-K.A.-R.E.
SEQUENTIAL ORDER OF LEARNING®

40

Yashu'a (Jesus) said: "Thou shalt love the Most High
Heavenly Father, thy Sustainer with all thy heart, and
with all thy soul, and with all thy mind. Thou shalt love
thy neighbour as thyself."

Mind Gardening in the Creative Garden of Will (Your Mind) to Grow a Living Water Mentality!

CHILDREN OF THE MOST HIGH:
PRISTINE YOUTH AND FAMILY SOLUTIONS, LLC.
SONS AND DAUGHTERS OF THE MOST HIGH PUBLISHERS ®

Oh, Gracious Most High Heavenly father, Holy is your name,
Your Will Be Done Now and Forever!

According to the children of the Most High, is the Creative Garden of Will (Your Mind) like a Magic Garden? Yes. How? Each person plants **mental seeds (thoughts)** in their **Creative Garden of Will (Your Mind) with each thought (mental seed)** that they have. The **Creative Garden of Will (Your Mind) is like a Magic Garden** because any **mental seeds (thoughts)** you plant in the **Creative Garden of Will (Your Mind),** they will grow. If you put **poison mental seeds (negative thoughts)** in it, they will grow. If you put **positive mental seeds (positive thoughts)** in it, they will grow.

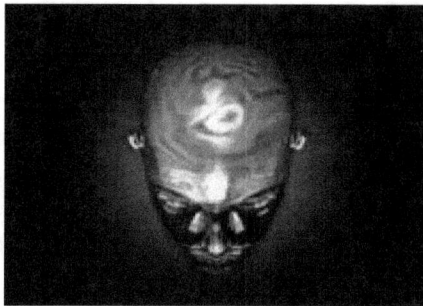

41

Yashu'a (Jesus) said: "Thou shalt love the Most High Heavenly Father, thy Sustainer with all thy heart, and with all thy soul, and with all thy mind. Thou shalt love thy neighbour as thyself."

Mind Gardening in the Creative Garden of Will (Your Mind) to Grow a Living Water Mentality!

CHILDREN OF THE MOST HIGH:
PRISTINE YOUTH AND FAMILY SOLUTIONS, LLC.
SONS AND DAUGHTERS OF THE MOST HIGH PUBLISHERS ®

Oh, Gracious Most High Heavenly father, Holy is your name,
Your Will Be Done Now and Forever!

Each child of the Most High has to willingly decide, out of love for the Most High and love of the Messiah Yashu'a (Jesus); whether or not they will utilize their **Creative Garden of Will (Your Mind)** to do their part in assisting in the process of creating what the Children of the Most High: Pristine Youth and Family Solutions, LLC. refer to as **a global True Vine "Yashu'a" (Jesus) Farm-And-See (which is phonetically pronounced as: Pharm-a-cy) Garden of Love.** As oppose to the present **global Devil's Web Pharmacy Garden of Poison Seeds** (Hughes, 2019).

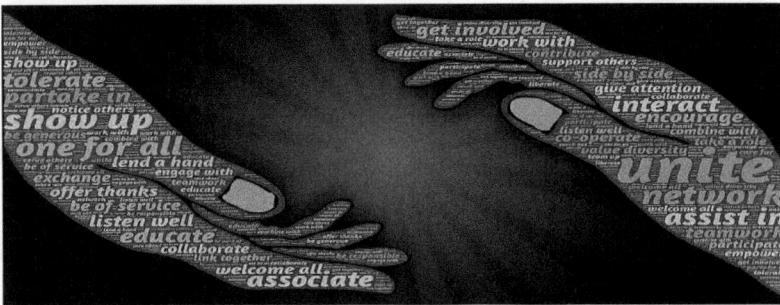

42

Yashu'a (Jesus) said: "Thou shalt love the Most High Heavenly Father, thy Sustainer with all thy heart, and with all thy soul, and with all thy mind. Thou shalt love thy neighbour as thyself."

Mind Gardening in the Creative Garden of Will (Your Mind) to Grow a Living Water Mentality!

CHILDREN OF THE MOST HIGH:
PRISTINE YOUTH AND FAMILY SOLUTIONS, LLC.
SONS AND DAUGHTERS OF THE MOST HIGH PUBLISHERS ®

*Oh, Gracious Most High Heavenly father, Holy is your name,
Your Will Be Done Now and Forever!*

THE DEVIL'S WEB

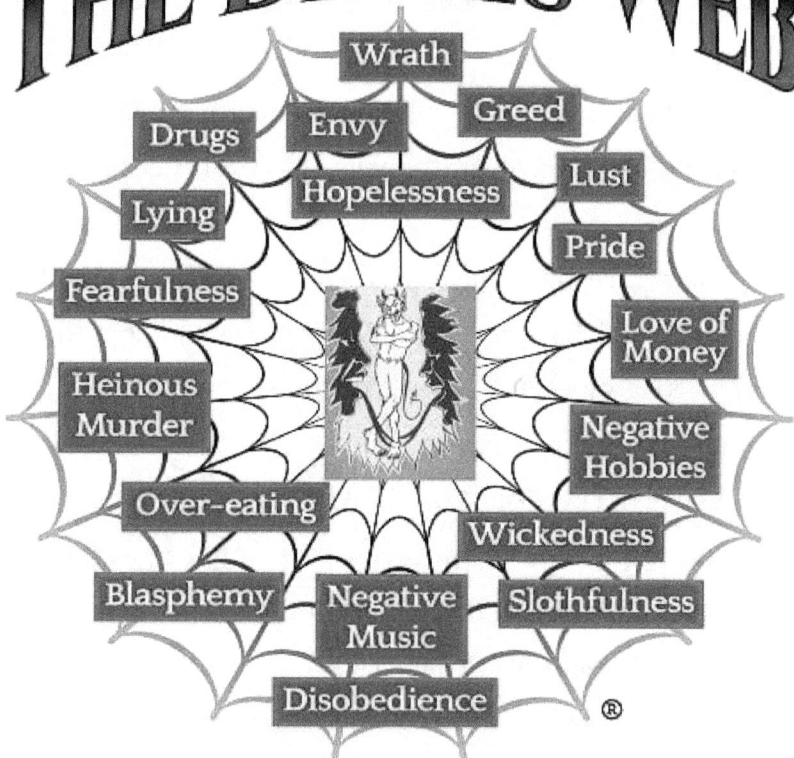

Wrath

Envy Greed

Drugs

Lust

Hopelessness

Lying

Pride

Fearfulness

Love of Money

Heinous Murder

Negative Hobbies

Over-eating

Wickedness

Blasphemy Negative Music Slothfulness

Disobedience ®

43

Yashu'a (Jesus) said: "Thou shalt love the Most High Heavenly Father, thy Sustainer with all thy heart, and with all thy soul, and with all thy mind. Thou shalt love thy neighbour as thyself."

Mind Gardening in the Creative Garden of Will (Your Mind) to Grow a Living Water Mentality!

CHILDREN OF THE MOST HIGH:
PRISTINE YOUTH AND FAMILY SOLUTIONS, LLC.
SONS AND DAUGHTERS OF THE MOST HIGH PUBLISHERS ®

Oh, Gracious Most High Heavenly father, Holy is your name,
Your Will Be Done Now and Forever!

However, the children of the Most High who eat of the True Vine (Yashu'a, Jesus) Fruits of the Spirit; when you "See" them, you see a reflection of the portion of the Most High that is in them working through their "**Spiritual Majesty**" gifts from the Most High to do the will of the Most High so that "Thy Will Be Done on Earth as it is in Heaven!" And those who see them, have a reminder and an opportunity to Glorify the Most High! **The True Vine (Yashu'a, Jesus) <u>Farm-And-See</u> Garden** grows **True Vine (Yashu'a, Jesus) Fruits of the Spirit** that feeds people mentally, spiritually, emotionally and physically. **The True Vine (Yashu'a, Jesus) <u>Farm-And-See</u> (which is phonetically pronounced as: <u>Pharm-a-cy</u>) Garden foundation is** rooted in the "**Will**" of the Most High Heavenly Father. The Messiah Yashu'a (Jesus) proceeded from the Most High Heavenly Father as the "**True Vine**" (Hughes, 2019).

Yashu'a (Jesus) said: "Thou shalt love the Most High Heavenly Father, thy Sustainer with all thy heart, and with all thy soul, and with all thy mind. Thou shalt love thy neighbour as thyself."

Mind Gardening in the Creative Garden of Will (Your Mind) to Grow a Living Water Mentality!

CHILDREN OF THE MOST HIGH:
PRISTINE YOUTH AND FAMILY SOLUTIONS, LLC.
SONS AND DAUGHTERS OF THE MOST HIGH PUBLISHERS ®

Oh, Gracious Most High Heavenly father, Holy is your name,
Your Will Be Done Now and Forever!

In the KJV bible book of John chapter 15 verses 1-12;18-25; Yashu'a (Jesus) said: "I am the true vine, and my Father is the husbandman. Every branch in me that beareth not fruit he "taketh away: and every branch that beareth fruit, he purgeth it, that it may bring forth more fruit. Now ye are clean through the word which I have spoken unto you. Abide in me, and I in you. As the branch cannot bear fruit of itself, except it abide in the vine; no more can ye, except ye abide in me. I am the vine, ye are the branches: He that abideth in me, and I in him, the same bringeth forth much fruit: for without me ye can do nothing. If a man [person] abide not in me, he is cast forth as a branch, and is withered; and men [human beings] gather them, and cast them into the fire, and they are burned."

45

Yashu'a (Jesus) said: "Thou shalt love the Most High Heavenly Father, thy Sustainer with all thy heart, and with all thy soul, and with all thy mind. Thou shalt love thy neighbour as thyself."

Mind Gardening in the Creative Garden of Will (Your Mind) to Grow a Living Water Mentality!

CHILDREN OF THE MOST HIGH:
PRISTINE YOUTH AND FAMILY SOLUTIONS, LLC.
SONS AND DAUGHTERS OF THE MOST HIGH PUBLISHERS ®

*Oh, Gracious Most High Heavenly father, Holy is your name,
Your Will Be Done Now and Forever!*

"If ye abide in me, and my words abide in you, ye shall ask what ye will, and it shall be done unto you. Herein is my Father glorified, that ye bear much fruit; so, shall ye be my disciples. As the Father hath loved me, so have I loved you: continue ye in my love. If ye keep my commandments, ye shall abide in my love; even as I have kept my Father's commandments, and abide in his love. These things have I spoken unto you, that my joy might remain in you, and that your joy might be full. This is my commandment, that ye love one another, as I have loved you. <u>If the world hates you, ye know that it hated me before it hated you. If ye were of the world, the world would love his own: but because ye are not of the world, but I have chosen you out of the world, therefore the world hateth you</u>. Remember the word that I said unto you, the servant is not greater than his lord."

46

Yashu'a (Jesus) said: "Thou shalt love the Most High Heavenly Father, thy Sustainer with all thy heart, and with all thy soul, and with all thy mind. Thou shalt love thy neighbour as thyself."

Mind Gardening in the Creative Garden of Will (Your Mind) to Grow a Living Water Mentality!

CHILDREN OF THE MOST HIGH:
PRISTINE YOUTH AND FAMILY SOLUTIONS, LLC.
SONS AND DAUGHTERS OF THE MOST HIGH PUBLISHERS ®

Oh, Gracious Most High Heavenly father, Holy is your name,
Your Will Be Done Now and Forever!

"If they have persecuted me, they will also persecute you; if they have kept my saying, they will keep yours also. But all these things will they do unto you for my name's sake, because they know not him that sent me. If I had not come and spoken unto them, they had not had sin: but now they have no cloke for their sin. He [a person] that hateth me hateth my Father also. If I had not done among them the works which none other man did, they had not had sin: but now have they both seen and hated both me and my Father. <u>But this cometh to pass, that the word might be fulfilled that is written in their law, they hated me without a cause.</u>" So, according to the **predominate mental seeds (thoughts)** that are sown in the **Creative Garden of Will (Your Mind)**, those **mental seeds (thoughts)** will determine if you are growing a **Magic Garden** that will yield harvests of the **Kingdom of God** inside of you, or if you will yield harvests of the **Kingdom of the Devil** inside of you.

47

Yashu'a (Jesus) said: "Thou shalt love the Most High Heavenly Father, thy Sustainer with all thy heart, and with all thy soul, and with all thy mind. Thou shalt love thy neighbour as thyself."

Mind Gardening in the Creative Garden of Will (Your Mind) to Grow a Living Water Mentality!

CHILDREN OF THE MOST HIGH:
PRISTINE YOUTH AND FAMILY SOLUTIONS, LLC.
SONS AND DAUGHTERS OF THE MOST HIGH PUBLISHERS ®

*Oh, Gracious Most High Heavenly father, Holy is your name,
Your Will Be Done Now and Forever!*

**Chapter 2: Know Thyself, and Know Whether You Value
"Mine" or the "Christ Mind" More?**

CHILDREN OF THE MOST HIGH:
PRISTINE YOUTH AND FAMILY SOLUTIONS, LLC.
SONS AND DAUGHTERS OF THE MOST HIGH PUBLISHERS ®

According to your most dominant and most frequent thoughts, who are you? What type of being are you by nature? What is the content of you character? Are you a legend in your own mind? Are you a victim of your own vanity? What does the phrase **"that thou art"** mean to you from a non-physical point of view, by the content of your character?

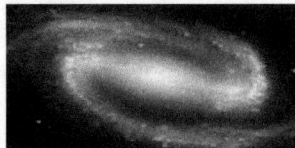

48

Yashu'a (Jesus) said: "Thou shalt love the Most High Heavenly Father, thy Sustainer with all thy heart, and with all thy soul, and with all thy mind. Thou shalt love thy neighbour as thyself."

Mind Gardening in the Creative Garden of Will (Your Mind) to Grow a Living Water Mentality!

CHILDREN OF THE MOST HIGH:
PRISTINE YOUTH AND FAMILY SOLUTIONS, LLC.
SONS AND DAUGHTERS OF THE MOST HIGH PUBLISHERS ®

Oh, Gracious Most High Heavenly father, Holy is your name,
Your Will Be Done Now and Forever!

According to the KJV bible, what are human beings? The KJV bible book of **Genesis chapter 2 verse 7** answers that question; it states: "And **the Lord God formed man of the dust of the ground, and breathed into his nostrils the breath of life; and man became a living soul**." **How**? the connection occurred when the **Yehovah (LORD) Elohiym (God)** breathed the **Khay** or **Hayy (Neshamaw Khayyeem** נשמה חיים - Divine Breath of Life) into the nostrils of אָדָם **'Adam** (the **KJV bible Hebrew Strong's Concordance#120** word **"Adam"** <u>means a</u>

Yashu'a (Jesus) said: "Thou shalt love the Most High Heavenly Father, thy Sustainer with all thy heart, and with all thy soul, and with all thy mind. Thou shalt love thy neighbour as thyself."

Mind Gardening in the Creative Garden of Will (Your Mind) to Grow a Living Water Mentality!

CHILDREN OF THE MOST HIGH:
PRISTINE YOUTH AND FAMILY SOLUTIONS, LLC.
SONS AND DAUGHTERS OF THE MOST HIGH PUBLISHERS ®

Oh, Gracious Most High Heavenly father, Holy is your name,
Your Will Be Done Now and Forever!

"**Human being**) and Adam became a **Nephesh Khay** which in the Aramic (Hebrew) language, **Nephesh** is "**Spirit**" and **Rooahk** or **Ruwach** "**Soul**". Why are the words **spirit** and **soul so confusing to differentiate in the English language?** The words **spirit** and **soul are confusing to differentiate in the English language** because the words **Nephesh** is "**Spirit**" and **Rooahk** or **Ruwah** "**Soul**" and **mind** are sometimes interchangeably translated in English as the same words.

50

Yashu'a (Jesus) said: "Thou shalt love the Most High Heavenly Father, thy Sustainer with all thy heart, and with all thy soul, and with all thy mind. Thou shalt love thy neighbour as thyself."

Mind Gardening in the Creative Garden of Will (Your Mind) to Grow a Living Water Mentality!

CHILDREN OF THE MOST HIGH:
PRISTINE YOUTH AND FAMILY SOLUTIONS, LLC.
SONS AND DAUGHTERS OF THE MOST HIGH PUBLISHERS ®

Oh, Gracious Most High Heavenly father, Holy is your name, Your Will Be Done Now and Forever!

For example: in the KJV bible book of Genesis chapter 1:1, the Aramic (Hebrew) language word **Rooahk** or **Ruwah** "Soul" is translated in English as "spirit" and in Genesis (KJV) chapter 2:7, the Aramaic (Hebrew) language word **Nephesh** which is "**Spirit**" is translated in English as "**Soul**".

Genesis (KJV) Chapter 1:1

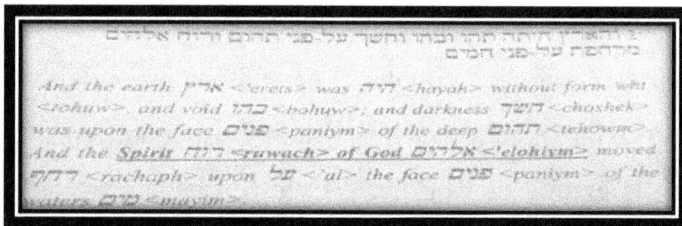

And the earth אָרֶץ <'erets> was הָיָה <hayah> without form and <tohuw>, and void בֹּהוּ <bohuw>; and darkness חֹשֶׁךְ <choshek> was upon the face פָּנִים <paniym> of the deep תְּהוֹם <tehowm> And the _Spirit_ רוּחַ <ruwach> of God אֱלֹהִים <'elohiym> moved רָחַף <rachaph> upon עַל <'al> the face פָּנִים <paniym> of the waters מַיִם <mayim>

Genesis (KJV) 2:7

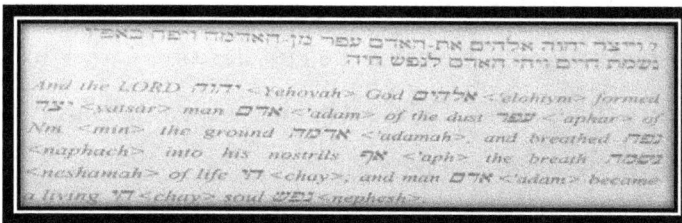

And the LORD יְהֹוָה <Yehovah> God אֱלֹהִים <'elohiym> formed יָצַר <yatsar> man אָדָם <'adam> of the dust עָפָר <aphar> of Nm. מִן <min> the ground אֲדָמָה <'adamah>, and breathed נָפַח <naphach> into his nostrils אַף <'aph> the breath נְשָׁמָה <neshamah> of life חַי <chay>; and man אָדָם <'adam> became a living חַי <chay> soul נֶפֶשׁ <nephesh>

Yashu'a (Jesus) said: "Thou shalt love the Most High Heavenly Father, thy Sustainer with all thy heart, and with all thy soul, and with all thy mind. Thou shalt love thy neighbour as thyself."

Mind Gardening in the Creative Garden of Will (Your Mind) to Grow a Living Water Mentality!

CHILDREN OF THE MOST HIGH:
PRISTINE YOUTH AND FAMILY SOLUTIONS, LLC.
SONS AND DAUGHTERS OF THE MOST HIGH PUBLISHERS ®

Oh, Gracious Most High Heavenly father, Holy is your name,
Your Will Be Done Now and Forever!

Are you a celestial being or a terrestrial being? What is the difference between celestial beings and terrestrial beings?

According to the Online American Heritage Dictionary (2020), the word "**Celestial**" comes from the Old Latin word "Caelum" meaning "Heaven" or that which relates to the heavens, and heaven is an Anglo-Saxon word, meaning "the region or expanse which surrounds the Planet Earth" and is ethereal, immortal, angelic, divine, or divination. The word "**Terrestrial**" is that which is within Earth's atmosphere, that which is earthly or worldly." **Celestial** beings are driven to think, do and feel from that which is divine, and those who are children of the Most High, define success as: "**the Most High's will being done**!" Celestial beings are not drawn to what society defines as fun, Celestial beings' idea of fun, is doing the "**Will**" of the Most High."

52

Yashu'a (Jesus) said: "Thou shalt love the Most High Heavenly Father, thy Sustainer with all thy heart, and with all thy soul, and with all thy mind. Thou shalt love thy neighbour as thyself."

Mind Gardening in the Creative Garden of Will (Your Mind) to Grow a Living Water Mentality!

CHILDREN OF THE MOST HIGH:
PRISTINE YOUTH AND FAMILY SOLUTIONS, LLC.
SONS AND DAUGHTERS OF THE MOST HIGH PUBLISHERS ®

Oh, Gracious Most High Heavenly father, Holy is your name, Your Will Be Done Now and Forever!

"**Terrestrial** beings are driven to think, do and feel from that which society defines as: power, money, lusts, intoxication, and fun as recreation (**re-creation** of that which **wrecks-creation**; and over time causes damage to your body, mind, and spirit and can lead to the destruction of your body that God (אֱלֹהִים 'Elohiym) **created**. After reading the aforementioned; according to your most dominant and most frequent thoughts, who are you? What type of being are you by nature? What is the content of you character?

What does the words **mine** and **mind** mean? According to Online American Heritage Dictionary (2020), **mine** is defined as: "**Used to indicate the one or ones belonging to me.**" **Mind** is defined as: "**Individual consciousness, memory, or recollection.**" <u>**Mine**</u> refers to the "**I**" principle that grows the "**I want** <u>to be seen</u> or <u>in-the-vis-u-al</u> (<u>in-di-vid-u-al</u>).

53

Yashu'a (Jesus) said: "Thou shalt love the Most High Heavenly Father, thy Sustainer with all thy heart, and with all thy soul, and with all thy mind. Thou shalt love thy neighbour as thyself."

Mind Gardening in the Creative Garden of Will (Your Mind) to Grow a Living Water Mentality!

CHILDREN OF THE MOST HIGH:
PRISTINE YOUTH AND FAMILY SOLUTIONS, LLC.
SONS AND DAUGHTERS OF THE MOST HIGH PUBLISHERS ®

Oh, Gracious Most High Heavenly father, Holy is your name,
Your Will Be Done Now and Forever!

<u>Mine</u> is also in reference to "**Individuality**." **Universal Love** is against **I**ndividuality, which is why the word "**Universe**" consists of the two syllables of "**Uni**" (**One**) **Verse** (**Against**) or "**ALL**" or "**The ALL**" is against "**I**ndividuality." "**Pride**", and the **Me**, **Myself** and **I Trinity** are the children of the "**EGO**, the KJV bible Greek Strong's Concordance#**1473** word: ἐγώ **egō** which means: **I, me, my**; a primary pronoun of the first person **I**" and are the greatest barriers to experiencing the Most High Heavenly Father through obedience to the "**Will**" and "**Commandments**" of the Most High. So, what did the Messiah Yashu'a (Jesus) mean when he said: "love the Most High Heavenly father with all of our mind and all of our heart?"

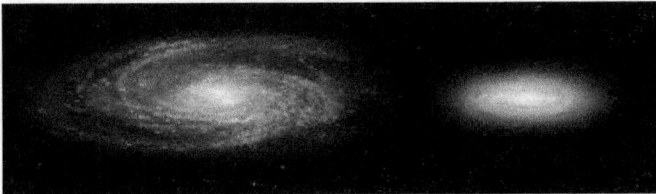

54

Yashu'a (Jesus) said: "Thou shalt love the Most High Heavenly Father, thy Sustainer with all thy heart, and with all thy soul, and with all thy mind. Thou shalt love thy neighbour as thyself."

Mind Gardening in the Creative Garden of Will (Your Mind) to Grow a Living Water Mentality!

CHILDREN OF THE MOST HIGH:
PRISTINE YOUTH AND FAMILY SOLUTIONS, LLC.
SONS AND DAUGHTERS OF THE MOST HIGH PUBLISHERS ®

Oh, Gracious Most High Heavenly father, Holy is your name,
Your Will Be Done Now and Forever!

According to the KJV bible book of Matthew chapter 22 verse 36; it states: "Master, which is the great commandment in the law? the Messiah Yashu'a (Jesus) said: "Thou shalt love the Lord thy God with all thy <u>heart</u>, and with all thy soul, and with all thy <u>mind</u>, KJV Matthew 22:37." According to the **KJV bible Greek Strong's Concordance "#2588, καρδία Kardia** is the word for "**heart**". **Kardia** means: that organ in the body of a human or animal which is the center of the circulation of the blood, and hence was regarded as the seat of physical life denotes the **center of all physical and spiritual life**. The KJV bible Greek Strong's Concordance #1271, **διάνοια Dianoia** is the word for "**mind**". **Dianoia** means: faculty of understanding, thinking and thoughts." According to the KJV bible book of Isaiah chapter 26 verse 3; it states with Aramic (Hebrew) excerpts: **26:3 יֵצֶר סָמוּךְ תִּצֹּר שָׁלוֹם שָׁלוֹם כִּי בְךָ בָּטוּחַ:**

Yashu'a (Jesus) said: "Thou shalt love the Most High Heavenly Father, thy Sustainer with all thy heart, and with all thy soul, and with all thy mind. Thou shalt love thy neighbour as thyself."

Mind Gardening in the Creative Garden of Will (Your Mind) to Grow a Living Water Mentality!

CHILDREN OF THE MOST HIGH: PRISTINE YOUTH AND FAMILY SOLUTIONS, LLC. SONS AND DAUGHTERS OF THE MOST HIGH PUBLISHERS ®

Oh, Gracious Most High Heavenly father, Holy is your name, Your Will Be Done Now and Forever!

"Thou wilt keep him in perfect peace, **whose mind** is stayed on thee: because he trusteth in thee." According to the **KJV bible Hebrew Strong's Concordance #3336**, is יֵצֶר **Yetser** for the phrase "**whose mind**." יֵצֶר **Yetser** means: form, framing, purpose, framework, thing framed, imagination, mind, work: framed purpose, imagination, device (intellectual framework)." According to the KJV bible book of 1st Corinthians chapter 2 verse 16; it states: "For who hath known **the mind** of the Lord, that he may instruct him? But we have **the mind** of Christ."

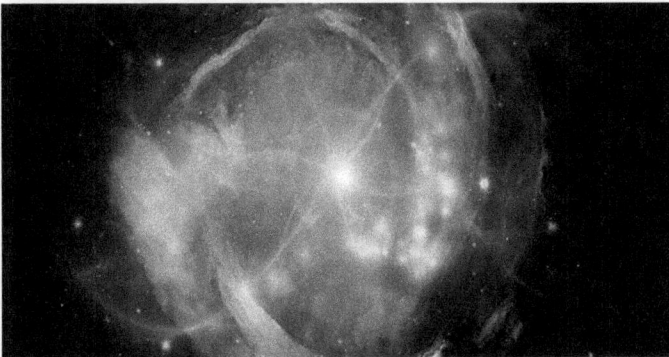

56

Yashu'a (Jesus) said: "Thou shalt love the Most High Heavenly Father, thy Sustainer with all thy heart, and with all thy soul, and with all thy mind. Thou shalt love thy neighbour as thyself."

Mind Gardening in the Creative Garden of Will (Your Mind) to Grow a Living Water Mentality!

CHILDREN OF THE MOST HIGH:
PRISTINE YOUTH AND FAMILY SOLUTIONS, LLC.
SONS AND DAUGHTERS OF THE MOST HIGH PUBLISHERS ®

*Oh, Gracious Most High Heavenly father, Holy is your name,
Your Will Be Done Now and Forever!*

The **KJV bible Greek Strong's Concordance#3563**, is νοῦς **Nous** for the phrase "**the mind**." νοῦς **Nous**, means: the mind, comprising alike the faculties of perceiving and understanding and those of feeling, judging, determining the intellectual faculty, the understanding reason in the narrower sense, as the capacity for spiritual truth, the higher powers of the soul, the faculty of perceiving divine things, of recognizing goodness and of hating evil the power of considering and judging soberly, calmly and impartially a particular mode of thinking and judging, thoughts, feelings, purposes, desires; the intellect, mind (divine thought, or will)." A person speaks as a reflection of how he or she thinks. So, the "**Christ Mind**" is reflected in the words of the Messiah Yashu'a (Jesus) when he said: "Thou shalt love the Lord thy God with all thy <u>heart</u>, and with all thy soul, and with all thy <u>mind</u>."

57

Yashu'a (Jesus) said: "Thou shalt love the Most High Heavenly Father, thy Sustainer with all thy heart, and with all thy soul, and with all thy mind. Thou shalt love thy neighbour as thyself."

Mind Gardening in the Creative Garden of Will (Your Mind) to Grow a Living Water Mentality!

CHILDREN OF THE MOST HIGH:
PRISTINE YOUTH AND FAMILY SOLUTIONS, LLC.
SONS AND DAUGHTERS OF THE MOST HIGH PUBLISHERS ®

*Oh, Gracious Most High Heavenly father, Holy is your name,
Your Will Be Done Now and Forever!*

The mind and the heart have to be as one in **active divine love** for the Most High Heavenly Father only! This occurs with each heartbeat, each breath, and when a person most frequent, moment to moment intentional thinking, mental focus, predominate thoughts, and heart divine love are only focused on the Most High Heavenly Father, the Creator of All of the boundless universes! Therefore, each child of the Most High has an opportunity to get to **"Know Thyself"** and will inevitably have to choose between, whether he or she values **"Mine"** or the **"Christ Mind"** more if he or she seeks to grow a **Living Water Mentality** - **M.I.N.D.** which will be expounded on in chapter 19. **M.I.N.D** are the acronyms for: Making, Intentional, Noble, Decisions!

Yashu'a (Jesus) said: "Thou shalt love the Most High Heavenly Father, thy Sustainer with all thy heart, and with all thy soul, and with all thy mind. Thou shalt love thy neighbour as thyself."

Mind Gardening in the Creative Garden of Will (Your Mind) to Grow a Living Water Mentality!

CHILDREN OF THE MOST HIGH:
PRISTINE YOUTH AND FAMILY SOLUTIONS, LLC.
SONS AND DAUGHTERS OF THE MOST HIGH PUBLISHERS ®

Oh, Gracious Most High Heavenly father, Holy is your name,
Your Will Be Done Now and Forever!

Chapter 3: The Mind and the Brain are not the Same Thing!

What is the difference between the brain and the mind?

59

Yashu'a (Jesus) said: "Thou shalt love the Most High Heavenly Father, thy Sustainer with all thy heart, and with all thy soul, and with all thy mind. Thou shalt love thy neighbour as thyself."

CHILDREN OF THE MOST HIGH:
PRISTINE YOUTH AND FAMILY SOLUTIONS, LLC.
SONS AND DAUGHTERS OF THE MOST HIGH PUBLISHERS ®

Oh, Gracious Most High Heavenly father, Holy is your name,
Your Will Be Done Now and Forever!

The Human Brain

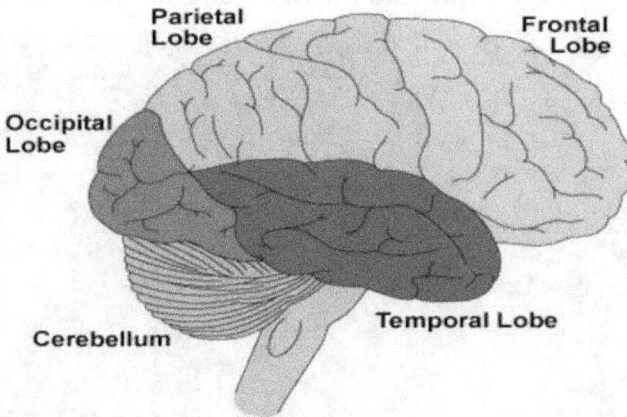

According to the Online American Heritage Dictionary (2020), the **brain** is defined as: "the portion of the vertebrate central nervous system that is enclosed within the cranium, continuous with the spinal cord, and composed of gray matter and white matter. It is the primary center for the regulation and control of bodily activities, receiving and interpreting sensory impulses, and transmitting information to the muscles and body organs."

Yashu'a (Jesus) said: "Thou shalt love the Most High Heavenly Father, thy Sustainer with all thy heart, and with all thy soul, and with all thy mind. Thou shalt love thy neighbour as thyself."

Mind Gardening in the Creative Garden of Will (Your Mind) to Grow a Living Water Mentality!

CHILDREN OF THE MOST HIGH:
PRISTINE YOUTH AND FAMILY SOLUTIONS, LLC.
SONS AND DAUGHTERS OF THE MOST HIGH PUBLISHERS ®

Oh, Gracious Most High Heavenly father, Holy is your name,
Your Will Be Done Now and Forever!

"It is also the seat of consciousness, thought, memory, and emotion. b. A functionally similar portion of the invertebrate nervous system." According to the National Institute of Health (2020), the brain is: "The brain is the most complex part of the human body. This three-pound organ is the seat of intelligence, interpreter of the senses, initiator of body movement, and controller of behavior. Lying in its bony shell and washed by protective fluid, the brain is the source of all the qualities that define our humanity. The brain is the crown jewel of the human body. The brain is like a committee of experts. All the parts of the brain work together, but each part has its own special properties. The brain can be divided into three basic units: the forebrain, the midbrain, and the hindbrain. The hindbrain includes the upper part of the spinal cord, the brain stem, and a wrinkled ball of tissue called the cerebellum (National Institute of Health, 2020)."

Yashu'a (Jesus) said: "Thou shalt love the Most High Heavenly Father, thy Sustainer with all thy heart, and with all thy soul, and with all thy mind. Thou shalt love thy neighbour as thyself."

Mind Gardening in the Creative Garden of Will (Your Mind) to Grow a Living Water Mentality!

CHILDREN OF THE MOST HIGH:
PRISTINE YOUTH AND FAMILY SOLUTIONS, LLC.
SONS AND DAUGHTERS OF THE MOST HIGH PUBLISHERS ®

*Oh, Gracious Most High Heavenly father, Holy is your name,
Your Will Be Done Now and Forever!*

According to the Online American Heritage Dictionary (2020), the **mind** is defined as: "Individual consciousness, memory, or recollection." In the KJV bible book of Romans chapter 8 verse 5; it states: "For they that are after the flesh do **mind** the things of the flesh; but they that are after the Spirit the things of the Spirit." In this verse, the KJV bible Greek Strong's Concordance "**#5426 φρονέω Phroneō (Fro-ne'-o)** for the word **mind**. φρονέω Phroneō means: **think**, regard, **mind**, be minded, **be of the same mind**, be like minded, to have understanding, **be wise**, to feel, to think, to have an opinion of one's self, think of one's self, **to be modest, not let one's opinion (though just) of himself or herself exceed the bounds of modesty, minds agreed together, cherish the same views, be harmonious, to direct one's mind to a thing, to seek, to strive for.**"

62

Yashu'a (Jesus) said: "Thou shalt love the Most High Heavenly Father, thy Sustainer with all thy heart, and with all thy soul, and with all thy mind. Thou shalt love thy neighbour as thyself."

Mind Gardening in the Creative Garden of Will (Your Mind) to Grow a Living Water Mentality!

CHILDREN OF THE MOST HIGH:
PRISTINE YOUTH AND FAMILY SOLUTIONS, LLC.
SONS AND DAUGHTERS OF THE MOST HIGH PUBLISHERS ®

*Oh, Gracious Most High Heavenly father, Holy is your name,
Your Will Be Done Now and Forever!*

In the KJV bible book of Romans chapter 8 verse 6; it states: "For to be **carnally minded** is **death**; but to be **spiritually minded** is **life and peace**." In this verse, the KJV bible Greek Strong's Concordance "**#5427 φρόνημα Phronēma (Fro'-na-mä**) for the word **minded. φρόνημα Phronēma means what one has in the mind, the thoughts and purposes, (mental) inclination or purpose: — (be, + be carnally, + be spiritually minded**." In the KJV bible book of Romans chapter 8 verse 7; it states: "Because the carnal **mind (φρόνημα Phronēma (Fro'-na-mä - what one has in the mind, the thoughts and purposes, (mental) inclination or purpose: — (be, + be carnally, + be spiritually minded)** is enmity against God: for it is not subject to the law of God, neither indeed can be."

63

Yashu'a (Jesus) said: "Thou shalt love the Most High Heavenly Father, thy Sustainer with all thy heart, and with all thy soul, and with all thy mind. Thou shalt love thy neighbour as thyself."

Mind Gardening in the Creative Garden of Will (Your Mind) to Grow a Living Water Mentality!

CHILDREN OF THE MOST HIGH:
PRISTINE YOUTH AND FAMILY SOLUTIONS, LLC.
SONS AND DAUGHTERS OF THE MOST HIGH PUBLISHERS ®

Oh, Gracious Most High Heavenly father, Holy is your name,
Your Will Be Done Now and Forever!

According to Neuroscientist, Dr. Newberg's research "The moment we encounter God, or the idea of God, our brain begins to change, p. 41). In the KJV bible book of 1st Corinthians chapter 2 verse 16; it states: "For who hath known **the mind** of the Lord, that he may instruct him? But we have **the mind of Christ**."

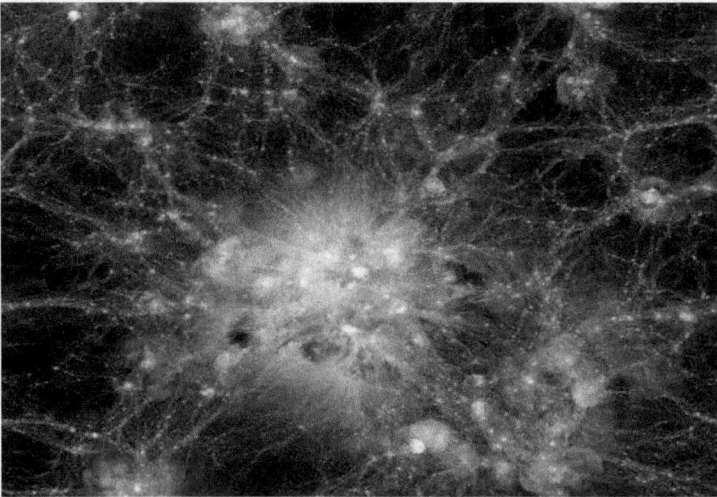

64

Yashu'a (Jesus) said: "Thou shalt love the Most High Heavenly Father, thy Sustainer with all thy heart, and with all thy soul, and with all thy mind. Thou shalt love thy neighbour as thyself."

Mind Gardening in the Creative Garden of Will (Your Mind) to Grow a Living Water Mentality!

CHILDREN OF THE MOST HIGH:
PRISTINE YOUTH AND FAMILY SOLUTIONS, LLC.
SONS AND DAUGHTERS OF THE MOST HIGH PUBLISHERS ®

Oh, Gracious Most High Heavenly father, Holy is your name,
Your Will Be Done Now and Forever!

The **KJV bible Greek Strong's Concordance#3563**, is νοῦς **Nous** for the phrase "**the mind**." νοῦς **Nous**, means: **the mind**, comprising alike the faculties of perceiving and understanding and those of feeling, judging, **determining the intellectual faculty**, the understanding reason in the narrower sense, as the **capacity for spiritual truth, the higher powers of the soul, the faculty of perceiving divine things**, of recognizing goodness and of hating evil the power of considering and judging soberly, **calmly** and impartially a particular mode of thinking and judging, thoughts, feelings, purposes, desires; the intellect, mind (**divine thought, or will**)." Therefore; the mind must be controlled in order to achieve union with the Most High Heavenly Father through the Messiah Yashu'a (Jesus).

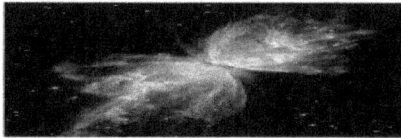

65

Yashu'a (Jesus) said: "Thou shalt love the Most High Heavenly Father, thy Sustainer with all thy heart, and with all thy soul, and with all thy mind. Thou shalt love thy neighbour as thyself."

Mind Gardening in the Creative Garden of Will (Your Mind) to Grow a Living Water Mentality!

CHILDREN OF THE MOST HIGH:
PRISTINE YOUTH AND FAMILY SOLUTIONS, LLC.
SONS AND DAUGHTERS OF THE MOST HIGH PUBLISHERS ®

Oh, Gracious Most High Heavenly father, Holy is your name, Your Will Be Done Now and Forever!

The Messiah Yashu'a (Jesus) said: "I am the way, the truth, and the life: no man cometh unto the Father, but by me, KJV bible John 14:6." **Thoughts initiate all actions**; **all actions and reactions occur in the mind as thought waves or an influx of thoughts**. All physical things that are made, are a reflection of thoughts. **For example**: a car. In order to make or build a car, a person or people have to have the image of a car in their mind first before it can be made or built physically. In the KJV bible book of Matthew chapter 6 verses 21-23; the Messiah Yashu'a (Jesus) said: "For where your treasure is, there will your heart be also. The light of the body is the eye: if therefore thine eye be single; thy whole body shall be full of light. But if thine eye be evil; thy whole body shall be full of darkness. If therefore the light that is in thee be darkness, how great is that darkness!" Therefore; **the brain** is the **physical organ** that **works in collaboration** with each person's individual **non-physical consciousness** known as **the mind** (νοῦς Nous).

66

Yashu'a (Jesus) said: "Thou shalt love the Most High Heavenly Father, thy Sustainer with all thy heart, and with all thy soul, and with all thy mind. Thou shalt love thy neighbour as thyself."

Mind Gardening in the Creative Garden of Will (Your Mind) to Grow a Living Water Mentality!

CHILDREN OF THE MOST HIGH:
PRISTINE YOUTH AND FAMILY SOLUTIONS, LLC.
SONS AND DAUGHTERS OF THE MOST HIGH PUBLISHERS ®

*Oh, Gracious Most High Heavenly father, Holy is your name,
Your Will Be Done Now and Forever!*

Chapter 4: The Most High Heavenly Father Created the Brain, So Don't Let the Devil Poison Your Heart and Mind with Feelings and Thoughts of Denial, Shame and Blame!

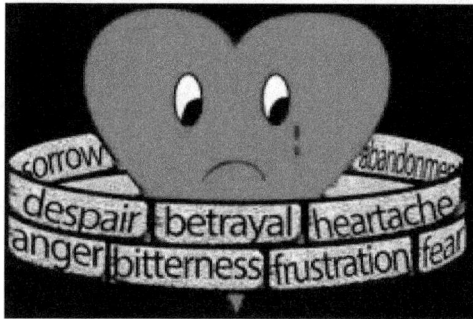

67

Yashu'a (Jesus) said: "Thou shalt love the Most High Heavenly Father, thy Sustainer with all thy heart, and with all thy soul, and with all thy mind. Thou shalt love thy neighbour as thyself."

Mind Gardening in the Creative Garden of Will (Your Mind) to Grow a Living Water Mentality!

CHILDREN OF THE MOST HIGH:
PRISTINE YOUTH AND FAMILY SOLUTIONS, LLC.
SONS AND DAUGHTERS OF THE MOST HIGH PUBLISHERS ®

*Oh, Gracious Most High Heavenly father, Holy is your name,
Your Will Be Done Now and Forever!*

In the previous chapter, we discussed and defined the **mind** and the **brain**; and explained how they are not the **same thing**. In this chapter, we will define: **thoughts**, and discuss **denial**, **shame** and **blame** from a biblical perspective. We will also explain why that matters to the children of the Most High as it relates to **not allowing the Devil to Poison our Hearts and Minds with Feelings and Thoughts of Denial, Shame and Blame!**

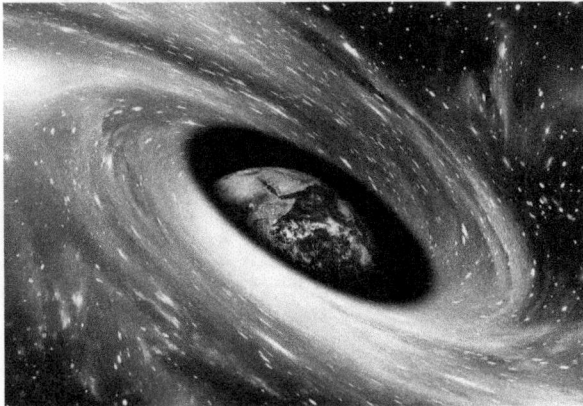

68

Yashu'a (Jesus) said: "Thou shalt love the Most High Heavenly Father, thy Sustainer with all thy heart, and with all thy soul, and with all thy mind. Thou shalt love thy neighbour as thyself."

Mind Gardening in the Creative Garden of Will (Your Mind) to Grow a Living Water Mentality!

CHILDREN OF THE MOST HIGH:
PRISTINE YOUTH AND FAMILY SOLUTIONS, LLC.
SONS AND DAUGHTERS OF THE MOST HIGH PUBLISHERS ®

Oh, Gracious Most High Heavenly father, Holy is your name,
Your Will Be Done Now and Forever!

In the KJV bible book of Genesis chapter 3 verses 1-15; it states: "**Now the serpent** was more subtil than any beast of the field **which the LORD God had made.** And he said unto the woman, **Yea, hath God said, Ye shall not eat of every tree of the garden**? (<u>the serpent is planting the seed</u> (<u>thought</u>) <u>in Eve's mind</u>) And the woman said unto the serpent, We may eat of the fruit of the trees of the garden: But of the fruit of the tree which is in the midst of the garden, God hath said, Ye shall not eat of it, neither shall ye touch it, lest ye die. And the serpent said unto the woman, Ye shall not surely die: For God doth know that in the day ye eat thereof, then your eyes shall be opened, and ye shall be as gods, knowing good and evil."

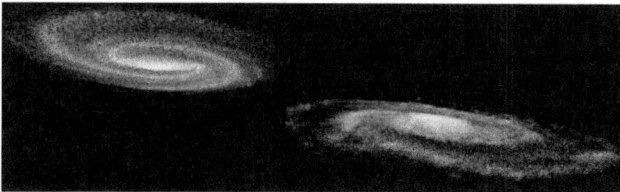

69

Yashu'a (Jesus) said: "Thou shalt love the Most High Heavenly Father, thy Sustainer with all thy heart, and with all thy soul, and with all thy mind. Thou shalt love thy neighbour as thyself."

Mind Gardening in the Creative Garden of Will (Your Mind) to Grow a Living Water Mentality!

CHILDREN OF THE MOST HIGH:
PRISTINE YOUTH AND FAMILY SOLUTIONS, LLC.
SONS AND DAUGHTERS OF THE MOST HIGH PUBLISHERS ®

*Oh, Gracious Most High Heavenly father, Holy is your name,
Your Will Be Done Now and Forever!*

"And when the woman saw that the tree was **good for food (Eating for pleasure, and not for sustaining the body. This can lead to gluttony which is a form of greed, that can become a negative habit**), and that it was **pleasant to the eyes (the serpent introduced Eve to desire through beauty**), and a tree to be **desired to make one wise (the serpent introduced Eve to desire for knowledge to be able to do what you want to do when you want to do it**), she took of the fruit thereof, and did eat, and gave also unto her husband with her; and he did eat (**Denial means: a refusal to comply with or satisfy a request**). And the eyes of them both were opened, and they knew that they were naked; and they sewed fig leaves together, and made themselves aprons."

70

Yashu'a (Jesus) said: "Thou shalt love the Most High Heavenly Father, thy Sustainer with all thy heart, and with all thy soul, and with all thy mind. Thou shalt love thy neighbour as thyself."

Mind Gardening in the Creative Garden of Will (Your Mind) to Grow a Living Water Mentality!

CHILDREN OF THE MOST HIGH:
PRISTINE YOUTH AND FAMILY SOLUTIONS, LLC.
SONS AND DAUGHTERS OF THE MOST HIGH PUBLISHERS ®

Oh, Gracious Most High Heavenly father, Holy is your name,
Your Will Be Done Now and Forever!

"And they heard the voice of the LORD God walking in the garden in the cool of the day: and **Adam and his wife hid themselves (this was an example of ignoring the confirmed facts or ignorance in action. To hide from God in God's garden, was not the smartest decision)** from the presence of the LORD God amongst the trees of the garden. And the LORD God called unto Adam, and said unto him, Where art thou? And he said, I heard thy voice in the garden, and **I was afraid, because I was naked; and I hid myself (Shame means: A painful emotion caused by the belief that one is, or is perceived by others to be, inferior or unworthy of affection or respect because of one's actions, thoughts, circumstances, or experiences)."**

71

Yashu'a (Jesus) said: "Thou shalt love the Most High Heavenly Father, thy Sustainer with all thy heart, and with all thy soul, and with all thy mind. Thou shalt love thy neighbour as thyself."

Mind Gardening in the Creative Garden of Will (Your Mind) to Grow a Living Water Mentality!

CHILDREN OF THE MOST HIGH:
PRISTINE YOUTH AND FAMILY SOLUTIONS, LLC.
SONS AND DAUGHTERS OF THE MOST HIGH PUBLISHERS ®

*Oh, Gracious Most High Heavenly father, Holy is your name,
Your Will Be Done Now and Forever!*

"And he said, who told thee that thou wast naked? Hast thou eaten of the tree, whereof I commanded thee that thou shouldest not eat? And the man said, **the woman whom thou gavest to be with me (<u>Blame</u> means: to place responsibility for something)**, she gave me of the tree, and I did eat. "And the LORD God said unto the woman, what is this that thou hast done? And the woman said, the serpent beguiled me (**<u>Blame</u> means: to place responsibility for something**), and I did eat. And the LORD God said unto the serpent, because thou hast done this, thou art cursed above all cattle, and above every beast of the field; upon thy belly shalt thou go, and dust shalt thou eat all the days of thy life. And I will put enmity between thee and the woman, and between thy seed and her seed; it shall bruise thy head, and thou shalt bruise his heel."

72

Yashu'a (Jesus) said: "Thou shalt love the Most High Heavenly Father, thy Sustainer with all thy heart, and with all thy soul, and with all thy mind. Thou shalt love thy neighbour as thyself."

Mind Gardening in the Creative Garden of Will (Your Mind) to Grow a Living Water Mentality!

Oh, Gracious Most High Heavenly father, Holy is your name,
Your Will Be Done Now and Forever!

In the KJV bible book of 1st Chronicles, chapter 28, verse 9; it states: "And thou, Solomon my son, **know** thou the **God (אֱלֹהִים 'Elohiym)** of thy father, **and serve** him with a **perfect heart** and **with a willing mind**: for the LORD **searcheth all hearts**, and understandeth all the imaginations of the **thoughts**: if thou seek him, he will be found of thee; but if thou forsake him, he will cast thee off forever. In the KJV bible Hebrew Strong's Concordance "#3054 is יָדַע Yada` for the word "**know**". יָדַע **Yada** means: to know, learn to know, to perceive and see, find out and discern, to know by experience, to have knowledge, be wise, be aware, teach, (can) tell, understand, have (understanding)."

73

Yashu'a (Jesus) said: "Thou shalt love the Most High Heavenly Father, thy Sustainer with all thy heart, and with all thy soul, and with all thy mind. Thou shalt love thy neighbour as thyself."

Mind Gardening in the Creative Garden of Will (Your Mind) to Grow a Living Water Mentality!

*Oh, Gracious Most High Heavenly father, Holy is your name,
Your Will Be Done Now and Forever!*

"The KJV bible Hebrew Strong's Concordance **#5647** is עָבַד `**Abad** for the words "**and serve**". עָבַד `**Abad** means: to work, serve (God). The KJV bible Hebrew Strong's Concordance **#8003** is שָׁלֵם **Shalem** for the words "**him with a perfect**". שָׁלֵם **Shalem** means: complete, safe, peaceful, perfect, whole, full, at peace, peace (of covenant of **peace, mind**). The KJV bible Hebrew Strong's Concordance "**#3820** is לֵב **Leb** for the word "**heart**". לֵב **Leb** (**Labe**) means: inner man, **mind, will, heart**, understanding, **inner part**, midst (of things), heart (of a person), soul, heart (of a person), mind, knowledge, **thinking, reflection, memory, inclination**, resolution, **determination (of will), conscience, heart (of moral character), as seat of emotions and passions, as seat of courage**."

Yashu'a (Jesus) said: "Thou shalt love the Most High Heavenly Father, thy Sustainer with all thy heart, and with all thy soul, and with all thy mind. Thou shalt love thy neighbour as thyself."

Mind Gardening in the Creative Garden of Will (Your Mind) to Grow a Living Water Mentality!

*Oh, Gracious Most High Heavenly father, Holy is your name,
Your Will Be Done Now and Forever!*

"The KJV bible Hebrew Strong's Concordance "**#4284** is

מַחֲשָׁבָה **Machashabah** for the words "**of the thoughts**". מַחֲשָׁבָה

Machashabah (Makh-ash-aw-baw') means: thought, device

plan, intentional plan (whether bad, a plot; or good, advice):

cunning (work), curious work, device(-sed), imagination,

invented, purposeful **thought**." Therefore, the aforementioned

verses provide examples of how t**he Most High Heavenly**

Father gave us a brain and the ability to think. The ability

to think is a gift that should not be misused and should not

be under used. The above verses also provide positive reasons

why the children of the Most High should not allow **the devil**

to poison our hearts and minds with feelings and thoughts

of denial, shame and blame!

*Yashu'a (Jesus) said: "Thou shalt love the Most High
Heavenly Father, thy Sustainer with all thy heart, and
with all thy soul, and with all thy mind. Thou shalt love
thy neighbour as thyself."*

Mind Gardening in the Creative Garden of Will (Your Mind) to Grow a Living Water Mentality!

CHILDREN OF THE MOST HIGH:
PRISTINE YOUTH AND FAMILY SOLUTIONS, LLC.
SONS AND DAUGHTERS OF THE MOST HIGH PUBLISHERS ®

Oh, Gracious Most High Heavenly father, Holy is your name, Your Will Be Done Now and Forever!

Chapter 5: Stop Waiting on the Devil to Give You God's Blessings! – Sin Mind Awareness!

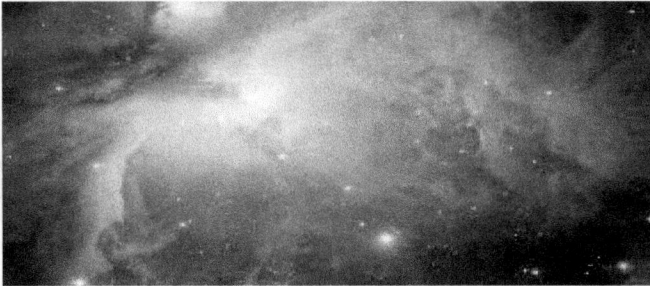

In the KJV bible book of John chapter 14 verses 12-15; the Messiah Yashu'a (Jesus) said: "Verily, verily, I say unto you, He that believeth on me, the works that I do shall he do also; and greater works than these shall he do; because I go unto my Father. And whatsoever ye shall ask in my name, that will I do, that the Father may be glorified in the Son. If ye shall ask any thing in my name, I will do it. If ye love me, keep my commandments."

76

Yashu'a (Jesus) said: "Thou shalt love the Most High Heavenly Father, thy Sustainer with all thy heart, and with all thy soul, and with all thy mind. Thou shalt love thy neighbour as thyself."

Mind Gardening in the Creative Garden of Will (Your Mind) to Grow a Living Water Mentality!

CHILDREN OF THE MOST HIGH:
PRISTINE YOUTH AND FAMILY SOLUTIONS, LLC.
SONS AND DAUGHTERS OF THE MOST HIGH PUBLISHERS ®

*Oh, Gracious Most High Heavenly father, Holy is your name,
Your Will Be Done Now and Forever!*

Therefore, all children of the Most High must **do for self**: physically, mentally, spiritually, emotionally, financially, personally, and professionally **NOW!!! Stop waiting on the devil to give you God's blessings! And Stop intentionally sinning!**

How does the KJV bible define the word "sin?"

According to the KJV bible book of Psalms chapter 51 verse 1-2; it states: "[To the chief Musician, A Psalm of David, when Nathan the prophet came unto him, after he had gone in to Bathsheba.] Have mercy upon me, O God, according to thy lovingkindness: according unto the multitude of thy tender mercies blot out my transgressions. Wash me thoroughly from mine iniquity, and cleanse me from my **sin**."

Yashu'a (Jesus) said: "Thou shalt love the Most High Heavenly Father, thy Sustainer with all thy heart, and with all thy soul, and with all thy mind. Thou shalt love thy neighbour as thyself."

Mind Gardening in the Creative Garden of Will (Your Mind) to Grow a Living Water Mentality!

CHILDREN OF THE MOST HIGH:
PRISTINE YOUTH AND FAMILY SOLUTIONS, LLC.
SONS AND DAUGHTERS OF THE MOST HIGH PUBLISHERS ®

Oh, Gracious Most High Heavenly father, Holy is your name, Your Will Be Done Now and Forever!

The word: *"sin"* "(is the KJV bible Hebrew Strong's Concordance#2403 word: *Chatta'ath* – Pronunciation **Khat·tä·ä'** חַטָּאת occurs **448** times in **389** verses, and Strong's Number 2403 matches the Hebrew חַטָּאת (**Chatta'ath**), which occurs 296 times in 272 verses in the Hebrew concordance in the King James Version of the bible and **means: "an offence (sometimes habitual sinfulness), and its penalty, occasion, sacrifice, or expiation; also (concretely) an offender:— punishment (of sin), purifying(-fication for sin), sin(-ner, offering).**"

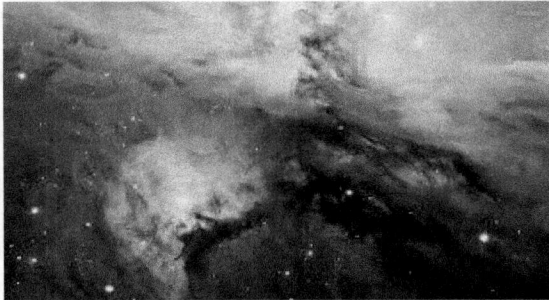

78

Yashu'a (Jesus) said: "Thou shalt love the Most High Heavenly Father, thy Sustainer with all thy heart, and with all thy soul, and with all thy mind. Thou shalt love thy neighbour as thyself."

Mind Gardening in the Creative Garden of Will (Your Mind) to Grow a Living Water Mentality!

CHILDREN OF THE MOST HIGH:
PRISTINE YOUTH AND FAMILY SOLUTIONS, LLC.
SONS AND DAUGHTERS OF THE MOST HIGH PUBLISHERS ®

Oh, Gracious Most High Heavenly father, Holy is your name,
Your Will Be Done Now and Forever!

מַטְאָה —(1) f. of the word מַטָא *a sinner* f., or *sinful*, Am. 9:8.

(2) i. q. מַטָאָה —(a) *sin*, Ex. 34:7.—(b) *penalty of sin* (like מַטָאָה No. 3), Isa. 5:18.

מַטָאָה constr. מַטָאָה plur. מַטָאוֹת f. ["*a miss, misstep, slip with the foot*, Pro. 13:6"].

(1) *sin*, Ex. 28:9; Isa. 6:27, etc. ["Rarely for the habit of sinning, *sinfulness*, Prov. 14:34; Isa. 3:9."] Also applied to that by which any one sins, e.g. idols, Hos. 10:8; Deut. 9:21; comp. 2 Ki. 13:2, *water of sin*, i.e. of expiation or purifying, Num. 8:7.

(2) *a sin offering*, Levit. 6:18, 23; as to its difference from אָשָׁם see that word.

(3) *penalty*, Lam. 3:39; Zec. 14:19; hence *calamity, misfortune*, Isa. 40:2; Prov. 10:16 (opp. to חַיִּים). [Is not this last sense wholly needless? and would not its introduction utterly mar the sense of the passages referred to in support of it?]

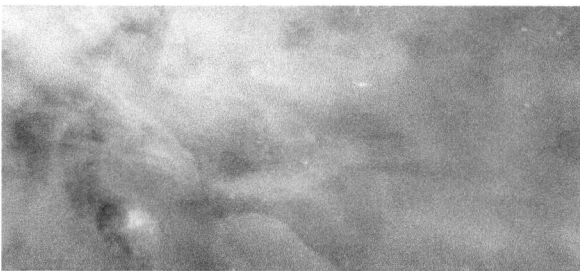

79

Yashu'a (Jesus) said: "Thou shalt love the Most High Heavenly Father, thy Sustainer with all thy heart, and with all thy soul, and with all thy mind. Thou shalt love thy neighbour as thyself."

Mind Gardening in the Creative Garden of Will (Your Mind) to Grow a Living Water Mentality!

CHILDREN OF THE MOST HIGH:
PRISTINE YOUTH AND FAMILY SOLUTIONS, LLC.
SONS AND DAUGHTERS OF THE MOST HIGH PUBLISHERS ®

Oh, Gracious Most High Heavenly father, Holy is your name, Your Will Be Done Now and Forever!

According to the KJV bible book of 1st John chapter 1 verse 9; it states: "If we confess our **sins**, he is faithful and just to forgive us our **sins**, and to cleanse us from all unrighteousness." In the KJV bible book of 1st John chapter 1 verses 9, the word "**sins**" in the "**KJV bible Greek Strong's Concordance #266 word:** ἁμαρτία **hamartia,** which means: to be without a share in, to miss the mark, to err, be mistaken to miss or **wander from the path of uprightness and honor, to do or go wrong, to wander from the law of God, violate God's law, sin that which is done wrong**, sin, an offence, **a violation of the divine law in thought or in act collectively**, the complex or aggregate of sins committed either by a single person or by many."

Yashu'a (Jesus) said: "Thou shalt love the Most High Heavenly Father, thy Sustainer with all thy heart, and with all thy soul, and with all thy mind. Thou shalt love thy neighbour as thyself."

Mind Gardening in the Creative Garden of Will (Your Mind) to Grow a Living Water Mentality!

CHILDREN OF THE MOST HIGH:
PRISTINE YOUTH AND FAMILY SOLUTIONS, LLC.
SONS AND DAUGHTERS OF THE MOST HIGH PUBLISHERS ®

Oh, Gracious Most High Heavenly father, Holy is your name,
Your Will Be Done Now and Forever!

According to the KJV bible book of Genesis chapter 4 verse 7; it states: "If (אִם 'im) thou doest well (יָטַב Yatab) shalt thou not be accepted (שְׂאֵת Sĕ'eth) and if thou doest not well (יָטַב Yatab) sin (חַטָּאת Chatta'ath) lieth (רָבַץ Rabats) at the door (פֶּתַח Pethach) And unto thee shall be his desire (תְּשׁוּקָה Tĕshuwqah) and thou shalt rule (מְשָׁל Mashal) over him." In the KJV bible book of Genesis chapter 4 verse 7, the word "**sin**" in the **KJV bible Hebrew Strong's Concordance #2403 word: חַטָּאת Chatta'ath**, which means: an offence (sometimes habitual sinfulness), sin, sinful, sin offering, condition of sin, guilt of sin, punishment for sin, purification from sins of ceremonial uncleanness, and its penalty, occasion, sacrifice, or expiation; also (concretely) an offender:—punishment (of sin), purifying(-fication for sin), sin(-ner, offering)."

Yashu'a (Jesus) said: "Thou shalt love the Most High Heavenly Father, thy Sustainer with all thy heart, and with all thy soul, and with all thy mind. Thou shalt love thy neighbour as thyself."

Mind Gardening in the Creative Garden of Will (Your Mind) to Grow a Living Water Mentality!

CHILDREN OF THE MOST HIGH:
PRISTINE YOUTH AND FAMILY SOLUTIONS, LLC.
SONS AND DAUGHTERS OF THE MOST HIGH PUBLISHERS ®

Oh, Gracious Most High Heavenly father, Holy is your name,
Your Will Be Done Now and Forever!

In the KJV bible book of Genesis chapter 4 verse 5 with Hebrew inserts; it states:

5: וְאֶל־קַיִן וְאֶל־מִנְחָתוֹ לֹא שָׁעָה וַיִּחַר לְקַיִן מְאֹד וַיִּפְּלוּ פָּנָיו

"But unto Cain and to his offering he had not respect. And Cain was very <u>wroth</u> (the word "wroth" is the KJV bible Hebrew Strong's Concordance#2734 חָרָה **Charah, which means: to be very angry**, to glow or grow warm; figuratively (usually) to blaze up, of anger, zeal, jealousy: —be angry, burn, be displeased, × earnestly, fret self, grieve, be (wax) hot, be incensed, kindle, × very, be wroth." his <u>countenance</u> (**Paniym** – Pronunciation **Pä·nēm'**) fell, and is defined as: "when a person face frowns when they don't get their way", and then he became **wroth or very angry**." So, according to the previous verses, we learn that when Cain was disrespectful to the **Yehovah (LORD)** and when he did not get his way, <u>**he became**</u>

Mind Gardening in the Creative Garden of Will (Your Mind) to Grow a Living Water Mentality!

CHILDREN OF THE MOST HIGH:
PRISTINE YOUTH AND FAMILY SOLUTIONS, LLC.
SONS AND DAUGHTERS OF THE MOST HIGH PUBLISHERS ®

Oh, Gracious Most High Heavenly father, Holy is your name,
Your Will Be Done Now and Forever!

very angry, and it led to him committing the **sin** of killing his brother Abel in the KJV bible book of Genesis chapter 4 verse 8. **Anger and alcohol can impair the prefrontal lobe of the brain which is responsible for making sound decisions and can negatively affect the body** (Hendricks, Bore, Aslinia, & Morriss, 2013).

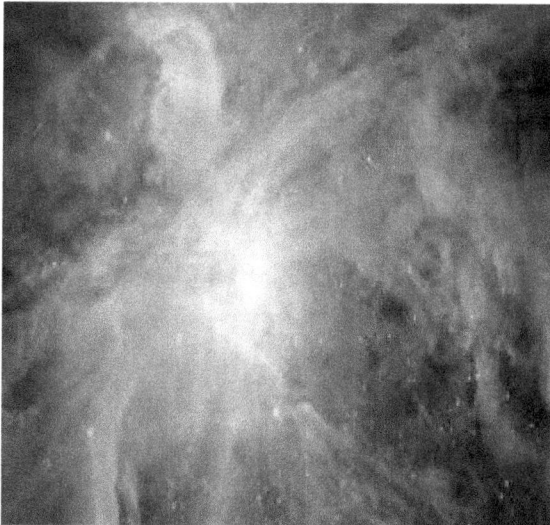

83

Yashu'a (Jesus) said: "Thou shalt love the Most High Heavenly Father, thy Sustainer with all thy heart, and with all thy soul, and with all thy mind. Thou shalt love thy neighbour as thyself."

Mind Gardening in the Creative Garden of Will (Your Mind) to Grow a Living Water Mentality!

CHILDREN OF THE MOST HIGH:
PRISTINE YOUTH AND FAMILY SOLUTIONS, LLC.
SONS AND DAUGHTERS OF THE MOST HIGH PUBLISHERS ®

Oh, Gracious Most High Heavenly father, Holy is your name,
Your Will Be Done Now and Forever!

Therefore; the aforementioned KJV bible verses teach us that **Sin Mind-Awareness** can prevent us from making negative decisions that can cause a life time of regrets! The verses also teach the children of the Most High that "**Sin**" "lays and waits at the door" for the essence (**soul**) of people in hopes that **the great dragon**, that **old serpent** called the **devil** and **satan** and **his angels** can seduce people to commit "**Sin**". Cain's encounter with "**Sin**" is a warning and sign for those who seek to grow a **Living Water Mentality** that the **devil** and **his angels** will do everything in their power to sway members of humanity **from the path back to the Most High Heavenly Father**!

84

Yashu'a (Jesus) said: "Thou shalt love the Most High Heavenly Father, thy Sustainer with all thy heart, and with all thy soul, and with all thy mind. Thou shalt love thy neighbour as thyself."

Mind Gardening in the Creative Garden of Will (Your Mind) to Grow a Living Water Mentality!

CHILDREN OF THE MOST HIGH:
PRISTINE YOUTH AND FAMILY SOLUTIONS, LLC.
SONS AND DAUGHTERS OF THE MOST HIGH PUBLISHERS ®

*Oh, Gracious Most High Heavenly father, Holy is your name,
Your Will Be Done Now and Forever!*

For Example: the **devil** and **his angels** <u>**can plant a negative thought in our minds**</u> via news media or person, place or thing, and a person may unfortunately act on that negative thought which could lead to that person's life and the lives of those closest to him or her being in ruins. **How does the Online American Heritage Dictionary** (2020) **define the word "sin?"** The Online American Heritage Dictionary (2020) defines the word "sin" as: "**sin**[1] (sĭn) *n.* **1.** A transgression of a religious or moral law, especially when deliberate. **2.** Theology: **a.** Deliberate disobedience to the known will of God. **b.** <u>A condition of estrangement from God resulting from such disobedience</u>. **3.** Something regarded as being shameful, deplorable, or utterly wrong. **Idioms: live in sin**; to cohabit in a sexual relationship without being married. [Middle English *sinne*, from Old English *synn*; see **es-** <u>in the Appendix of Indo-European roots</u>]."

85

Yashu'a (Jesus) said: "Thou shalt love the Most High Heavenly Father, thy Sustainer with all thy heart, and with all thy soul, and with all thy mind. Thou shalt love thy neighbour as thyself."

Mind Gardening in the Creative Garden of Will (Your Mind) to Grow a Living Water Mentality!

CHILDREN OF THE MOST HIGH:
PRISTINE YOUTH AND FAMILY SOLUTIONS, LLC.
SONS AND DAUGHTERS OF THE MOST HIGH PUBLISHERS ®

*Oh, Gracious Most High Heavenly father, Holy is your name,
Your Will Be Done Now and Forever!*

Therefore; it is imperative that all children of the Most High; stop waiting on the devil to give you God's blessings! And stop intentional, disobedience through sinning! For more information **on how to eliminate the habit of disobedience** seek out the Children of the Most High: Pristine Youth and Solution, LLC. book below:

86

Yashu'a (Jesus) said: "Thou shalt love the Most High Heavenly Father, thy Sustainer with all thy heart, and with all thy soul, and with all thy mind. Thou shalt love thy neighbour as thyself."

Mind Gardening in the Creative Garden of Will (Your Mind) to Grow a Living Water Mentality!

CHILDREN OF THE MOST HIGH:
PRISTINE YOUTH AND FAMILY SOLUTIONS, LLC.
SONS AND DAUGHTERS OF THE MOST HIGH PUBLISHERS ®

Oh, Gracious Most High Heavenly father, Holy is your name, Your Will Be Done Now and Forever!

Chapter 6: As it Relates to How You Are Living Your Life: Are you Playing Fearful Checkers? Demonic Chess? Or Creating Children of the Most High Chess Moves?"

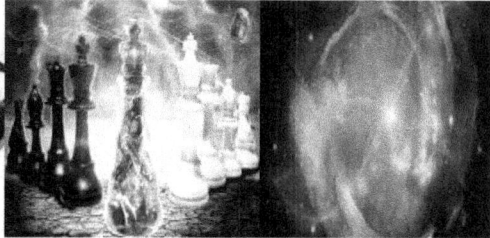

What is Life? The Online American Heritage Dictionary (2020), defines the word "life" as: **the time for which something exists or functions.** The word "life" is mentioned for the first time in the KJV bible book of Genesis chapter 1 verse 20; and it states: "And God said, Let the waters bring forth abundantly the moving creature that hath **life**, and fowl that may fly above the earth in the open firmament of heaven."

Yashu'a (Jesus) said: "Thou shalt love the Most High Heavenly Father, thy Sustainer with all thy heart, and with all thy soul, and with all thy mind. Thou shalt love thy neighbour as thyself."

Mind Gardening in the Creative Garden of Will (Your Mind) to Grow a Living Water Mentality!

CHILDREN OF THE MOST HIGH:
PRISTINE YOUTH AND FAMILY SOLUTIONS, LLC.
SONS AND DAUGHTERS OF THE MOST HIGH PUBLISHERS ®

Oh, Gracious Most High Heavenly father, Holy is your name,
Your Will Be Done Now and Forever!

The KJV bible Hebrew Strong's Concordance#**2416** word for

life is: **Khah-Ee** חַי (**Khay** or **Chay**) and means **living**, **alive**.

The Ashuric/Syriac (Arabic) Word For "Life" Is Hayaat (حياة) In Greek The Word Is Zoe (Ζωη); Meaning *"The Time You Spend*

alive or living; the time for which something exists or functions.

What is the game of checkers?

88

Yashu'a (Jesus) said: "Thou shalt love the Most High
Heavenly Father, thy Sustainer with all thy heart, and
with all thy soul, and with all thy mind. Thou shalt love
thy neighbour as thyself."

Mind Gardening in the Creative Garden of Will (Your Mind) to Grow a Living Water Mentality!

CHILDREN OF THE MOST HIGH:
PRISTINE YOUTH AND FAMILY SOLUTIONS, LLC.
SONS AND DAUGHTERS OF THE MOST HIGH PUBLISHERS ®

Oh, Gracious Most High Heavenly father, Holy is your name,
Your Will Be Done Now and Forever!

According to checkers.com (2020), "The board game called "Checkers" in North America and "Draughts" (pronounced as "drafts") in Europe is one of the oldest games known to man. The history of checkers can be traced to the very cradle of civilization, where vestiges of the earliest form of the game was unearthed in an archeological dig in the ancient city of Ur in southern Mesopotamia, which is now modern-day Iraq. Using a slightly different board, no one is sure of the exact rules of the game which was carbon dated at 3000 B.C. A similar game using a 5x5 board, called Alquerque is known to have existed in ancient Egypt as far back as 1400 B.C. This Egyptian version was so popular that man played it for thousands of years. **Then, in the year 1100 A.D., an innovative Frenchman thought of <u>playing the game on a chess board</u> and increased the number** of pieces for each player to 12."

Yashu'a (Jesus) said: "Thou shalt love the Most High Heavenly Father, thy Sustainer with all thy heart, and with all thy soul, and with all thy mind. Thou shalt love thy neighbour as thyself."

Mind Gardening in the Creative Garden of Will (Your Mind) to Grow a Living Water Mentality!

*Oh, Gracious Most High Heavenly father, Holy is your name,
Your Will Be Done Now and Forever!*

"This modified game was then called **"Fierges"** or **"Ferses**," but it was more appropriately called as **"Le Jeu Plaisant De Dames**," because it was considered a women's social game. Later, the game was made more challenging by making jumps mandatory and so, this newer version was referred to as **"Jeu Force**." As early as the mid-1500s, books were written on the game and in 1756, an English mathematician wrote a treatise on draughts. Now, with its own written rules, the game settled in England where it was known as **"Draughts"** and in America where it was called **"Checkers**." According to Britannica Encyclopedia (2020), "**Checkers**, also called **draughts**, board game, one of the world's oldest games. Checkers is played by two persons who oppose each other across a board of 64 light and dark squares, the same as a chessboard."

90

Yashu'a (Jesus) said: "Thou shalt love the Most High Heavenly Father, thy Sustainer with all thy heart, and with all thy soul, and with all thy mind. Thou shalt love thy neighbour as thyself."

Mind Gardening in the Creative Garden of Will (Your Mind) to Grow a Living Water Mentality!

CHILDREN OF THE MOST HIGH:
PRISTINE YOUTH AND FAMILY SOLUTIONS, LLC.
SONS AND DAUGHTERS OF THE MOST HIGH PUBLISHERS ®

Oh, Gracious Most High Heavenly father, Holy is your name,
Your Will Be Done Now and Forever!

"The 24 playing pieces are disk-shaped and of contrasting colors (whatever their colors, they are identified as black and white). At the start of the game, each contestant has 12 pieces arranged on the board. While the actual playing is always done on the dark squares, the board is often shown in reverse for clarity. The notation used in describing the game is based on numbering the squares on the board. The black pieces always occupy squares 1 to 12, and the white pieces invariably rest on squares 21 to 32. Play consists of advancing a piece diagonally forward to an adjoining vacant square. Black moves first. If an opponent's piece is in such an adjoining vacant square, with a vacant space beyond, it must be captured and removed by jumping over it to the empty square. If this square presents the same situation, successive jumps forward in a straight or zigzag direction must be completed in the same play."

91

Yashu'a (Jesus) said: "Thou shalt love the Most High
Heavenly Father, thy Sustainer with all thy heart, and
with all thy soul, and with all thy mind. Thou shalt love
thy neighbour as thyself."

Mind Gardening in the Creative Garden of Will (Your Mind) to Grow a Living Water Mentality!

CHILDREN OF THE MOST HIGH:
PRISTINE YOUTH AND FAMILY SOLUTIONS, LLC.
SONS AND DAUGHTERS OF THE MOST HIGH PUBLISHERS ®

Oh, Gracious Most High Heavenly father, Holy is your name,
Your Will Be Done Now and Forever!

"When there is more than one way to jump, the player has a choice. When a piece first enters the king row, the opponent's back row, it must be crowned by the opponent, who places another piece of the same color on it. The piece, now called a king, has the added privilege of moving and jumping backward; if it moved to the last row with a capture, it must continue capturing backward if possible. A win is scored when an opponent's pieces are all captured or blocked so that they cannot move. When neither side can force a victory and the trend of play becomes repetitious, a draw game is declared."

What is the game of chess?

92

Yashu'a (Jesus) said: "Thou shalt love the Most High Heavenly Father, thy Sustainer with all thy heart, and with all thy soul, and with all thy mind. Thou shalt love thy neighbour as thyself."

Mind Gardening in the Creative Garden of Will (Your Mind) to Grow a Living Water Mentality!

CHILDREN OF THE MOST HIGH:
PRISTINE YOUTH AND FAMILY SOLUTIONS, LLC.
SONS AND DAUGHTERS OF THE MOST HIGH PUBLISHERS ®

*Oh, Gracious Most High Heavenly father, Holy is your name,
Your Will Be Done Now and Forever!*

According to the Encyclopedia Britannica (2020), "Chess, one of the oldest and most popular board games, played by two opponents on a checkered board with specially designed pieces of contrasting colors, commonly white and black. White moves first, after which the players alternate turns in accordance with fixed rules, each player attempting to force the opponent's principal piece, the King, into checkmate a position where it is unable to avoid capture. Chess first appeared in India about the 6th century ad and by the 10th century had spread from Asia to the Middle East and Europe). Chess is derived from the **Persian** word **Sha** which means **King**. Chess is a game of skill and mental expertise and is called the **Game of Life**. The game itself is one of the oldest games which pure mental skill must be used which rules out chance. The game of chess is like warfare."

Yashu'a (Jesus) said: "Thou shalt love the Most High Heavenly Father, thy Sustainer with all thy heart, and with all thy soul, and with all thy mind. Thou shalt love thy neighbour as thyself."

Mind Gardening in the Creative Garden of Will (Your Mind) to Grow a Living Water Mentality!

CHILDREN OF THE MOST HIGH:
PRISTINE YOUTH AND FAMILY SOLUTIONS, LLC.
SONS AND DAUGHTERS OF THE MOST HIGH PUBLISHERS ®

*Oh, Gracious Most High Heavenly father, Holy is your name,
Your Will Be Done Now and Forever!*

"It consists of an organized attack and defense, each conducted with a definite object in view. The main objective of chess is to kill the king or **Sha Maut**, which means the "**King is Dead**." **What does the words: "fearful" and "demonic" mean?** According to the Online American Heritage Dictionary (2020), the word: "**fearful**" means: "**1. a.** Experiencing fear; frightened: fearful about losing one's job; fearful of a scornful response. **b.** Inclined to feel anxiety or apprehension; timid; nervous. **c.** Indicating anxiety or fear: **2.** Causing or capable of causing fear; frightening: a fearful howling. **3.** Extreme, as in degree or extent. Used especially of something negative: a fearful blunder; fearful poverty." According to the Online American Heritage Dictionary (2020), the word: "**demonic**" means: "Of, relating to, or suggestive of a demon."

Yashu'a (Jesus) said: "Thou shalt love the Most High Heavenly Father, thy Sustainer with all thy heart, and with all thy soul, and with all thy mind. Thou shalt love thy neighbour as thyself."

Mind Gardening in the Creative Garden of Will (Your Mind) to Grow a Living Water Mentality!

CHILDREN OF THE MOST HIGH:
PRISTINE YOUTH AND FAMILY SOLUTIONS, LLC.
SONS AND DAUGHTERS OF THE MOST HIGH PUBLISHERS ®

Oh, Gracious Most High Heavenly father, Holy is your name,
Your Will Be Done Now and Forever!

"**Demon** is defined as: 1. An evil supernatural being; **a devil**. 2. A persistently tormenting person, force, or passion: the demon of drug addiction. 3. Variant of daimon." According the KJV bible book of 2nd Timothy chapter 1 verse 7; it states: "For God hath not given us the spirit of fear; but of power, and of love, and of a sound mind." So, a person who lives their life in a manner that is synonymous to playing **fearful checkers, stunts their own mental and spiritual growth by being poisoned by the spirit of fear**! According to the Children of the Most High: Pristine Youth and Family Solutions, LLC., what is **F.E.A.R.**? **F.E.A.R.** are the acronyms for <u>F</u>aint-Hearted <u>E</u>xamples <u>A</u>mplifying <u>R</u>eality (**F.E.A.R.**).

95

Yashu'a (Jesus) said: "Thou shalt love the Most High Heavenly Father, thy Sustainer with all thy heart, and with all thy soul, and with all thy mind. Thou shalt love thy neighbour as thyself."

Mind Gardening in the Creative Garden of Will (Your Mind) to Grow a Living Water Mentality!

CHILDREN OF THE MOST HIGH:
PRISTINE YOUTH AND FAMILY SOLUTIONS, LLC.
SONS AND DAUGHTERS OF THE MOST HIGH PUBLISHERS ®

Oh, Gracious Most High Heavenly father, Holy is your name,
Your Will Be Done Now and Forever!

Why would a person live their life in a manner that is synonymous to playing **demonic chess**?

According to the KJV bible book of Ecclesiastes chapter 8 verse 11; it states: "Because sentence against an evil work is not executed speedily, therefore the heart of the sons of men is fully set in them to do evil." In the KJV bible book of John chapter 8 verse 44; Yashu'a (Jesus) said: "Ye are of your father the devil, and the lusts of your father ye will do. He was a murderer from the beginning, and abode not in the truth, because there is no truth in him. When he speaketh a lie, he speaketh of his own: for he is a liar, and the father of it."

Yashu'a (Jesus) said: "Thou shalt love the Most High Heavenly Father, thy Sustainer with all thy heart, and with all thy soul, and with all thy mind. Thou shalt love thy neighbour as thyself."

Mind Gardening in the Creative Garden of Will (Your Mind) to Grow a Living Water Mentality!

CHILDREN OF THE MOST HIGH:
PRISTINE YOUTH AND FAMILY SOLUTIONS, LLC.
SONS AND DAUGHTERS OF THE MOST HIGH PUBLISHERS ®

Oh, Gracious Most High Heavenly father, Holy is your name,
Your Will Be Done Now and Forever!

Therefore, **a person who lives their life in a manner that is synonymous to playing demonic chess,** there is **no truth in them**, and <u>their ending of their evil living will be according to their works</u>! In the KJV bible book of 2nd Corinthians chapter 11 verses 13-15; it states: "For such are false apostles, deceitful workers, **transforming themselves** into the apostles of Christ. And no marvel; for Satan himself is transformed into an angel of light. Therefore, it is no great thing if **his ministers** also be transformed as the ministers of righteousness; <u>whose end shall be according to their works</u>."

97

Yashu'a (Jesus) said: "Thou shalt love the Most High Heavenly Father, thy Sustainer with all thy heart, and with all thy soul, and with all thy mind. Thou shalt love thy neighbour as thyself."

Mind Gardening in the Creative Garden of Will (Your Mind) to Grow a Living Water Mentality!

CHILDREN OF THE MOST HIGH:
PRISTINE YOUTH AND FAMILY SOLUTIONS, LLC.
SONS AND DAUGHTERS OF THE MOST HIGH PUBLISHERS ®

Oh, Gracious Most High Heavenly father, Holy is your name, Your Will Be Done Now and Forever!

How does the Children of the Most High: Pristine Youth and Family Solutions LLC., define: "Creating Children of the Most High Chess Moves?"

"Creating Children of the Most High Chess Moves" are when a **child of the Most High (not to be confused with a child of the devil)** <u>creates a positive new reality from their mental thoughts</u> for themselves and others from the **True Vine Yashu'a (Jesus) Children of the Most High (God) Mind as a Mental Artist**. This ability is initiated through the intentional utilization of a person's: **"will"**, **spiritual majesty**, **potential diversification** through an **overstanding** of how your physical brain works with your non-physical mind, combined with **divine love, the True Vine Yashu'a (Jesus) Art of Spiritual Warfare, true-prayer supplication** and **true-faith** in the Most High Heavenly Father.

98

Yashu'a (Jesus) said: "Thou shalt love the Most High Heavenly Father, thy Sustainer with all thy heart, and with all thy soul, and with all thy mind. Thou shalt love thy neighbour as thyself."

Mind Gardening in the Creative Garden of Will (Your Mind) to Grow a Living Water Mentality!

CHILDREN OF THE MOST HIGH:
PRISTINE YOUTH AND FAMILY SOLUTIONS, LLC.
SONS AND DAUGHTERS OF THE MOST HIGH PUBLISHERS ®

Oh, Gracious Most High Heavenly father, Holy is your name,
Your Will Be Done Now and Forever!

Chapter 7: Develop Your Mind Skills on the Battlefield of "Wills"!

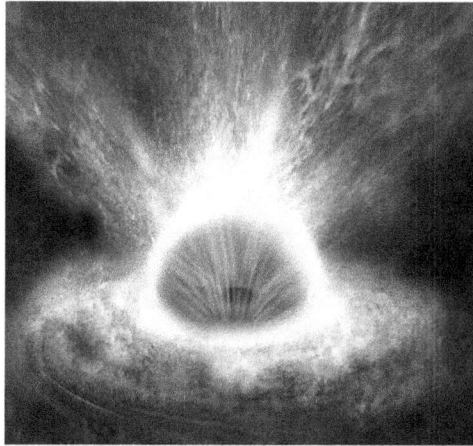

In the KJV bible book of Matthew, chapter 6 verses 9-10; Yashu'a (Jesus) said: "After this manner therefore pray ye: Our Father which art in heaven, Hallowed be thy name. Thy kingdom come. Thy will be done in earth, as *it is* in heaven."

Yashu'a (Jesus) said: "Thou shalt love the Most High Heavenly Father, thy Sustainer with all thy heart, and with all thy soul, and with all thy mind. Thou shalt love thy neighbour as thyself."

Mind Gardening in the Creative Garden of Will (Your Mind) to Grow a Living Water Mentality!

CHILDREN OF THE MOST HIGH:
PRISTINE YOUTH AND FAMILY SOLUTIONS, LLC.
SONS AND DAUGHTERS OF THE MOST HIGH PUBLISHERS ®

Oh, Gracious Most High Heavenly father, Holy is your name,
Your Will Be Done Now and Forever!

The KJV bible Greek Strong's Concordance for the word: "**will**" in this verse is "**#2307 θέλημα thelēma. θέλημα thelēma (the'-lā-mä)**, is defined as: "what one wishes or has determined shall be done; purpose of God; of what God wishes to be done by us; commands, precepts, choice, inclination, and desire." The word for "**Will**" in **Galilean Ashuric/Syriac (Arabic)** is: "**Mashiyya**". Mashiyya (مشيьا) Which Comes From The Root Word Shayaa-A (شاء) Or Yashaa-A (يشاء) And Means: "By Which One deliberately chooses or decides upon a course of action; an instance of exercising this faculty; a deliberate decision or conclusion; choice. "**Will**" is to do what one chooses, to have one's way and to see fit to one's own thinking (Hughes, 2019).

100

Yashu'a (Jesus) said: "Thou shalt love the Most High Heavenly Father, thy Sustainer with all thy heart, and with all thy soul, and with all thy mind. Thou shalt love thy neighbour as thyself."

Mind Gardening in the Creative Garden of Will (Your Mind) to Grow a Living Water Mentality!

CHILDREN OF THE MOST HIGH:
PRISTINE YOUTH AND FAMILY SOLUTIONS, LLC.
SONS AND DAUGHTERS OF THE MOST HIGH PUBLISHERS ®

Oh, Gracious Most High Heavenly father, Holy is your name,
Your Will Be Done Now and Forever!

How can a portion of the Most High be in a person and a person not know that it exists within him or her? In the KJV bible book of John chapter 1 verses 1-5; answers that question for us. In the KJV bible book of John chapter 1 verses 1-5; it states: "In the beginning was the Word, and the Word was with God, and the Word was God. The same was in the beginning with God. All things were made by him; and without him was not anything made that was made. In him was life (**breath of life from the Lord God**); and the life (**from the Lord God made people into living souls**) was the light (**Neshamaw Khayyeem נשמה חיים - Divine Breath of Life**) of <u>men</u> (meaning human beings). The **KJV bible Hebrew Strong's Concordance#444** word for "men" is: ἄνθρωπος anthrōpos which means a human being)."

Yashu'a (Jesus) said: "Thou shalt love the Most High Heavenly Father, thy Sustainer with all thy heart, and with all thy soul, and with all thy mind. Thou shalt love thy neighbour as thyself."

Mind Gardening in the Creative Garden of Will (Your Mind) to Grow a Living Water Mentality!

CHILDREN OF THE MOST HIGH:
PRISTINE YOUTH AND FAMILY SOLUTIONS, LLC.
SONS AND DAUGHTERS OF THE MOST HIGH PUBLISHERS ®

Oh, Gracious Most High Heavenly father, Holy is your name,
Your Will Be Done Now and Forever!

"And the light **(portion of the Most High that exists in every person)** shineth in darkness **(is inside the body of every person)**; and the darkness **(the body and the mind in many people lack of the knowledge of how a portion of the Most High exists in every person)** comprehended it not." How did <u>**the light shineth in darkness; and the darkness comprehended it not**</u> get inside of us? The KJV bible book of **Genesis chapter 2 verse 7** answers that question; it states: "And the Lord God formed man of the dust of the ground, and breathed into his nostrils the breath of life; and man became a living soul." So, the portion of the Most High Heavenly Father which is a: **"Spiritual Majesty"** is usually not allowed to function in our lives due to many of us living most days according to people other than yourself, places and worldly things and other people plans for our lives that may not have

Yashu'a (Jesus) said: "Thou shalt love the Most High Heavenly Father, thy Sustainer with all thy heart, and with all thy soul, and with all thy mind. Thou shalt love thy neighbour as thyself."

Mind Gardening in the Creative Garden of Will (Your Mind) to Grow a Living Water Mentality!

CHILDREN OF THE MOST HIGH:
PRISTINE YOUTH AND FAMILY SOLUTIONS, LLC.
SONS AND DAUGHTERS OF THE MOST HIGH PUBLISHERS ®

Oh, Gracious Most High Heavenly father, Holy is your name,
Your Will Be Done Now and Forever!

our best interest; rather than becoming aware of the Most High's pre-ordained plan for each of our lives and learning to only live by the "**Will**" and commandments of the Most High. **Spiritual Majesty** is an inner quality that when it is intentionally organized and directed towards positive accomplishments it activates our higher potential that helps us to conquer adverse situations. Also, when our **Spiritual Majesty** is intentionally organized and directed towards positive accomplishments, it activates the ability to create positive life achievements that afford us the opportunity to get more out of life by sacrificing through our works in a positive healthy manner to give more to life.

103

Yashu'a (Jesus) said: "Thou shalt love the Most High Heavenly Father, thy Sustainer with all thy heart, and with all thy soul, and with all thy mind. Thou shalt love thy neighbour as thyself."

Mind Gardening in the Creative Garden of Will (Your Mind) to Grow a Living Water Mentality!

CHILDREN OF THE MOST HIGH:
PRISTINE YOUTH AND FAMILY SOLUTIONS, LLC.
SONS AND DAUGHTERS OF THE MOST HIGH PUBLISHERS ®

Oh, Gracious Most High Heavenly father, Holy is your name, Your Will Be Done Now and Forever!

What is the True Vine Yashu'a (Jesus) Art of Spiritual Warfare? The True Vine (Yashu'a, Jesus) Art of Spiritual Warfare is: A disciplined, waging of mental, spiritual and emotional war skill that is attained by rigorous study and practice of the Doctrine of the Most High that was taught by the True Vine (Yashu'a, Jesus) against all wickedness. Without a foe a soldier never knows his or her strength, and the **True Vine Yashu'a (Jesus) Children of the Most High (God) Mind** must be developed by the exercise of experience, evidence, reason, strength, and the willingness to change over time. So, the carnal nature is a foe that the children of the Most High Heavenly Father must fight. In order to overcome the foe of the carnal nature, a child of the Most High must decrease and the Messiah Yashu'a (Jesus) must increase in them as the strength of him manifest.

Yashu'a (Jesus) said: "Thou shalt love the Most High Heavenly Father, thy Sustainer with all thy heart, and with all thy soul, and with all thy mind. Thou shalt love thy neighbour as thyself."

Mind Gardening in the Creative Garden of Will (Your Mind) to Grow a Living Water Mentality!

CHILDREN OF THE MOST HIGH:
PRISTINE YOUTH AND FAMILY SOLUTIONS, LLC.
SONS AND DAUGHTERS OF THE MOST HIGH PUBLISHERS ®

*Oh, Gracious Most High Heavenly father, Holy is your name,
Your Will Be Done Now and Forever!*

Those of us who are successful in this battle will regain our lost eternal heritage; but we must do it in a conflict that cannot be told in words! **What is True-Prayer Supplication**? True-Prayer Supplication occurs through the combination of spoken words from a sincere heart, mind focused on the Most High only, and internal meditation. This occurs by allowing the Most High's words and laws being placed in our hearts. When this occurs, it puts our minds in alignment with the "**Will**" of the Most High as stated in the KJV bible book of Hebrews chapter 8 verse 10; it states: "For this is the covenant that I will make with the house of Israel after those days, saith the Lord; I will put my laws into their mind, and write them in their hearts: and I will be to them a God, and they shall be to me a people." Thus, when we pray the Most High's words and obey the Most High's laws that are placed in our hearts; the Most High's "**Will**", becomes our will.

Yashu'a (Jesus) said: "Thou shalt love the Most High Heavenly Father, thy Sustainer with all thy heart, and with all thy soul, and with all thy mind. Thou shalt love thy neighbour as thyself."

Mind Gardening in the Creative Garden of Will (Your Mind) to Grow a Living Water Mentality!

CHILDREN OF THE MOST HIGH:
PRISTINE YOUTH AND FAMILY SOLUTIONS, LLC.
SONS AND DAUGHTERS OF THE MOST HIGH PUBLISHERS ®

*Oh, Gracious Most High Heavenly father, Holy is your name,
Your Will Be Done Now and Forever!*

Our True-Prayer Supplications must be directed through the portion of the Most High that exists in us as stated in the KJV bible book of John chapter 1 verses 1-5. However, this should not ever be misinterpreted as praying to yourself as the Most High (that would be BLASPHEMY!). **What is True-Faith? True-Faith is unshakable moral conviction of the truth and trust in the Most High Heavenly Father, the Messiah Yashu'a (Jesus), the Most High Heavenly Father's Angelic-Beings or Messengers of the Most High who are sent to certain members of humanity to teach us how to obey the Most High's laws and to learn and teach the Most High's Doctrine only. This specific learning and teaching of the Most High's Doctrine is taught through the B.A.-K.A.-R.E. Sequential Learning Habits of Success as a pathway** for the Most High's "**Will**" to be done.

Yashu'a (Jesus) said: "Thou shalt love the Most High Heavenly Father, thy Sustainer with all thy heart, and with all thy soul, and with all thy mind. Thou shalt love thy neighbour as thyself."

Mind Gardening in the Creative Garden of Will (Your Mind) to Grow a Living Water Mentality!

CHILDREN OF THE MOST HIGH:
PRISTINE YOUTH AND FAMILY SOLUTIONS, LLC.
SONS AND DAUGHTERS OF THE MOST HIGH PUBLISHERS ®

Oh, Gracious Most High Heavenly father, Holy is your name,
Your Will Be Done Now and Forever!

Also, <u>**True-Faith must be grounded in substantiated facts that are strongly supported through, evidence, experience and reason**</u>. So, the Most High Heavenly Father gave many members of humanity the gift of the ability to think, which **behooves** us to not misuse it or under use the gift of the ability to think! One of the most powerful forces in the universe is: "**Thought**" because thought initiates all actions which is maximized through divine love for the Most High Heavenly Father, true-prayer supplication and true-faith in the Most High. The highest level of knowledge throughout the boundless universes is: "**LOVE**" and **the Most High Heavenly Father is "LOVE"**.

107

Yashu'a (Jesus) said: "Thou shalt love the Most High Heavenly Father, thy Sustainer with all thy heart, and with all thy soul, and with all thy mind. Thou shalt love thy neighbour as thyself."

Mind Gardening in the Creative Garden of Will (Your Mind) to Grow a Living Water Mentality!

CHILDREN OF THE MOST HIGH:
PRISTINE YOUTH AND FAMILY SOLUTIONS, LLC.
SONS AND DAUGHTERS OF THE MOST HIGH PUBLISHERS ®

Oh, Gracious Most High Heavenly father, Holy is your name,
Your Will Be Done Now and Forever!

Therefore, it is a person's divine love for the Most High Heavenly Father, their **true-prayer supplication and true-faith** in the Most High who have accepted the Messiah Yashu'a (Jesus) as savior **that have the ability to create children of the Most High chess moves**. This occurs through the spirit of the Messiah Yashu'a (Jesus) in us that guides our will to be a reflection of the Most High Heavenly Father's **"Will"** which activates our mental ability to create. So, a child of the Most High who lives their life in a manner that is synonymous to **creating children of the Most High chess moves**, he or she **creates a new physical reality from their mental thoughts for themselves and others** from the **True Vine Yashu'a (Jesus) Children of the Most High (God) Mind** as a **Mental Artist**.

Yashu'a (Jesus) said: "Thou shalt love the Most High Heavenly Father, thy Sustainer with all thy heart, and with all thy soul, and with all thy mind. Thou shalt love thy neighbour as thyself."

Mind Gardening in the Creative Garden of Will (Your Mind) to Grow a Living Water Mentality!

CHILDREN OF THE MOST HIGH:
PRISTINE YOUTH AND FAMILY SOLUTIONS, LLC.
SONS AND DAUGHTERS OF THE MOST HIGH PUBLISHERS ®

*Oh, Gracious Most High Heavenly father, Holy is your name,
Your Will Be Done Now and Forever!*

Chapter 8: Aroma of the Death Mind!

In the KJV bible book of James chapter 1 verse 8; it states: "A **double minded** man is unstable in all his ways." The KJV bible book of James chapter 4 verse 8; it states: "<u>**Draw nigh to God, and he will draw nigh to you. Cleanse your hands, ye sinners; and purify your hearts**</u>, ye *double minded*." In both of the previous verses, the KJV bible Greek Strong's Concordance "**#1374** is δίψυχος Dipsychos (Dip'-soo-khos) the word for the words "<u>**double minded**</u>". δίψυχος Dipsychos means: double minded, wavering, uncertain, doubting, <u>**divided in interest namely, between God and the world**</u>."

Yashu'a (Jesus) said: "Thou shalt love the Most High Heavenly Father, thy Sustainer with all thy heart, and with all thy soul, and with all thy mind. Thou shalt love thy neighbour as thyself."

Mind Gardening in the Creative Garden of Will (Your Mind) to Grow a Living Water Mentality!

CHILDREN OF THE MOST HIGH:
PRISTINE YOUTH AND FAMILY SOLUTIONS, LLC.
SONS AND DAUGHTERS OF THE MOST HIGH PUBLISHERS ®

*Oh, Gracious Most High Heavenly father, Holy is your name,
Your Will Be Done Now and Forever!*

In the KJV bible book of James chapter 2 verse 26; it states: "For as the body without the spirit is dead, so faith without works is dead also." The KJV bible Greek Strong's Concordance "**#3498** is the word: **νεκρός Nekros** for the word "**dead**" in this verse. **νεκρός Nekros (Nek-ros')**, means: (a corpse); **dead (literally or figuratively**; and is also a noun). **One that has breathed his or her last breath; lifeless, deceased, departed, one whose soul is in heaven or hell, destitute of life, without life, inanimate; <u>spiritually dead</u>, destitute of a life that recognizes and is devoted to God, <u>because given up to trespasses and sins inactive as respects doing right</u>, destitute of force or power, inactive, inoperative.**"

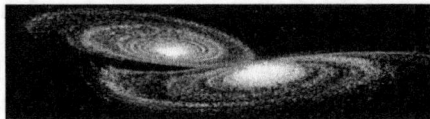

110

Yashu'a (Jesus) said: "Thou shalt love the Most High Heavenly Father, thy Sustainer with all thy heart, and with all thy soul, and with all thy mind. Thou shalt love thy neighbour as thyself."

Mind Gardening in the Creative Garden of Will (Your Mind) to Grow a Living Water Mentality!

CHILDREN OF THE MOST HIGH:
PRISTINE YOUTH AND FAMILY SOLUTIONS, LLC.
SONS AND DAUGHTERS OF THE MOST HIGH PUBLISHERS ®

Oh, Gracious Most High Heavenly father, Holy is your name,
Your Will Be Done Now and Forever!

According to the KJV bible book of Romans chapter 12 verse 2; it states: "And be not conformed to this world: **but be ye transformed by the renewing of your mind**, that ye may prove what [is] that good, and acceptable, and perfect, will of God." The KJV bible Greek Strong's Concordance word for the words "**by the renewing**" in this verse is **#342 ἀνακαίνωσις Anakainōsis. Anakainōsis** means: "**a renewal, renovation, complete change for the better**." What is the difference between **unconscious** and **conscious** as it relates to the renewal of the mind? **Unconscious** is the opposite of conscious. According to the Online American Heritage Dictionary (2020), **unconscious** is defined as: "1. Lacking awareness and the capacity for sensory perception; not conscious. 2. Occurring in the absence of conscious awareness or thought: unconscious resentment; unconscious fears."

Yashu'a (Jesus) said: "Thou shalt love the Most High Heavenly Father, thy Sustainer with all thy heart, and with all thy soul, and with all thy mind. Thou shalt love thy neighbour as thyself."

Mind Gardening in the Creative Garden of Will (Your Mind) to Grow a Living Water Mentality!

CHILDREN OF THE MOST HIGH:
PRISTINE YOUTH AND FAMILY SOLUTIONS, LLC.
SONS AND DAUGHTERS OF THE MOST HIGH PUBLISHERS ®

Oh, Gracious Most High Heavenly father, Holy is your name,
Your Will Be Done Now and Forever!

"**Conscious** is defined as: "1. a. Characterized by or having an awareness of one's environment and one's own existence, sensations, and thoughts. See Synonyms at aware. b. Mentally perceptive or alert; awake: 2. Capable of thought, will, or perception: the development of conscious life on the planet. 3. Intentionally conceived or done; made a conscious effort to speak more clearly. 4. Inwardly attentive or sensitive to something; 5. Showing awareness of or preoccupation with something." Positiveness always overcomes the negative, and courage always overcomes timidity. Yashu'a (Jesus) is also is in charge of the Resurrection at the end of the world.

112

Yashu'a (Jesus) said: "Thou shalt love the Most High Heavenly Father, thy Sustainer with all thy heart, and with all thy soul, and with all thy mind. Thou shalt love thy neighbour as thyself."

Mind Gardening in the Creative Garden of Will (Your Mind) to Grow a Living Water Mentality!

CHILDREN OF THE MOST HIGH:
PRISTINE YOUTH AND FAMILY SOLUTIONS, LLC.
SONS AND DAUGHTERS OF THE MOST HIGH PUBLISHERS ®

Oh, Gracious Most High Heavenly father, Holy is your name,
Your Will Be Done Now and Forever!

In the KJV bible book of John chapter 11 verses 25-26; Yashu'a (Jesus) said: "I am the resurrection, and the life: he that believeth in me, though he were dead, yet shall he live. And whosoever liveth and believeth in me shall never die. Believest thou this?" So, the "**Aroma of the Death Mind**" is **double minded <u>and is preoccupied with the 9 Deadly Venoms of Desires of the great dragon, that old serpent, called the devil and satan that deceived the whole world</u>**. The 9 Deadly Venoms of the Desires of the great dragon, that old serpent called the devil and satan which deceiveth the whole world are: **Slothful**, **Wrath**, **Pride**, **Greed**, **Lust**, **Hopeless-Fear-Disobedience**, **Lying**, **Heinous Murder**, and **Wickedness**. These 9 Deadly Venoms of the Desires of are the root causes that prevent the acquisition of the **True Vine (Yashu'a, Jesus) Living Water Mentality**.

113

Yashu'a (Jesus) said: "Thou shalt love the Most High Heavenly Father, thy Sustainer with all thy heart, and with all thy soul, and with all thy mind. Thou shalt love thy neighbour as thyself."

Mind Gardening in the Creative Garden of Will (Your Mind) to Grow a Living Water Mentality!

CHILDREN OF THE MOST HIGH:
PRISTINE YOUTH AND FAMILY SOLUTIONS, LLC.
SONS AND DAUGHTERS OF THE MOST HIGH PUBLISHERS ®

Oh, Gracious Most High Heavenly father, Holy is your name,
Your Will Be Done Now and Forever!

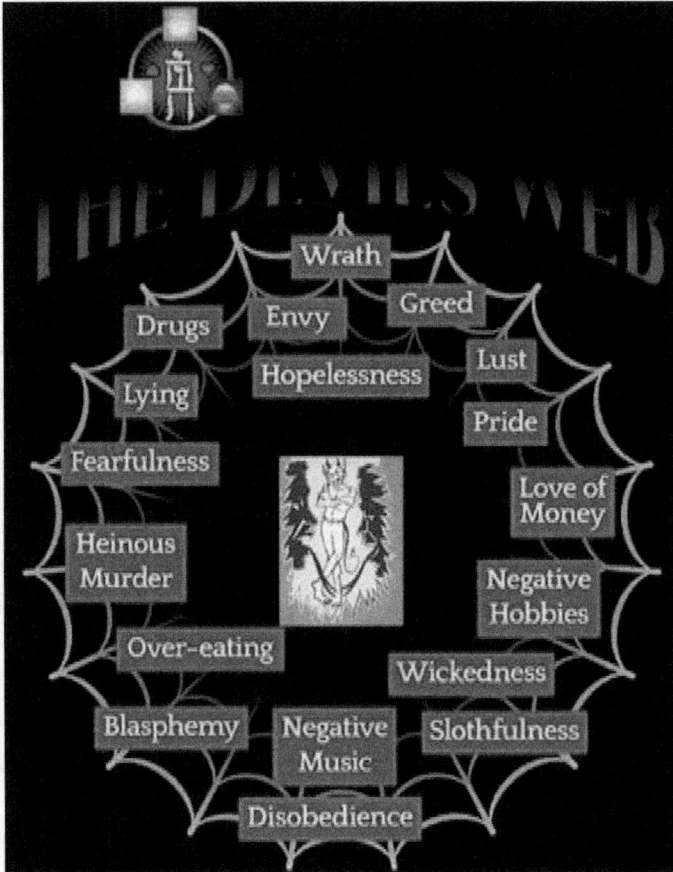

114

Yashu'a (Jesus) said: "Thou shalt love the Most High Heavenly Father, thy Sustainer with all thy heart, and with all thy soul, and with all thy mind. Thou shalt love thy neighbour as thyself."

Mind Gardening in the Creative Garden of Will (Your Mind) to Grow a Living Water Mentality!

CHILDREN OF THE MOST HIGH:
PRISTINE YOUTH AND FAMILY SOLUTIONS, LLC.
SONS AND DAUGHTERS OF THE MOST HIGH PUBLISHERS ®

*Oh, Gracious Most High Heavenly father, Holy is your name,
Your Will Be Done Now and Forever!*

In the KJV bible book of Revelation chapter 12 verses 7-9; it states: "And there was war in heaven: **Michael and his angels** (ἄγγελος **Angelos, meaning Messengers** according to the **KJV bible Greek Strong's Concordance#32**) fought against the **dragon**; and **the dragon fought and his angels** (ἄγγελος **Angelos, meaning Messengers**, according to the KJV bible Greek **Strong's Concordance#32**, And prevailed not; neither was their place found any more in heaven. And the **great dragon** was cast out, that **old serpent**, **called the Devil, and Satan**, which deceiveth the whole world: he was cast out into the earth, and his **angels** (ἄγγελος **Angelos, meaning Messengers**) were cast out with him."

115

Yashu'a (Jesus) said: "Thou shalt love the Most High Heavenly Father, thy Sustainer with all thy heart, and with all thy soul, and with all thy mind. Thou shalt love thy neighbour as thyself."

Mind Gardening in the Creative Garden of Will (Your Mind) to Grow a Living Water Mentality!

CHILDREN OF THE MOST HIGH:
PRISTINE YOUTH AND FAMILY SOLUTIONS, LLC.
SONS AND DAUGHTERS OF THE MOST HIGH PUBLISHERS ®

Oh, Gracious Most High Heavenly father, Holy is your name,
Your Will Be Done Now and Forever!

However; the children of the Most High can overcome the "**Aroma of the Death Mindedness**" through the application of the **9X9 True Vine (Yashu'a, Jesus) B.A.-K.A.-R.E. Sequential Order of Learning Habits of Success <u>in action</u>. What is the Children of the Most High Pristine Youth and Family Solutions, LLC. 9X9 True Vine "Yashu'a" (Jesus) B.A.-K.A.-R.E. Sequential Order of Learning Habits of Success?**

116

Yashu'a (Jesus) said: "Thou shalt love the Most High Heavenly Father, thy Sustainer with all thy heart, and with all thy soul, and with all thy mind. Thou shalt love thy neighbour as thyself."

Mind Gardening in the Creative Garden of Will (Your Mind) to Grow a Living Water Mentality!

CHILDREN OF THE MOST HIGH:
PRISTINE YOUTH AND FAMILY SOLUTIONS, LLC.
SONS AND DAUGHTERS OF THE MOST HIGH PUBLISHERS ®

*Oh, Gracious Most High Heavenly father, Holy is your name,
Your Will Be Done Now and Forever!*

The Children of the Most High Pristine Youth and Family Solutions, LLC. 9X9 True Vine "Yashu'a" (Jesus) B.A.-K.A.-R.E. Sequential Order of Learning Habits of Success are the intentional, non-formal education sequential steps to teaching **youth and adults'** the True Vine Yashu'a (Jesus) doctrine of the Most High. This is taught to them in an effort to create an opportunity for them to learn how to apply the doctrine of the Most High in all that they aspire to do and to teach them how to create positive predetermined goals that may help then to achieve positive success. When we say **"positive success", we mean according to what positive success means to them**.

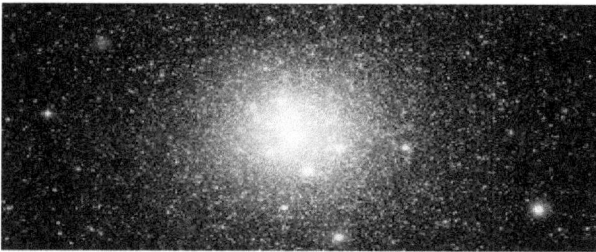

117

Yashu'a (Jesus) said: "Thou shalt love the Most High Heavenly Father, thy Sustainer with all thy heart, and with all thy soul, and with all thy mind. Thou shalt love thy neighbour as thyself."

Mind Gardening in the Creative Garden of Will (Your Mind) to Grow a Living Water Mentality!

CHILDREN OF THE MOST HIGH:
PRISTINE YOUTH AND FAMILY SOLUTIONS, LLC.
SONS AND DAUGHTERS OF THE MOST HIGH PUBLISHERS ®

*Oh, Gracious Most High Heavenly father, Holy is your name,
Your Will Be Done Now and Forever!*

We also seek to teach youth and adults' the True Vine Yashu'a (Jesus) doctrine of the Most High in an effort to learn how to work together with members of humanity to create a world where all children of the Most High youth and all adults are happy, healthy, and balanced mentally, spiritually, physically, emotionally, financially, personally, professionally, and socially. The True Vine "Yashu'a" (Jesus) B.A.-K.A.-R.E. Sequential Order of Learning Habits of Success must be taught in proper sequential order in an effort to not confuse the mind of the learner. **BA** is the Ancient African word for **Soul**, **KA** is the Ancient African word for **Spirit**, **RE** (pronounced as RAY) is the Ancient African word for **Sun**. Psalms (KJV) 84:11 with Hebrew inserts:

כִּי שֶׁמֶשׁ וּמָגֵן יְהוָה אֱלֹהִים חֵן וְכָבוֹד יִתֵּן יְהוָה לֹא
יִמְנַע־טוֹב לַהֹלְכִים בְּתָמִים:

118

Yashu'a (Jesus) said: "Thou shalt love the Most High Heavenly Father, thy Sustainer with all thy heart, and with all thy soul, and with all thy mind. Thou shalt love thy neighbour as thyself."

Mind Gardening in the Creative Garden of Will (Your Mind) to Grow a Living Water Mentality!

CHILDREN OF THE MOST HIGH:
PRISTINE YOUTH AND FAMILY SOLUTIONS, LLC.
SONS AND DAUGHTERS OF THE MOST HIGH PUBLISHERS ®

Oh, Gracious Most High Heavenly father, Holy is your name,
Your Will Be Done Now and Forever!

In the KJV bible book of **Psalms chapter 84 verse 11**; it states: "For **the LORD (Yĕhovah, יְהוָה, Yahuwa)** God (**Elohiym אֱלֹהִים**) is a "**Sun**" **Shemesh שֶׁמֶשׁ** and "**Shield**" **Magen מָגֵן**: the **LORD (Yĕhovah, Yahuwa)** will give grace and glory: no good thing will he withhold from them that walk uprightly **Tamiym תָּמִים**." The **"Sun" (RE)** is the light of star that sustains all life on the planet earth. In the **True Vine (Yashu'a, Jesus) B.A.-K.A.-R.E. Sequential Order of Learning Habits of Success**, the **RE (Sun)** connects to the body as the light (**RE**) that shines in the darkness (**Body**) that the darkness (**Body**) does not comprehend in the KJV bible book of John chapter 1 verse 5, and as Yashu'a (Jesus) said in the KJV bible book of Matthew chapter 6 verse 22 "**the light (RE) of the body is the eye: if therefore thine eye be single, thy whole body shall be full of light.**"

119

Yashu'a (Jesus) said: "Thou shalt love the Most High Heavenly Father, thy Sustainer with all thy heart, and with all thy soul, and with all thy mind. Thou shalt love thy neighbour as thyself."

Mind Gardening in the Creative Garden of Will (Your Mind) to Grow a Living Water Mentality!

CHILDREN OF THE MOST HIGH:
PRISTINE YOUTH AND FAMILY SOLUTIONS, LLC.
SONS AND DAUGHTERS OF THE MOST HIGH PUBLISHERS ®

Oh, Gracious Most High Heavenly father, Holy is your name,
Your Will Be Done Now and Forever!

So, **B.A.-K.A.-R.E.** translates in English as: **The <u>Soul</u> and <u>Spirit</u>, <u>Sun-Light of Life</u> of Yĕhovah**, **Yahuwa, Yahweh, Yahovah, Jehovah (Lord God),** and **Yahayyu** in Modern Hebrew translates as **Existing One** or **Living One** that sustains all life on the planet earth, and it also translates as: "**Glorious is the Spirit of the Lord God (RE).**" The acronyms of "**B.A.-K.A.-R.E.**" in **English** stands for: **B**ecome, **A**ware, **K**nowledge, **A**pply, **R**eflect, **E**xperience. Therefore, **the True Vine (Yashu'a, Jesus) B.A.-K.A.-R.E. Sequential Order of Learning Habits of Success, <u>children of the Most High</u> youth and adult learners**; **B**ecome **A**ware of the meaning of the KJV bible book of Hosea chapter 4 verse 6: "**My people (<u>children of the Most High</u>)** are being destroyed for lack of not knowing **God's (אלהים Elôhîym) A**ll **W**ise **R**ight **A**nd **E**xact (**A.W.A.R.E.**) knowledge."

120

Yashu'a (Jesus) said: "Thou shalt love the Most High Heavenly Father, thy Sustainer with all thy heart, and with all thy soul, and with all thy mind. Thou shalt love thy neighbour as thyself."

Mind Gardening in the Creative Garden of Will (Your Mind) to Grow a Living Water Mentality!

CHILDREN OF THE MOST HIGH:
PRISTINE YOUTH AND FAMILY SOLUTIONS, LLC.
SONS AND DAUGHTERS OF THE MOST HIGH PUBLISHERS ®

Oh, Gracious Most High Heavenly father, Holy is your name,
Your Will Be Done Now and Forever!

By learning **God's (אלהים Elôhîym) All Wise Abundant Right Exact (A.W.A.R.E)** Knowledge with a sincere-heart and focused mind, they acquire the **God's (אלהים Elôhîym) All Wise Abundant Right Exact (A.W.A.R.E) K**nowledge which affords youth and adult learners the opportunity to **A**pply **God's (אלהים Elôhîym) A.W.A.R.E.** knowledge in order to be capable of growing the **True Vine (Yashu'a, Jesus) Living Water Mentality M.I.N.D.** (**M**aking **I**ntentional **N**oble **D**ecisions) in **A.C.T.I.O.N.** (**A**ctivated, **C**onscious, **T**imely, **I**ntentions, **O**bligated, **N**ow)!

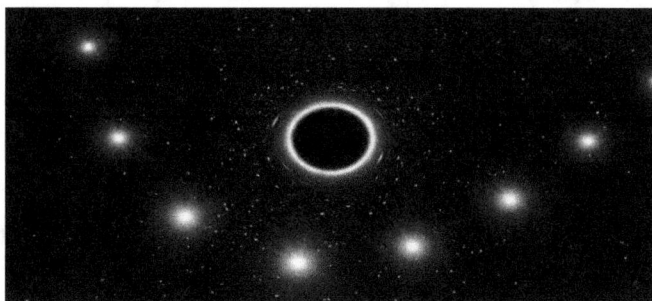

121

Yashu'a (Jesus) said: "Thou shalt love the Most High Heavenly Father, thy Sustainer with all thy heart, and with all thy soul, and with all thy mind. Thou shalt love thy neighbour as thyself."

Mind Gardening in the Creative Garden of Will (Your Mind) to Grow a Living Water Mentality!

CHILDREN OF THE MOST HIGH:
PRISTINE YOUTH AND FAMILY SOLUTIONS, LLC.
SONS AND DAUGHTERS OF THE MOST HIGH PUBLISHERS ®

Oh, Gracious Most High Heavenly father, Holy is your name,
Your Will Be Done Now and Forever!

As the **Children of the Most High Pristine Youth and Family Solutions, LLC. 9X9 True Vine "Yashu'a" (Jesus) B.A.-K.A.-R.E. Sequential Order** of **Learning Habits of Success** continues to be applied and practiced over time by youth and adult learners, opportunities will occur for them to **R**eflect on their **E**xperiences as they share and process what they learned with others; in an ongoing process that may help children of the Most High youth and adults to develop new skills that enables them to best respond to daily life situations that may lead to successful outcomes. This also affords children of the Most High youth and adults' opportunities to create new ways of how to utilize their newly acquired knowledge to successfully achieve all of their positive life aspirations and predetermined positive life goals.

122

Yashu'a (Jesus) said: "Thou shalt love the Most High Heavenly Father, thy Sustainer with all thy heart, and with all thy soul, and with all thy mind. Thou shalt love thy neighbour as thyself."

Mind Gardening in the Creative Garden of Will (Your Mind) to Grow a Living Water Mentality!

CHILDREN OF THE MOST HIGH:
PRISTINE YOUTH AND FAMILY SOLUTIONS, LLC.
SONS AND DAUGHTERS OF THE MOST HIGH PUBLISHERS ®

*Oh, Gracious Most High Heavenly father, Holy is your name,
Your Will Be Done Now and Forever!*

The **Children of the Most High Pristine Youth and Family Solutions, LLC. 9X9 True Vine "Yashu'a" (Jesus) B.A.-K.A.-R.E. Sequential Order of Learning Habits of Success** also teaches children of the Most High youth and adults how to be aware of the children of the devil who advocate, teach and preach <u>**the great dragon, that old serpent, called the Devil, and Satan, which deceiveth the whole world and his angels**</u> (ἄγγελος Angelos, meaning Messengers), **messages** of the **9 Deadly Venoms of the Desires** of the great dragon, that old serpent, called the Devil, and Satan, which deceiveth the whole world. The **9 Deadly Venoms of Desires** are: **Slothful, Wrath, Pride, Greed, Lust, Hopeless Fear Disobedience, Lying, Heinous Murde**r, and **Wickedness.**

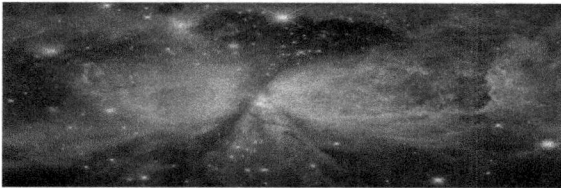

123

Yashu'a (Jesus) said: "Thou shalt love the Most High Heavenly Father, thy Sustainer with all thy heart, and with all thy soul, and with all thy mind. Thou shalt love thy neighbour as thyself."

Mind Gardening in the Creative Garden of Will (Your Mind) to Grow a Living Water Mentality!

CHILDREN OF THE MOST HIGH:
PRISTINE YOUTH AND FAMILY SOLUTIONS, LLC.
SONS AND DAUGHTERS OF THE MOST HIGH PUBLISHERS ®

*Oh, Gracious Most High Heavenly father, Holy is your name,
Your Will Be Done Now and Forever!*

Chapter 9: 9 Deadly Venoms Mental Life or Death Match in the Arena of the True Vine (Yashu'a, Jesus) Mind!

The **9 Deadly Venoms of the Desires of the great dragon, that old serpent called the devil and satan which deceiveth the whole world** are: **Slothful, Wrath, Pride, Greed, Lust, Hopeless-Fear-Disobedience, Lying, Heinous Murde**r, and **Wickedness.**

124

Yashu'a (Jesus) said: "Thou shalt love the Most High Heavenly Father, thy Sustainer with all thy heart, and with all thy soul, and with all thy mind. Thou shalt love thy neighbour as thyself."

Mind Gardening in the Creative Garden of Will (Your Mind) to Grow a Living Water Mentality!

CHILDREN OF THE MOST HIGH:
PRISTINE YOUTH AND FAMILY SOLUTIONS, LLC.
SONS AND DAUGHTERS OF THE MOST HIGH PUBLISHERS ®

Oh, Gracious Most High Heavenly father, Holy is your name,
Your Will Be Done Now and Forever!

These **9 Deadly Venoms of the Desires** are the root causes that prevent the growth of the **Living Water Mentality**. **What is venom?** According to the Online American Heritage Dictionary (2020), venom is defined as: **1.** A poisonous secretion of an animal, such as a snake, spider, or scorpion, usually transmitted to prey or to attackers by a bite or sting. **Is there a correlation between venom, Leviathan, the old Serpent and the Dragon mentioned in the Bible that can adversely impact a person's the growth of the Living Water Mentality?** In the KJV bible book of **Job chapter 41 verse 1**; it states: "Canst thou draw out **leviathan** with a hook? or his tongue with a cord which thou lettest down?" "Thou brakest the heads of **leviathan** in pieces, and gavest him to be meat to the people inhabiting the wilderness, In the book of **KJV bible Psalms 74:14**."

Yashu'a (Jesus) said: "Thou shalt love the Most High Heavenly Father, thy Sustainer with all thy heart, and with all thy soul, and with all thy mind. Thou shalt love thy neighbour as thyself."

Mind Gardening in the Creative Garden of Will (Your Mind) to Grow a Living Water Mentality!

CHILDREN OF THE MOST HIGH:
PRISTINE YOUTH AND FAMILY SOLUTIONS, LLC.
SONS AND DAUGHTERS OF THE MOST HIGH PUBLISHERS ®

*Oh, Gracious Most High Heavenly father, Holy is your name,
Your Will Be Done Now and Forever!*

In the KJV bible book of **Psalms** chapter **104** verse **26:** "There go the ships: there is that **leviathan**, whom thou hast made to play therein." "In that day the LORD with his sore and great and strong sword shall punish **leviathan** the piercing serpent, even leviathan that crooked serpent; and he shall slay the dragon that is in the sea, KJV bible **Isaiah** chapter **27** verse **1:**"

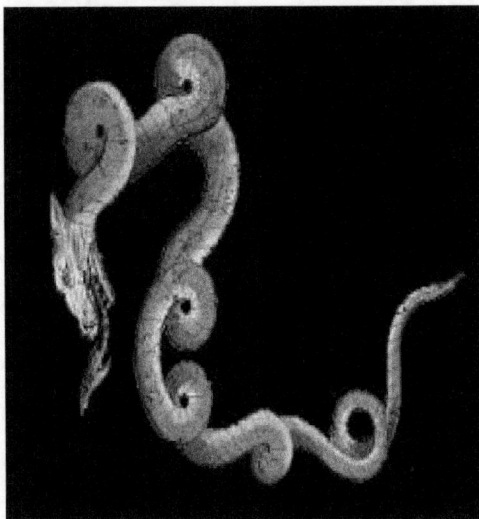

126

Yashu'a (Jesus) said: "Thou shalt love the Most High Heavenly Father, thy Sustainer with all thy heart, and with all thy soul, and with all thy mind. Thou shalt love thy neighbour as thyself."

Mind Gardening in the Creative Garden of Will (Your Mind) to Grow a Living Water Mentality!

CHILDREN OF THE MOST HIGH:
PRISTINE YOUTH AND FAMILY SOLUTIONS, LLC.
SONS AND DAUGHTERS OF THE MOST HIGH PUBLISHERS ®

Oh, Gracious Most High Heavenly father, Holy is your name, Your Will Be Done Now and Forever!

Leviathan: From *The Klein's Comprehensive Etymological Dictionary Of The English Language.*

Late Latin From Hebrew **Liwayathan**, *"Serpent, Dragon, `Leviathan"*, Prop, Tortuous, Which Is Related To `Liwya, *"Wreath" From* Base **L-W-H**, *"To Wind, Turn, Twist"*, Whence Also Arab, Lawa, *"The Wound, Turned, Twisted"*, To Surround, Encircle.

Leviathan: From the *Webster's New Twentieth Century Dictionary Unabridged, Second Edition*

*(Noun) Middle English - **Leuyethan**, Late Latin (Ecclesiastic) Hebrew **Liwayathan**, base akin to Akkadian - **Lawu**, to surround, Arabic: **Liyatu**, Snake. 1. A large and powerful aquatic animal described in **Job Chapter 4**, and mentioned in other passages or*

scriptures: variously thought of as a whale or a reptile. 2. Anything huge of its kind.

Leviathan: From The *Webster's Second College Edition, New World Dictionary.*

*(Noun) Middle English - **Leuyethan**, Late Latin (Ecclesiastic) Hebrew **Liwayathan**, base akin to Akkadian - **Lawu**, to surround, Arabic: **Liyatu**, Snake. 1. Bible, a sea monster, variously thought of as a reptile or a whale. 2. Anything huge or very powerful. 3. a political treatise by Thomas Hobbes (1651 A.D.) dealing with the organization of the state.*

Yashu'a (Jesus) said: "Thou shalt love the Most High Heavenly Father, thy Sustainer with all thy heart, and with all thy soul, and with all thy mind. Thou shalt love thy neighbour as thyself."

CHILDREN OF THE MOST HIGH:
PRISTINE YOUTH AND FAMILY SOLUTIONS, LLC.
SONS AND DAUGHTERS OF THE MOST HIGH PUBLISHERS ®

Oh, Gracious Most High Heavenly father, Holy is your name,
Your Will Be Done Now and Forever!

The KJV bible Hebrew Strong's Concordance "**#3882** is לִוְיָתָן

Livyathan for the word: "**Leviathan**" in the aforementioned

bible verses. לִוְיָתָן **Livyâthân, Liv-yaw-thawn'**; is a wreathed

animal, i.e. a serpent (especially the crocodile or some other

large sea-monster); figuratively, **the constellation of the**

dragon; also, as a symbol of Babylon: —**Leviathan,**

mourning."

לִוְיָתָן (with the adj. termination ן-, like נְחֻשְׁתָן
brazen, from נְחֹשֶׁת, עֶקְלָתוֹן from עֲקַלָּה), prop. an
(animal), *wreathed, twisted in folds.*

(1) *a serpent* of a larger kind, Job 3:8 (as to this
place see the root עוּר Pilel); Isa. 27:1 (where it is
the symbol of the hostile kingdom of Babylon).

(2) specially, *a crocodile*, Job 40:25, seq.

(3) any *very large aquatic creature*, Ps. 104:
26; used for a fierce enemy, Psa. 74:14; comp. תַּנִּין
Isa. 51:9; Ezek. 29:3; 32:2, 3. Bochart, Hieroz.
P. ii. lib. v. cap. 16—18.

Yashu'a (Jesus) said: "Thou shalt love the Most High
Heavenly Father, thy Sustainer with all thy heart, and
with all thy soul, and with all thy mind. Thou shalt love
thy neighbour as thyself."

Mind Gardening in the Creative Garden of Will (Your Mind) to Grow a Living Water Mentality!

CHILDREN OF THE MOST HIGH:
PRISTINE YOUTH AND FAMILY SOLUTIONS, LLC.
SONS AND DAUGHTERS OF THE MOST HIGH PUBLISHERS ®

Oh, Gracious Most High Heavenly father, Holy is your name,
Your Will Be Done Now and Forever!

In the KJV bible book of **Revelation** chapter **12** verses **7-9**; it states: "And there was war in heaven: **Michael and his angels** (ἄγγελος **Angelos,** meaning **Messengers**, the KJV bible Greek Strong's#32) fought against the **dragon**; and **the dragon fought and his angels** (ἄγγελος **Angelos, meaning Messengers**, the KJV bible Greek Strong's# 32), And prevailed not; neither was their place found any more in heaven. And the **great dragon** was cast out, that **old serpent, called the Devil, and Satan**, which deceiveth the whole world: he was cast out into the earth, and his **angels** (ἄγγελος **Angelos**, meaning **Messengers**, the KJV bible Greek Strong's#32) were cast out with him.

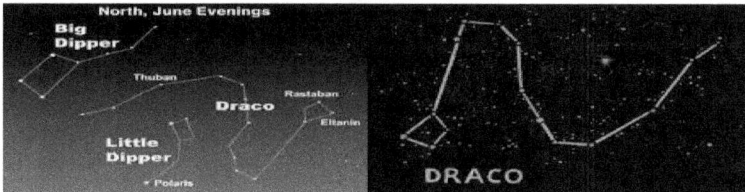

129

Yashu'a (Jesus) said: "Thou shalt love the Most High Heavenly Father, thy Sustainer with all thy heart, and with all thy soul, and with all thy mind. Thou shalt love thy neighbour as thyself."

Mind Gardening in the Creative Garden of Will (Your Mind) to Grow a Living Water Mentality!

CHILDREN OF THE MOST HIGH:
PRISTINE YOUTH AND FAMILY SOLUTIONS, LLC.
SONS AND DAUGHTERS OF THE MOST HIGH PUBLISHERS ®

Oh, Gracious Most High Heavenly father, Holy is your name,
Your Will Be Done Now and Forever!

So, the answer to the question: Is there a correlation between venom, **Leviathan**, the **old Serpent** and the **Dragon** mentioned in the bible that can adversely impact a person's growth into the **Living Water Mentality**? **YES!!!** By biblical definitions, the **old** cunning **Serpent** and the **Dragon** called **Satan** and the **Devil** deceived the whole world. **Are some of the people of this world under some type of Serpent's spell or spell of Leviathan**? Why do we ask this? It would seem unlikely that the **whole world** or everybody on the planet with the many intellectuals in the world would simultaneously be deceived unless the whole world was under some type of hypnotic spell (**which deceiveth the whole world**). **The spell of leviathan is another name for that great dragon, that old serpent called the devil and satan that deceiveth the whole world.**

130

Yashu'a (Jesus) said: "Thou shalt love the Most High Heavenly Father, thy Sustainer with all thy heart, and with all thy soul, and with all thy mind. Thou shalt love thy neighbour as thyself."

Mind Gardening in the Creative Garden of Will (Your Mind) to Grow a Living Water Mentality!

CHILDREN OF THE MOST HIGH:
PRISTINE YOUTH AND FAMILY SOLUTIONS, LLC.
SONS AND DAUGHTERS OF THE MOST HIGH PUBLISHERS ®

*Oh, Gracious Most High Heavenly father, Holy is your name,
Your Will Be Done Now and Forever!*

According to the bible, **Leviathan** is in the atmosphere of the planet earth. "**Levi**" means "**Law**" and "**athan**" means "**sin**". Could **Leviathan** be the **law** that governed the **serpent** in the Garden of Eden in the KJV bible book of Genesis chapter 3 verse 1? "Now the **serpent** was more subtil than any beast of the field which the LORD God had made. And he said unto the woman, Yea, hath God said, Ye shall not eat of every tree of the garden, KJV bible Genesis 3:1." Many theologians and practitioners of Judaism, Christianity and Islam refer to the **Serpent** in the KJV bible book of Genesis as another title for **Lucifer** as mentioned in the KJV bible book of Isaiah chapter 14 verses 12-16. So, Lucifer is sometimes referred to as a serpent. The pluralization of **Lucifer** is **Luciferians** or is sometimes referred to as **Legions**.

Yashu'a (Jesus) said: "Thou shalt love the Most High Heavenly Father, thy Sustainer with all thy heart, and with all thy soul, and with all thy mind. Thou shalt love thy neighbour as thyself."

Mind Gardening in the Creative Garden of Will (Your Mind) to Grow a Living Water Mentality!

CHILDREN OF THE MOST HIGH:
PRISTINE YOUTH AND FAMILY SOLUTIONS, LLC.
SONS AND DAUGHTERS OF THE MOST HIGH PUBLISHERS ®

*Oh, Gracious Most High Heavenly father, Holy is your name,
Your Will Be Done Now and Forever!*

In the KJV bible book of Isaiah chapter 14 verses 12-16; it states: "How art thou fallen from heaven, O **Lucifer**, son of the morning! [how] art thou cut down to the ground, which didst weaken the nations! For thou hast said in thine heart, I will ascend into heaven, I will exalt my throne above the stars of God: I will sit also upon the mount of the congregation, in the sides of the north: I will ascend above the heights of the clouds; I will be like the Most High. Yet thou shalt be brought down to hell, to the sides of the pit. They that see thee shall narrowly look upon thee, [and] consider thee, [saying, is] this the man that made the earth to tremble, that did shake kingdoms." In the KJV bible book of Mark chapter 5 verse 9; Yashu'a (Jesus) asked him (**the unclean spirits inside the man that was possessed**): "What [is] thy name? And he answered, saying, my name [is] **Legion**: **for we are many**."

Yashu'a (Jesus) said: "Thou shalt love the Most High Heavenly Father, thy Sustainer with all thy heart, and with all thy soul, and with all thy mind. Thou shalt love thy neighbour as thyself."

Mind Gardening in the Creative Garden of Will (Your Mind) to Grow a Living Water Mentality!

CHILDREN OF THE MOST HIGH:
PRISTINE YOUTH AND FAMILY SOLUTIONS, LLC.
SONS AND DAUGHTERS OF THE MOST HIGH PUBLISHERS ®

Oh, Gracious Most High Heavenly father, Holy is your name,
Your Will Be Done Now and Forever!

The **KJV bible Greek Strong's Concordance#3003**, defines: "λεγιών **Legion**" as a body of soldiers whose number differed at different times that can invade the body, mind and spirit. The **KJV bible Hebrew Strong's Concordance#03882**, defines: "Leviathan" לִוְיָתָן **Livyâthân, Liv-yaw-thawn'; as a sea monster, dragon from Lawwaw meaning: to unite, to remain.** In the KJV bible book of Isaiah chapter 27 verse 1; **Leviathan** is literally called the: "**piercing serpent**". The **KJV bible Strong's Hebrew Concordance# 5175**, defines: "**Serpent**" as נָחָשׁ **nachash or Nakhash** which is the same word used the KJV bible book of **Genesis chapter 3 verse 1** for "**the devil.**"

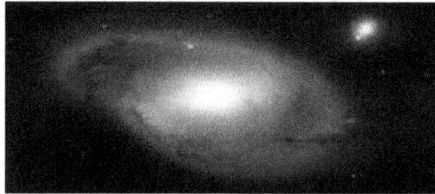

133

Yashu'a (Jesus) said: "Thou shalt love the Most High Heavenly Father, thy Sustainer with all thy heart, and with all thy soul, and with all thy mind. Thou shalt love thy neighbour as thyself."

Mind Gardening in the Creative Garden of Will (Your Mind) to Grow a Living Water Mentality!

CHILDREN OF THE MOST HIGH:
PRISTINE YOUTH AND FAMILY SOLUTIONS, LLC.
SONS AND DAUGHTERS OF THE MOST HIGH PUBLISHERS ®

Oh, Gracious Most High Heavenly father, Holy is your name, Your Will Be Done Now and Forever!

נָחָשׁ m. — (1) *a serpent,* so called from its hissing (see the root) Gen. 3:1, seq.; Ex. 4:3; 7:15; 2 Ki. 18:4. Used of the constellation of the serpent or dragon in the northern part of the sky, Arab. جبّـ Job 26:13.

THE DEVIL IS LUSTS, LIES, AND DELUSIONS;
AND THE MOST HIGH IS LOVE AND TRUTH WITHOUT CONFUSION!

THE DEVIL IS LUSTS, LIES, AND DELUSIONS;
—AND—
THE MOST HIGH IS LOVE AND TRUTH WITHOUT CONFUSION!

Is Your Heart Ruled by Lust or Ruled by the Love of God?

BY WOODIE HUGHES JR.

134

Yashu'a (Jesus) said: "Thou shalt love the Most High Heavenly Father, thy Sustainer with all thy heart, and with all thy soul, and with all thy mind. Thou shalt love thy neighbour as thyself."

Mind Gardening in the Creative Garden of Will (Your Mind) to Grow a Living Water Mentality!

CHILDREN OF THE MOST HIGH:
PRISTINE YOUTH AND FAMILY SOLUTIONS, LLC.
SONS AND DAUGHTERS OF THE MOST HIGH PUBLISHERS ®

*Oh, Gracious Most High Heavenly father, Holy is your name,
Your Will Be Done Now and Forever!*

In the KJV bible book of Mathew chapter 10 verse 1; the Messiah Yashu'a (Jesus): **"called unto him his twelve disciples, he gave them power against unclean spirits, to cast them out, and to heal all manner of sickness and all manner of disease."** In the previous verse when is said: **"all manner of sickness** and **all manner of disease."** The KJV Greek bible Strong's Concordance **"#3956 πᾶς Pas** for the words: **"all manner." πᾶς Pas** means: **every, any, all, the whole, everyone, all things,** everything collectively, **some of all types, including all of the forms of declension."** Therefore; πᾶς **Pas** is inclusive of **all of the forms of declension,** inclusive of **mental or Leviathan minded spell or influences** that prevent a child of the Most High **mind** from being able to grow into the **Living Water Mentality (which will be expounded on in chapter 19).**

Yashu'a (Jesus) said: "Thou shalt love the Most High Heavenly Father, thy Sustainer with all thy heart, and with all thy soul, and with all thy mind. Thou shalt love thy neighbour as thyself."

Mind Gardening in the Creative Garden of Will (Your Mind) to Grow a Living Water Mentality!

CHILDREN OF THE MOST HIGH:
PRISTINE YOUTH AND FAMILY SOLUTIONS, LLC.
SONS AND DAUGHTERS OF THE MOST HIGH PUBLISHERS ®

Oh, Gracious Most High Heavenly father, Holy is your name, Your Will Be Done Now and Forever!

The word "**unclean**" in this verse is KJV bible Greek Strong's Concordance#169 word: "**ἀκάθαρτος Akathartos- meaning:** not cleansed, unclean; in a ceremonial sense: that which must be abstained from according to the Levitical law; **in a moral sense: unclean in thought and life**; impure spiritually, emotionally, **mentally** (ceremonially, morally (lewd-**crude and offensive in a sexual way**, vulgar, filthy, obscene, pornographic, wicked (evil or morally wrong), indecent) or specially, (**demonic**): foul, unclean).**"

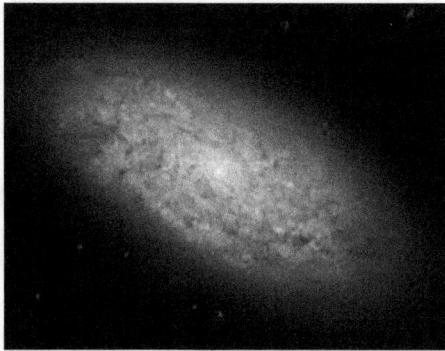

136

Yashu'a (Jesus) said: "Thou shalt love the Most High Heavenly Father, thy Sustainer with all thy heart, and with all thy soul, and with all thy mind. Thou shalt love thy neighbour as thyself."

Mind Gardening in the Creative Garden of Will (Your Mind) to Grow a Living Water Mentality!

CHILDREN OF THE MOST HIGH:
PRISTINE YOUTH AND FAMILY SOLUTIONS, LLC.
SONS AND DAUGHTERS OF THE MOST HIGH PUBLISHERS ®

Oh, Gracious Most High Heavenly father, Holy is your name,
Your Will Be Done Now and Forever!

According to the aforementioned KJV bible verses, **Leviathan, the great dragon** is a **Legion** of **unclean** spirits also known as the **Sex Spirit Force** called **Pórnē, Por'-nay πόρνη** and pronounced as: **"Pornay"** that the Messiah Yashu'a (Jesus) spoke about in the KJV bible book of John chapter 8 verse 41 below with Greek inserts. ὑμεῖς ποιεῖτε τὰ ἔργα τοῦ πατρὸς ὑμῶν εἶπον οὖν αὐτῷ Ἡμεῖς ἐκ πορνείας οὐ γεγεννήμεθα ἕνα πατέρα ἔχομεν τὸν θεόν **(KJV bible book of John chapter 8 verse 41).** In the KJV bible book of John chapter 8 verses 41; Yashu'a (Jesus) stated: "Ye do the deeds of your father. Then said they to him, we be not born of **Fornication**; we have one Father, even God."

137

Yashu'a (Jesus) said: "Thou shalt love the Most High Heavenly Father, thy Sustainer with all thy heart, and with all thy soul, and with all thy mind. Thou shalt love thy neighbour as thyself."

Mind Gardening in the Creative Garden of Will (Your Mind) to Grow a Living Water Mentality!

CHILDREN OF THE MOST HIGH:
PRISTINE YOUTH AND FAMILY SOLUTIONS, LLC.
SONS AND DAUGHTERS OF THE MOST HIGH PUBLISHERS ®

Oh, Gracious Most High Heavenly father, Holy is your name,
Your Will Be Done Now and Forever!

In the above-mentioned verse, the word "**fornication**" is the **KJV bible Greek Strong's Concordance#4202 πορνεία Porneia which means defined as illicit sexual intercourse, adultery, fornication, homosexuality, lesbianism, intercourse with animals etc.** "The word "**fornication**" πορνεία **Porneia,** is from the root word '**Pornay**", **KJV bible Greek Strong's Concordance#4202 πόρνη pórnē, por'-nay;** which means an idolater: —harlot, whore." In the KJV bible book of John chapter 8 verses 44; Yashu'a (Jesus) stated: "Ye are of *your* father the devil, and the <u>lusts</u> of your father ye will do. He was a <u>murderer</u> from the beginning, and abode not in the truth, because there is no truth in him. When he speaketh a lie, he speaketh of his own: for he is a <u>liar</u>, and the father of it." **Having <u>a mentality of lusts, murderer, and a liar; is adverse to the Living Water Mentality</u>.**

Yashu'a (Jesus) said: "Thou shalt love the Most High Heavenly Father, thy Sustainer with all thy heart, and with all thy soul, and with all thy mind. Thou shalt love thy neighbour as thyself."

Mind Gardening in the Creative Garden of Will (Your Mind) to Grow a Living Water Mentality!

CHILDREN OF THE MOST HIGH:
PRISTINE YOUTH AND FAMILY SOLUTIONS, LLC.
SONS AND DAUGHTERS OF THE MOST HIGH PUBLISHERS ®

*Oh, Gracious Most High Heavenly father, Holy is your name,
Your Will Be Done Now and Forever!*

The KJV bible book of John chapter 8 verses 44 with Greek inserts: ὑμεῖς ἐκ πατρὸς τοῦ διαβόλου ἐστὲ καὶ τὰς ἐπιθυμίας τοῦ πατρὸς ὑμῶν θέλετε ποιεῖν ἐκεῖνος ἀνθρωποκτόνος ἦν ἀπ᾽ ἀρχῆς καὶ ἐν τῇ ἀληθείᾳ οὐχ ἔστηκεν ὅτι οὐκ ἔστιν ἀλήθεια ἐν αὐτῷ ὅταν λαλῇ τὸ ψεῦδος ἐκ τῶν ἰδίων λαλεῖ ὅτι ψεύστης ἐστὶν καὶ ὁ πατὴρ αὐτοῦ.

In the above-mentioned verse, the word "**lusts**" is the **KJV bible Greek Strong's Concordance "#1939 word: ἐπιθυμία Epithymia**, which means: **desire, craving, longing, desire for what is forbidden, lust**." So far, the KJV bible has established that **Leviathan**, <u>the great dragon</u> is a **Legion** (a body of soldiers or many unclean spiritual soldiers that can invade the body, mind and spirit) also known as the **Sex Spirit Force** called **Pórnē, Por'-nay πόρνη** and pronounced as: **"Pornay"** that the Messiah Yashu'a (Jesus) spoke about in the KJV bible book of John chapter 8 verses 41-44.

139

Yashu'a (Jesus) said: "Thou shalt love the Most High Heavenly Father, thy Sustainer with all thy heart, and with all thy soul, and with all thy mind. Thou shalt love thy neighbour as thyself."

Mind Gardening in the Creative Garden of Will (Your Mind) to Grow a Living Water Mentality!

CHILDREN OF THE MOST HIGH:
PRISTINE YOUTH AND FAMILY SOLUTIONS, LLC.
SONS AND DAUGHTERS OF THE MOST HIGH PUBLISHERS ®

*Oh, Gracious Most High Heavenly father, Holy is your name,
Your Will Be Done Now and Forever!*

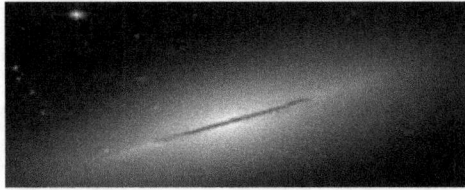

The bible also teaches us that this **Lucifer** who leads this **Legion** of **Luciferians, that old serpent (Leviathan)** who also **lived** during the time in the KJV bible book of **Genesis chapter 3 verse 1 called the Devil** (and **devil** spelled backwards is the word: "**lived**"). So, this devil and his angels convey messages to humanity to influence humanity through the **Deadly Venom of the Desire** of "**Lust**" as the **Sex Spirit Force called Pornay**. This old dragon, was called the **devil** and **satan**. So, **Lucifer controls a Legion** of **Leviathans** or **Luciferians** and is also the leader as **Satan** over a **Legion** called **Satanists**. Therefore, it is essential for all children of the Most High who are in the process of growing into the **Living Water Mentality**, do their best to not get trapped in the devil's web.

140

Yashu'a (Jesus) said: "Thou shalt love the Most High Heavenly Father, thy Sustainer with all thy heart, and with all thy soul, and with all thy mind. Thou shalt love thy neighbour as thyself."

Mind Gardening in the Creative Garden of Will (Your Mind) to Grow a Living Water Mentality!

CHILDREN OF THE MOST HIGH:
PRISTINE YOUTH AND FAMILY SOLUTIONS, LLC.
SONS AND DAUGHTERS OF THE MOST HIGH PUBLISHERS ®

*Oh, Gracious Most High Heavenly father, Holy is your name,
Your Will Be Done Now and Forever!*

THE DEVIL'S WEB

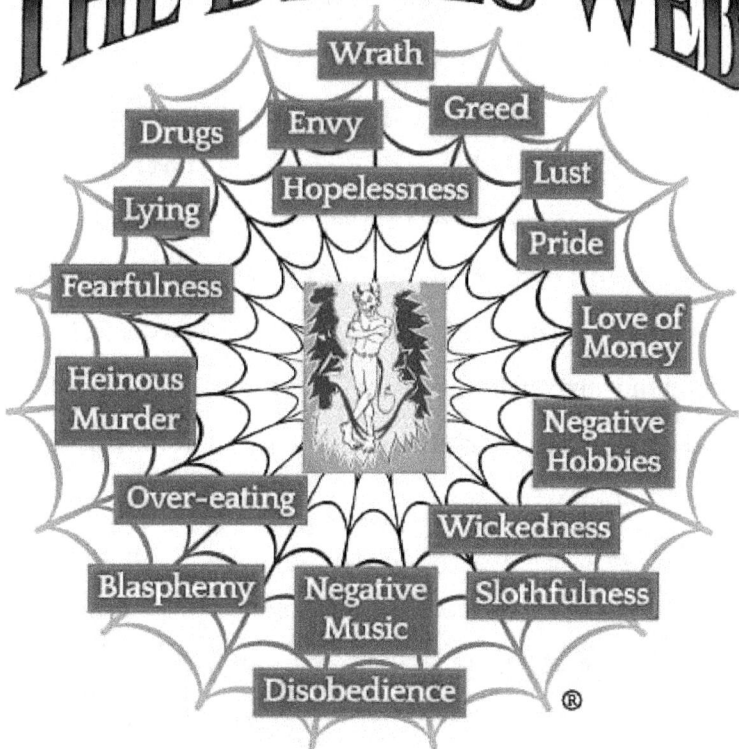

Wrath

Envy

Greed

Drugs

Hopelessness

Lust

Lying

Pride

Fearfulness

Love of Money

Heinous Murder

Negative Hobbies

Over-eating

Wickedness

Blasphemy

Negative Music

Slothfulness

Disobedience

®

141

*Yashu'a (Jesus) said: "Thou shalt love the Most High
Heavenly Father, thy Sustainer with all thy heart, and
with all thy soul, and with all thy mind. Thou shalt love
thy neighbour as thyself."*

Mind Gardening in the Creative Garden of Will (Your Mind) to Grow a Living Water Mentality!

CHILDREN OF THE MOST HIGH:
PRISTINE YOUTH AND FAMILY SOLUTIONS, LLC.
SONS AND DAUGHTERS OF THE MOST HIGH PUBLISHERS ®

*Oh, Gracious Most High Heavenly father, Holy is your name,
Your Will Be Done Now and Forever!*

How does a person guard their heart and mind against the **Luciferians** and **Satanists**? A person guards their heart and mind against the **Luciferians** and **Satanists** by being obedient the Most High Heavenly Father! By doing so, a person learns to study the KJV bible **Hebrew** and **Greek Strong's Concordance hidden meanings of the etymology of the English translated words or the translated words of any other language that their scriptures were translated into**. By researching the **original root meanings of the original languages that the scriptures were revealed in**, it affords a **person an opportunity to acquire the original messages that Michael and his angels** according the KJV bible book of Revelation chapter 12, conveys to members of humanity.

142

Yashu'a (Jesus) said: "Thou shalt love the Most High Heavenly Father, thy Sustainer with all thy heart, and with all thy soul, and with all thy mind. Thou shalt love thy neighbour as thyself."

Mind Gardening in the Creative Garden of Will (Your Mind) to Grow a Living Water Mentality!

CHILDREN OF THE MOST HIGH:
PRISTINE YOUTH AND FAMILY SOLUTIONS, LLC.
SONS AND DAUGHTERS OF THE MOST HIGH PUBLISHERS ®

Oh, Gracious Most High Heavenly father, Holy is your name, Your Will Be Done Now and Forever!

Thus, affording one to learn that the **Satanists** seek **mind** control and dominance and the **Luciferians** seek to control the energy of others. They are best described as "**Spiritual Vampires**" who draw energy from others which also can occur to a person who is striving to be positive while listening to negative speaking people or a negative speaking person.

143

Yashu'a (Jesus) said: "Thou shalt love the Most High Heavenly Father, thy Sustainer with all thy heart, and with all thy soul, and with all thy mind. Thou shalt love thy neighbour as thyself."

Mind Gardening in the Creative Garden of Will (Your Mind) to Grow a Living Water Mentality!

CHILDREN OF THE MOST HIGH:
PRISTINE YOUTH AND FAMILY SOLUTIONS, LLC.
SONS AND DAUGHTERS OF THE MOST HIGH PUBLISHERS ®

*Oh, Gracious Most High Heavenly father, Holy is your name,
Your Will Be Done Now and Forever!*

Consequently, the messages of the great dragon, called the devil and satan are a part of a **Lucifer Conspiracy**. This **Lucifer** or **Luciferian Conspiracy** has succeeded under the **biblical disguise** of "**Leviathan**" by inflicting the **spell of Leviathan** which is **another name for the great dragon, that old serpent called the devil and satan** who controls what we see and hear in the media, on television, on the internet, on the radio and on the satellite radio. How? By utilizing what we see and hear in the media, on television, on the internet, on the radio and on the satellite radio to effect members of humanity in four ways:

1. **Meretricious Effect**: Making people unable to see the truth by masking it in lies and deception as apparently attractive, but in reality, having no value or moral integrity.

Yashu'a (Jesus) said: "Thou shalt love the Most High Heavenly Father, thy Sustainer with all thy heart, and with all thy soul, and with all thy mind. Thou shalt love thy neighbour as thyself."

Mind Gardening in the Creative Garden of Will (Your Mind) to Grow a Living Water Mentality!

*Oh, Gracious Most High Heavenly father, Holy is your name,
Your Will Be Done Now and Forever!*

2. **Death-Dealing Effect**: Capable of causing death as the master orchestrator of chaos, conflict and illusions which causes 100% preventable global confusion amongst members of humanity. **F**aint-hearted **E**xamples **A**mplifying **R**eality **(F.E.A.R.) Effect**. So, always remember that true-faith and trust in the Most High through the True Vine (Yashu'a, Jesus), increases your courage over time. Beware to not **enter fear** in your mind and heart, so that it will not **interfere** with acquiring and sustaining a peace of mind that won't depart; because you are uniquely and wonderfully made, allow the Most High to recreate anew you and don't be afraid! The **F**aint-hearted **E**xamples **A**mplifying **R**eality **(F.E.A.R)** is strengthened through the **H.O.B.A. effect which is the Habit of Being Afraid (H.O.B.A.).**

Yashu'a (Jesus) said: "Thou shalt love the Most High Heavenly Father, thy Sustainer with all thy heart, and with all thy soul, and with all thy mind. Thou shalt love thy neighbour as thyself."

Mind Gardening in the Creative Garden of Will (Your Mind) to Grow a Living Water Mentality!

CHILDREN OF THE MOST HIGH:
PRISTINE YOUTH AND FAMILY SOLUTIONS, LLC.
SONS AND DAUGHTERS OF THE MOST HIGH PUBLISHERS ®

Oh, Gracious Most High Heavenly father, Holy is your name,
Your Will Be Done Now and Forever!

In the KJV bible book of Revelation chapter 13 verses 15 and 18; it states: "And he had power to give life unto the image of the beast, that the image of the beast should both speak, and cause that as many as would not worship the image of the beast should be killed. Here is wisdom. Let him that hath understanding count the number of **the beast**: for it **is the number of a man**; and his number is **Six hundred threescore and six (666)**."

3. **Culture Of Accepting Lies (C.O.A.L) Effect**: As the Messiah Yashu'a (Jesus) said: "Ye are of your father the devil, and the lusts of your father ye will do. He was a murderer from the beginning, and abode not in the truth, because there is no truth in him. When he speaketh a lie, he speaketh of his own: for he is a liar, and the father of it."

146

Yashu'a (Jesus) said: "Thou shalt love the Most High Heavenly Father, thy Sustainer with all thy heart, and with all thy soul, and with all thy mind. Thou shalt love thy neighbour as thyself."

Oh, Gracious Most High Heavenly father, Holy is your name, Your Will Be Done Now and Forever!

4. **Death-Dealing Effect**: Capable of causing death as the master orchestrator of chaos, conflict and illusions which causes 100% preventable global confusion amongst members of humanity. Beware to not **enter fear** in your **mind and heart**, so that it will not **interfere** with acquiring and sustaining a peace of mind that won't depart; because you are uniquely and wonderfully made, allow the Most High to recreate anew you and don't be afraid! So, the children of the Most High must ensure that when they **pray**, that they don't become the **prey** of leviathan spiritual forces.

147

Yashu'a (Jesus) said: "Thou shalt love the Most High Heavenly Father, thy Sustainer with all thy heart, and with all thy soul, and with all thy mind. Thou shalt love thy neighbour as thyself."

Mind Gardening in the Creative Garden of Will (Your Mind) to Grow a Living Water Mentality!

CHILDREN OF THE MOST HIGH:
PRISTINE YOUTH AND FAMILY SOLUTIONS, LLC.
SONS AND DAUGHTERS OF THE MOST HIGH PUBLISHERS ®

Oh, Gracious Most High Heavenly father, Holy is your name,
Your Will Be Done Now and Forever!

How does the poisonous venom Serpent's spell or the spell of Leviathan manifest in the <u>minds and hearts</u> of people? The poisonous venom **Serpent's spell** or the **spell of Leviathan** manifest in people <u>minds and hearts</u> through the dragon and his angels' messages. <u>**The great dragon that was cast out of heaven who is also known as: that old serpent, called the Devil, and Satan, which deceiveth the whole world and his angels**</u> (ἄγγελος **Angelos**, meaning: "**Messengers**" <u>**can only be messengers if they have a message or messages for the people on earth**</u>.

148

Yashu'a (Jesus) said: "Thou shalt love the Most High Heavenly Father, thy Sustainer with all thy heart, and with all thy soul, and with all thy mind. Thou shalt love thy neighbour as thyself."

Mind Gardening in the Creative Garden of Will (Your Mind) to Grow a Living Water Mentality!

CHILDREN OF THE MOST HIGH:
PRISTINE YOUTH AND FAMILY SOLUTIONS, LLC.
SONS AND DAUGHTERS OF THE MOST HIGH PUBLISHERS ®

*Oh, Gracious Most High Heavenly father, Holy is your name,
Your Will Be Done Now and Forever!*

Chapter 10: Highjacked Peace of Mind: Breaking Free from the Prison of the Reprobate-Mind!

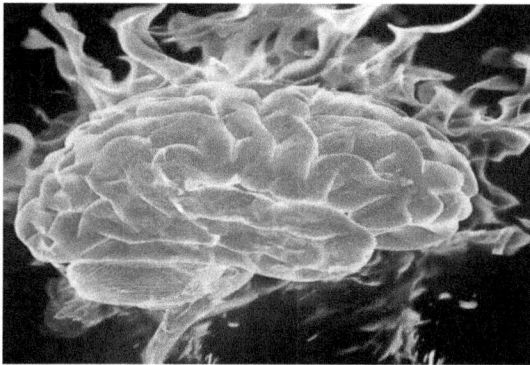

In the KJV bible book of Romans chapter 1 verse 28; it states: "And even as they did not like to retain God in their knowledge, God gave them over to a **reprobate mind**, to do those things which are not convenient." **Are the Mystery Harlots, Sorcery, Witchcraft, and Familiar Spirits, Root Causes of the Reprobate Mind?**

Yashu'a (Jesus) said: "Thou shalt love the Most High Heavenly Father, thy Sustainer with all thy heart, and with all thy soul, and with all thy mind. Thou shalt love thy neighbour as thyself."

Mind Gardening in the Creative Garden of Will (Your Mind) to Grow a Living Water Mentality!

CHILDREN OF THE MOST HIGH:
PRISTINE YOUTH AND FAMILY SOLUTIONS, LLC.
SONS AND DAUGHTERS OF THE MOST HIGH PUBLISHERS ®

Oh, Gracious Most High Heavenly father, Holy is your name,
Your Will Be Done Now and Forever!

The KJV Greek Strong's Concordance "**#96 ἀδόκιμος Adokimos (Aä-do'-ke-mos)** is the word for "**reprobate.**" ἀδόκιμος **Adokimos** means: **worthless (literally or morally):** **castaway, rejected, reprobate.**" The "**reprobate.**" ἀδόκιμος **Adokimos - worthless (literally or morally):** mind is grown in the Global Devil's Web **Pharmacy** Garden of Poison Seeds.

150

Yashu'a (Jesus) said: "*Thou shalt love the Most High Heavenly Father, thy Sustainer with all thy heart, and with all thy soul, and with all thy mind. Thou shalt love thy neighbour as thyself.*"

Mind Gardening in the Creative Garden of Will (Your Mind) to Grow a Living Water Mentality!

CHILDREN OF THE MOST HIGH:
PRISTINE YOUTH AND FAMILY SOLUTIONS, LLC.
SONS AND DAUGHTERS OF THE MOST HIGH PUBLISHERS ®

*Oh, Gracious Most High Heavenly father, Holy is your name,
Your Will Be Done Now and Forever!*

As oppose to being a child of the Most High who utilizes their **Creative Garden of Will (Your Mind)** to do their part in assisting in the process of creating a **Global True Vine "Yashu'a" (Jesus) Farm-And-See** (which is phonetically pronounced as: **Pharm-a-cy**) **Garden of Love, Living Water Mentality.** The **Global Devil's Web Farm-And-See (Pharm-a-cy) Garden of Poison Seeds** is the habitation of devils, the hold of every foul spirit, and a cage of every unclean and hateful bird, slaves (inclusive of human trafficking), and souls of people inclusive of all nations of people were deceived by **sorceries** which is a **Mystery** to those who do not know.

151

Yashu'a (Jesus) said: "Thou shalt love the Most High Heavenly Father, thy Sustainer with all thy heart, and with all thy soul, and with all thy mind. Thou shalt love thy neighbour as thyself."

Mind Gardening in the Creative Garden of Will (Your Mind) to Grow a Living Water Mentality!

CHILDREN OF THE MOST HIGH:
PRISTINE YOUTH AND FAMILY SOLUTIONS, LLC.
SONS AND DAUGHTERS OF THE MOST HIGH PUBLISHERS ®

*Oh, Gracious Most High Heavenly father, Holy is your name,
Your Will Be Done Now and Forever!*

In the KJV bible book of Revelation chapter 17 verse 5; and states: "And upon her forehead was a name written, **MYSTERY**, BABYLON THE GREAT, THE MOTHER OF **HARLOTS** AND ABOMINATIONS OF THE EARTH." The KJV bible Greek Strong's Concordance word for "**MYSTERY**" is#3466 and is the word μυστήριον mystērion which means **a hidden or secret thing, not obvious to the understanding**. The KJV bible Greek Strong's Concordance word for "**HARLOTS**" is#4204 and is the word πόρνη **pornē** which means **a prostitute, a harlot, an idolater, one who yields themselves to defilement for the sake of gain**.

152

Yashu'a (Jesus) said: "Thou shalt love the Most High Heavenly Father, thy Sustainer with all thy heart, and with all thy soul, and with all thy mind. Thou shalt love thy neighbour as thyself."

Mind Gardening in the Creative Garden of Will (Your Mind) to Grow a Living Water Mentality!

CHILDREN OF THE MOST HIGH:
PRISTINE YOUTH AND FAMILY SOLUTIONS, LLC.
SONS AND DAUGHTERS OF THE MOST HIGH PUBLISHERS ®

Oh, Gracious Most High Heavenly father, Holy is your name,
Your Will Be Done Now and Forever!

Porne is the **etymological root word** for "**Pornography**" which the Online American Heritage Dictionary (2020) defines to as: "Sexually explicit writing, images, video, or other material whose primary purpose is to cause sexual arousal. Lurid or sensational material. Often used in combination: violence pornography. [French pornographie, from pornographe, pornographer, from Late Greek pornographos, writing about prostitutes: **pornē**, prostitute; see per-5 in the Appendix of Indo-European roots + graphein, to write; see -GRAPHY."

153

Yashu'a (Jesus) said: "Thou shalt love the Most High Heavenly Father, thy Sustainer with all thy heart, and with all thy soul, and with all thy mind. Thou shalt love thy neighbour as thyself."

Mind Gardening in the Creative Garden of Will (Your Mind) to Grow a Living Water Mentality!

CHILDREN OF THE MOST HIGH:
PRISTINE YOUTH AND FAMILY SOLUTIONS, LLC.
SONS AND DAUGHTERS OF THE MOST HIGH PUBLISHERS ®

Oh, Gracious Most High Heavenly father, Holy is your name,
Your Will Be Done Now and Forever!

So, the **MYSTERY** name of the **Harlot** in the KJV bible book of Revelation chapter 17 that gave birth to the Global Devil's Web Pharmacy Garden of Poison Seeds is "**Porne**" or **Pornography**. "**Porne**" is rooted in "**Lusts**", which is the 3rd of the 9 Deadly Venoms of Desires of the great dragon, that old serpent called the devil and satan. This is what the Messiah Yashu'a (Jesus) warned us about in the KJV bible book of John chapter 8:44; where he said to the Jews of his day and time: "**Ye are of your father the devil, and the <u>lusts</u> of your father ye will do. <u>He</u> was a murderer from the beginning, and abode not in the truth, because there is no truth in <u>him</u>. When <u>he</u> speaketh a lie, <u>he</u> speaketh of <u>his</u> own: for <u>he</u> is a liar, and the father of it.**" Also, the words, **he**, **him** and **his** refers to **<u>one</u> individual** (phonetically is: **<u>in-the-visual</u>** or "**I want to be seen or <u>in-the-visual</u> (<u>individual</u>)** feeling of **P**ower") which denotes

154

Yashu'a (Jesus) said: "Thou shalt love the Most High Heavenly Father, thy Sustainer with all thy heart, and with all thy soul, and with all thy mind. Thou shalt love thy neighbour as thyself."

Mind Gardening in the Creative Garden of Will (Your Mind) to Grow a Living Water Mentality!

CHILDREN OF THE MOST HIGH:
PRISTINE YOUTH AND FAMILY SOLUTIONS, LLC.
SONS AND DAUGHTERS OF THE MOST HIGH PUBLISHERS ®

*Oh, Gracious Most High Heavenly father, Holy is your name,
Your Will Be Done Now and Forever!*

the "**I**" **principle** which grows in Devil's Web Pharmacy Garden of Poison Seeds, and it is rooted in "**Pride**", which is the 1st of the 9 Deadly Venoms of Desires of the great dragon, that old serpent called the devil and satan. The "**I**" **principle** <u>**destroys the possibility of achieving a peace of mind**</u>. The mind must be controlled in order to achieve peace. Pure peace is devoid of <u>d</u>esire, <u>i</u>gnorance and <u>e</u>motions. A man once stated to Siddhartha Gautama "Buddha", "**I want happiness.**" Buddha said, "First remove "**I**," that's **Ego**, then remove "**want**," that's **Desire**. See now, you are left with only "**Happiness**." Siddhartha Gautama "Buddha" also said: "**Desire is the lead to all suffering**." Therefore; when we surrender our ego, we become eligible to become an instrument of doing the Most High Heavenly Father's "**Will**" on earth.

155

Yashu'a (Jesus) said: "Thou shalt love the Most High Heavenly Father, thy Sustainer with all thy heart, and with all thy soul, and with all thy mind. Thou shalt love thy neighbour as thyself."

Mind Gardening in the Creative Garden of Will (Your Mind) to Grow a Living Water Mentality!

CHILDREN OF THE MOST HIGH:
PRISTINE YOUTH AND FAMILY SOLUTIONS, LLC.
SONS AND DAUGHTERS OF THE MOST HIGH PUBLISHERS ®

Oh, Gracious Most High Heavenly father, Holy is your name,
Your Will Be Done Now and Forever!

At that point, our only focus or predominant, most frequent thoughts are on the Most High through **divine love** to serve the Most High. **Divine love** or pure love is free from all lusts.

It is not possible to grow a **Living Water Mentality** without surrendering the **"I"** principle and converting the **"EGO"** into the eternal obedient service to the **"Will"** of the Most High Heavenly Father. By surrendering the **"I"** principle, over time with a lot of personal hard work on yourself, a person may become free from all of the 9 Deadly Venoms of the Desires of the great dragon, that old serpent called the devil and satan.

156

Yashu'a (Jesus) said: "Thou shalt love the Most High Heavenly Father, thy Sustainer with all thy heart, and with all thy soul, and with all thy mind. Thou shalt love thy neighbour as thyself."

Mind Gardening in the Creative Garden of Will (Your Mind) to Grow a Living Water Mentality!

CHILDREN OF THE MOST HIGH:
PRISTINE YOUTH AND FAMILY SOLUTIONS, LLC.
SONS AND DAUGHTERS OF THE MOST HIGH PUBLISHERS ®

*Oh, Gracious Most High Heavenly father, Holy is your name,
Your Will Be Done Now and Forever!*

In the KJV bible book of Revelation chapter 18 verses 1, 2, 13 and 23 states: "And after these things I saw another angel come down from heaven, having great power; and the earth was lightened with his glory. And he cried mightily with a strong voice, saying, Babylon the great is fallen, is fallen, and **is become the habitation of devils, and the hold of every foul spirit, and a cage of every unclean and hateful bird**." And cinnamon, and odours, and ointments, and frankincense, and wine, and oil, and fine flour, and wheat, and beasts, and sheep, and horses, and chariots, and **slaves, and souls of men**. And the light of a candle shall shine no more at all in thee; and the voice of the bridegroom and of the bride shall be heard no more at all in thee: for thy merchants were the great men of the earth; for by thy **sorceries** were all nations deceived."

Yashu'a (Jesus) said: "Thou shalt love the Most High Heavenly Father, thy Sustainer with all thy heart, and with all thy soul, and with all thy mind. Thou shalt love thy neighbour as thyself."

Mind Gardening in the Creative Garden of Will (Your Mind) to Grow a Living Water Mentality!

CHILDREN OF THE MOST HIGH:
PRISTINE YOUTH AND FAMILY SOLUTIONS, LLC.
SONS AND DAUGHTERS OF THE MOST HIGH PUBLISHERS ®

*Oh, Gracious Most High Heavenly father, Holy is your name,
Your Will Be Done Now and Forever!*

In the KJV bible book of Revelation chapter 18 verse 23; the word for **"sorceries"** is the KJV bible Greek Strong's Concordance#5331word: **φαρμακεία pharmakeia** which is the original Greek root word of where the word **"Pharmacy and Pharmaceuticals" originates from.** In the KJV bible book of Galatians chapter 5 verses 19-21; states: "Now the works of the flesh are manifest, which are these; Adultery, fornication, uncleanness, lasciviousness, Idolatry, **witchcraft**, hatred, variance, emulations, wrath, strife, seditions, heresies, Envyings, murders, drunkenness, reveling, and such like: of the which I tell you before, as I have also told you in time past, that they which do such things shall not inherit the kingdom of God."

158

Yashu'a (Jesus) said: "Thou shalt love the Most High Heavenly Father, thy Sustainer with all thy heart, and with all thy soul, and with all thy mind. Thou shalt love thy neighbour as thyself."

Mind Gardening in the Creative Garden of Will (Your Mind) to Grow a Living Water Mentality!

*Oh, Gracious Most High Heavenly father, Holy is your name,
Your Will Be Done Now and Forever!*

In the KJV bible book of Galatians chapter 5 verse 20; the word for "**witchcraft**" is the KJV bible Greek Strong's Concordance#5331word: **φαρμακεία pharmakeia** which is the original Greek root word of where the word **"Pharmacy and Pharmaceuticals" originates from. The Pharmaceutical companies** make opioids and pain medication that many people have become **addicted** to which grows the opioids "**addiction**" crisis in America. **However, in fairness, many people have taken opioids as prescribed by their medical physicians and did not become addicted to opioids or other pain medications. Leviathan**, as a sex force, utilizes **Porne to grow** "**Lusts**", the 3rd of the 9 Deadly Venoms of Desires of the great dragon, that old serpent called the devil and satan in the **global Devil's Web Pharmacy Garden of Poison Seeds**. For more information, seek out the book: "Spiritual Trillionaire" entitled:

Yashu'a (Jesus) said: "Thou shalt love the Most High Heavenly Father, thy Sustainer with all thy heart, and with all thy soul, and with all thy mind. Thou shalt love thy neighbour as thyself."

Mind Gardening in the Creative Garden of Will (Your Mind) to Grow a Living Water Mentality!

CHILDREN OF THE MOST HIGH:
PRISTINE YOUTH AND FAMILY SOLUTIONS, LLC.
SONS AND DAUGHTERS OF THE MOST HIGH PUBLISHERS ®

Oh, Gracious Most High Heavenly father, Holy is your name, Your Will Be Done Now and Forever!

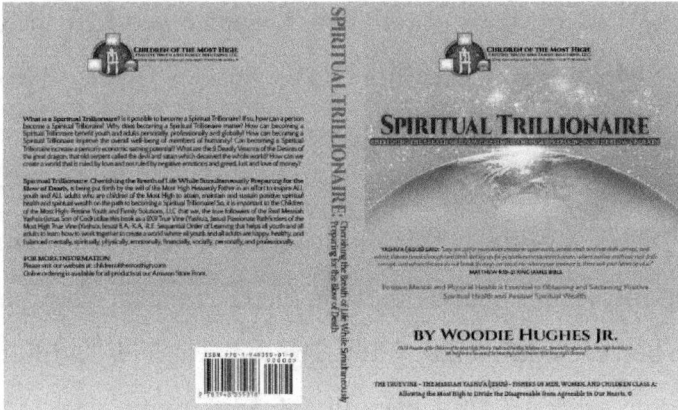

In the KJV bible book of Leviticus chapter 19 verse 31; states: "Regard **not them that have familiar spirits**, neither seek after **wizards** "to be defiled by them: I [am] the LORD your God." In the KJV bible book of Leviticus chapter 20 verse 6; states: "And the soul that turneth after **such as have familiar spirits**, and after **wizards**, to go a whoring after them, I will even set my face against that soul, and will cut him off from among his people."

160

Yashu'a (Jesus) said: "Thou shalt love the Most High Heavenly Father, thy Sustainer with all thy heart, and with all thy soul, and with all thy mind. Thou shalt love thy neighbour as thyself."

Mind Gardening in the Creative Garden of Will (Your Mind) to Grow a Living Water Mentality!

CHILDREN OF THE MOST HIGH:
PRISTINE YOUTH AND FAMILY SOLUTIONS, LLC.
SONS AND DAUGHTERS OF THE MOST HIGH PUBLISHERS ®

*Oh, Gracious Most High Heavenly father, Holy is your name,
Your Will Be Done Now and Forever!*

"In the KJV bible book of Leviticus chapter 19 verse 31, and Leviticus chapter 20 verse 6; the word for "wizards" is the KJV bible Hebrew Strong's Concordance#3045 word: **"Yiddehonee"** יִדְּעֹנִי yidd@`oniy **which means soothsayer, necromancer, a knowing one; specifically, a conjurer; (by implication) a ghost; wizard."**

יִדְּעֹנִי m. pl. יִדְּעֹנִים—(1) properly knowing, wise, hence *a prophet, a wizard,* always used in a bad sense of false prophets. Lev. 19:31; 20:6; Deut. 18:11; 1 Sa. 28:3, 9 (comp. عَالِم prop. knowing, a magician, like the Germ. weiſer Mann, kluge Frau, used of wizards uttering words to the deluded people.)

(2) *a spirit of divination, a spirit of python* with which these soothsayers were believed to be in communication. Lev. 20:27; comp. אוֹב.

161

Mind Gardening in the Creative Garden of Will (Your Mind) to Grow a Living Water Mentality!

CHILDREN OF THE MOST HIGH:
PRISTINE YOUTH AND FAMILY SOLUTIONS, LLC.
SONS AND DAUGHTERS OF THE MOST HIGH PUBLISHERS ®

Oh, Gracious Most High Heavenly father, Holy is your name,
Your Will Be Done Now and Forever!

In the above KJV bible book of Leviticus chapter 19 verse 31, and Leviticus chapter 20 verse 6; the word for phrases "**not them that have familiar spirits** and **such as have familiar spirits**" is the KJV bible Hebrew Strong's Concordance#178 word: אוֹב **'owb** which means **ghost, spirit of a dead one**. So, in summary, the aforementioned information explains the correlation between what the bible refers to as **sorcery**, **witchcraft**, **familiar spirits** and the **Mystery name of the Harlot** who gave birth to the **Global Devil's Web Pharmacy (Far-From-Mercy) Garden of Poison Seeds** as it relates to a child of the Most High person growing the **Living Water Mentality in their Creative Garden of "Will" (Your Mind)**.

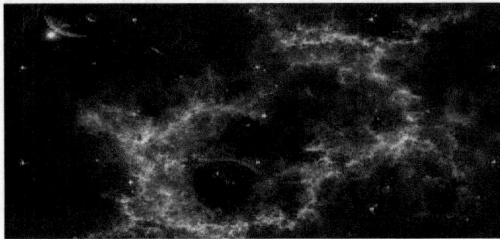

162

Yashu'a (Jesus) said: "Thou shalt love the Most High Heavenly Father, thy Sustainer with all thy heart, and with all thy soul, and with all thy mind. Thou shalt love thy neighbour as thyself."

Mind Gardening in the Creative Garden of Will (Your Mind) to Grow a Living Water Mentality!

CHILDREN OF THE MOST HIGH:
PRISTINE YOUTH AND FAMILY SOLUTIONS, LLC.
SONS AND DAUGHTERS OF THE MOST HIGH PUBLISHERS ®

Oh, Gracious Most High Heavenly father, Holy is your name,
Your Will Be Done Now and Forever!

It also clarifies **why God (אֱלֹהִים 'Elohiym)** is against the children of the Most High utilizing or experimenting with **Ouija boards or spirit boards, porne, soothsayers, necromancers, sorceries, witchcraft, familiar spirits and overcoming the "I" principle, as it relates to preventing a person from being able to acquire, maintain and sustain positive spiritual health and positive spiritual wealth**. So, it is crucial that all aspiring **Spiritual Trillionaires** set True Vine (Yashu'a, Jesus) P.A.S.S.I.O.N.A.T.E. P.A.T.H.F.I.N.D.E.R.S. of the Most High **Predetermined S.M.A.R.T. (Single-Minded, Achievable, Reasonable, Timed) Goals** for themselves to intentionally grow the **Living Water Mentality in their Creative Garden of "Will" (Your Mind)**.

Yashu'a (Jesus) said: "Thou shalt love the Most High Heavenly Father, thy Sustainer with all thy heart, and with all thy soul, and with all thy mind. Thou shalt love thy neighbour as thyself."

Mind Gardening in the Creative Garden of Will (Your Mind) to Grow a Living Water Mentality!

CHILDREN OF THE MOST HIGH:
PRISTINE YOUTH AND FAMILY SOLUTIONS, LLC.
SONS AND DAUGHTERS OF THE MOST HIGH PUBLISHERS ®

Oh, Gracious Most High Heavenly father, Holy is your name,
Your Will Be Done Now and Forever!

"Sometimes people hold a core belief that is very strong. When they are presented with evidence that works against that belief, the new evidence cannot be accepted. It would create a feeling that is extremely uncomfortable, called **cognitive dissonance**. And because it is so important to protect the core belief, they will rationalize, ignore and even deny anything that doesn't fit in with the core belief, (Fanon, 1970)." **The disciplined person's mind, learns to not allow emotions to control their thoughts**, **but; rather controls their emotions through their disciplined repetitive thoughts to control your emotions and to not allow your emotions to control you!** For example: overreacting to words and/or making assumptions or jumping to conclusions, are clear evidence of a mind that is controlled by emotions rather than disciplined repetitive thoughts to control your emotions and to not allow your emotions to control you!

Yashu'a (Jesus) said: "Thou shalt love the Most High Heavenly Father, thy Sustainer with all thy heart, and with all thy soul, and with all thy mind. Thou shalt love thy neighbour as thyself."

Mind Gardening in the Creative Garden of Will (Your Mind) to Grow a Living Water Mentality!

CHILDREN OF THE MOST HIGH:
PRISTINE YOUTH AND FAMILY SOLUTIONS, LLC.
SONS AND DAUGHTERS OF THE MOST HIGH PUBLISHERS ®

Oh, Gracious Most High Heavenly father, Holy is your name,
Your Will Be Done Now and Forever!

Therefore; in order to grow the **Living Water Mentality** in the **Creative Garden of "Will" (Your Mind)**, it requires a child of the Most High **to commit themselves with a sincere and compassionate heart to the service of the Most High Heavenly Father ONLY! Service** is the vehicle by which a child of the Most High Heavenly Father travels in life. **Love** is the zeal and speed of the vehicle by which a child of the Most High travels in life, and **Wisdom** is the way that a child of the Most High Heavenly Father travels in life. This way of thinking frees the **Highjacked Mind**, and **Breaks Free** the **Reprobate-Mind** from being a prisoner to the **habit of worthless immoral thinking**, and frees the **trapped-mind** from the biblical **Mystery Harlots**, **Sorcery**, **Witchcraft**, and **Familiar Spirits**, which are **Root Causes of the Reprobate-Mind** that prevents a child of the Most High from **having a Peace of Mind!** "Thou wilt keep him in **perfect peace**, whose **mind** is stayed on thee: because he trusteth in thee, KJV bible Isaiah 26:3."

Yashu'a (Jesus) said: "Thou shalt love the Most High Heavenly Father, thy Sustainer with all thy heart, and with all thy soul, and with all thy mind. Thou shalt love thy neighbour as thyself."

Mind Gardening in the Creative Garden of Will (Your Mind) to Grow a Living Water Mentality!

CHILDREN OF THE MOST HIGH:
PRISTINE YOUTH AND FAMILY SOLUTIONS, LLC.
SONS AND DAUGHTERS OF THE MOST HIGH PUBLISHERS ®

Oh, Gracious Most High Heavenly father, Holy is your name,
Your Will Be Done Now and Forever!

Chapter 11: 9 True Vine (Yashu'a, Jesus) Heart and Mind Total Trust in the Most High Heavenly Father, Unshakable Foundation of a Spiritual Trillionaire Trust-Mind!

166

Yashu'a (Jesus) said: "Thou shalt love the Most High Heavenly Father, thy Sustainer with all thy heart, and with all thy soul, and with all thy mind. Thou shalt love thy neighbour as thyself."

Mind Gardening in the Creative Garden of Will (Your Mind) to Grow a Living Water Mentality!

CHILDREN OF THE MOST HIGH:
PRISTINE YOUTH AND FAMILY SOLUTIONS, LLC.
SONS AND DAUGHTERS OF THE MOST HIGH PUBLISHERS ®

Oh, Gracious Most High Heavenly father, Holy is your name,
Your Will Be Done Now and Forever!

"Every word of **God** (אֱלוֹהַּ 'Elowahh) is pure (צָרַף Tsaraph): he is a shield **unto them that put their trust** in him, KJV Proverbs 30:5." In the KJV Hebrew bible Strong's Concordance "**#2620** חָסָה **Chacah** for the phrase "**unto them that put their trust**" and means: **to seek refuge in God, flee for protection in God, to put trust in God, confide or hope in God.**"

חָסָה [fut. יֶחֱסֶה and יֶחְסֶה] properly TO FLEE (see the root חוּס), specially *to take refuge, to flee* some where *for refuge*, followed by בְּ of the place, as בְּצֵל 'פ under the shadow (protection) of some one, Jud. 9:15; Isa. 30:2; בְּצֵל כַּנְפֵי יְ׳ under the shadow of the wings of God, Ps. 57:2; 61:5; hence *to trust* in some one, especially in God, followed by בְּ, Psalm 2:12; 5:12; 7:2; 25:20; 31:2; 37:40, etc. Absol. Psal. 17:7. Prov. 14:32, חֹסֶה בְמוֹתוֹ צַדִּיק " the righteous confides (in God) in his death," i. e. when dying, or as about to die.

Derivatives, חָסוּת, מַחֲסֶה, מַחְסֶיָה, and—

167

Yashu'a (Jesus) said: "Thou shalt love the Most High Heavenly Father, thy Sustainer with all thy heart, and with all thy soul, and with all thy mind. Thou shalt love thy neighbour as thyself."

Mind Gardening in the Creative Garden of Will (Your Mind) to Grow a Living Water Mentality!

CHILDREN OF THE MOST HIGH:
PRISTINE YOUTH AND FAMILY SOLUTIONS, LLC.
SONS AND DAUGHTERS OF THE MOST HIGH PUBLISHERS ®

Oh, Gracious Most High Heavenly father, Holy is your name,
Your Will Be Done Now and Forever!

In the KJV bible book of Matthew chapter 22 verses 37-38; the Messiah Yashu'a (Jesus) said: "Thou shalt love the Lord thy God with all thy heart, and with all thy soul, and with all thy mind. This is the first and great commandment." "**Trust** (בָּטַח **Batach (Baw-takh)**) in the **LORD** (יְהֹוָה **Yahayyu, Yehovah) with all thine heart**; and lean not unto thine own understanding, KJV Proverbs 3:5." In the KJV Hebrew bible Strong's Concordance "**#952** is בָּטַח **Batach** for the word "**Trust**" and means: **to confide in, be confident or sure, to cause to trust, make secure, to feel safe.**" So, there is a strong correlation between the **True Vine (Yashu'a, Jesus)** having a **total, unshakable foundation** of **trust in the Most High Heavenly Father, and loving the Most High Heavenly Father with all of his heart, all of his mind, all of his spirit, and all of his soul**; are the **essential elements** of **the True Vine (Yashu'a, Jesus) Trust-Mind** of a **Spiritual Trillionaire!**

168

Yashu'a (Jesus) said: "Thou shalt love the Most High
Heavenly Father, thy Sustainer with all thy heart, and
with all thy soul, and with all thy mind. Thou shalt love
thy neighbour as thyself."

Mind Gardening in the Creative Garden of Will (Your Mind) to Grow a Living Water Mentality!

CHILDREN OF THE MOST HIGH:
PRISTINE YOUTH AND FAMILY SOLUTIONS, LLC.
SONS AND DAUGHTERS OF THE MOST HIGH PUBLISHERS ®

Oh, Gracious Most High Heavenly father, Holy is your name,
Your Will Be Done Now and Forever!

I. בָּטַח—(1) TO CONFIDE IN any one, TO SET ONE'S HOPE AND CONFIDENCE upon any one. (Ch. and Samar. id., but of rare occurrence. Arab. بطح

to throw one down on his back, to throw in the face; whence Heb. בְּ בָּטַח perhaps pr. to throw oneself or one's cares on any one; compare גָּלַל עַל Psa. 22:9). Followed by בְּ Prov. 11:28; Psa. 28:7; עַל 2 Ki. 18:20, 21, 24; אֶל Ps. 4:6; 31:7. Sometimes with a dat. pleon. Jer. 7:4, אַל־תִּבְטְחוּ לָכֶם אֶל־דִּבְרֵי הַשֶּׁקֶר "set not your hope in lying words." Jer. 7:8; 2 Kings 18:21. It is rarely put absol. Job 6:20. In such cases, it is mostly equivalent to—

(2) *to be secure, to fear nothing for oneself.* Jud. 18:7, 10, 27; Jer. 12:5. Job 40:23, יִבְטַח כִּי־יָגִיחַ יַרְדֵּן אֶל־פִּיהוּ "he fears nothing, although Jordan should break forth at his mouth." Pro. 11:15, שֹׂנֵא תֹקְעִים בֹּטֵחַ "he who hates suretiships lives securely," has no cause of fear. Opp. to רַע יֵרוֹעַ. And so— (*a*) it is used in a good sense of the security of the righteous, Isa. 12:2; Pro. 28:1; Job 11:18.—(*b*) in a bad sense, of men who set all their hope and confidence in worldly things, and do not fear God and the Divine displeasure. Isa. 32:9, 10, 11; Pro. 14:16. Comp. שַׁאֲנָן, שָׁלָה, שְׁלָוָה.—Part. בָּטוּחַ *trusting*, with an active signification, Isa. 26:3, כִּי בְךָ בָּטוּחַ "because he trusteth in thee;" Ps. 112:7.

HIPHIL, fut. apoc. יַבְטַח—(1) *to cause to trust*, or *confide, to persuade to trust*, followed by אֶל־ and עַל. Isa. 36:15; Jer. 28:15; 29:31.

(2) absol. *to make secure*, Ps. 22:10.
Derived nouns, מִבְטָח, בַּטֻּחוֹת, בִּטָּחוֹן, בִּטְחָה, בֶּטַח.

II. בָּטַח transp. i. q. טָבַח, طبخ *to cook*, to *ripen*, whence אֲבַטִּים *melon*, which see.

169

Yashu'a (Jesus) said: "Thou shalt love the Most High Heavenly Father, thy Sustainer with all thy heart, and with all thy soul, and with all thy mind. Thou shalt love thy neighbour as thyself."

Mind Gardening in the Creative Garden of Will (Your Mind) to Grow a Living Water Mentality!

CHILDREN OF THE MOST HIGH:
PRISTINE YOUTH AND FAMILY SOLUTIONS, LLC.
SONS AND DAUGHTERS OF THE MOST HIGH PUBLISHERS ®

Oh, Gracious Most High Heavenly father, Holy is your name, Your Will Be Done Now and Forever!

What is a Spiritual Trillionaire?

In the KJV bible Greek Strong's Concordance "**#4151** is the word for "**spirit**" which is: "**Pneuma πνεῦμα (Spirit)**". The original Greek word for "**Spirit**" is "**Pneuma**" (pronounced as: **Pnyoo' - mah**); means: a movement of air (a gentle blast), of the wind, hence the wind itself; breath of nostrils or mouth. In the **original Aramic/Hebrew**, the word: "**Nefesh**, pronounced as: **Neh-Fesh**, means: "**spirit**", and in the **original Aramic/Hebrew** word: "**Rooahk**, pronounce as **Roo-Akh**, means: **Soul**." However, in the English translation of the KJV of the bible and other bibles, **spirit**, **soul** and **mind** <u>are sometimes utilized interchangeably</u> like in the KJV of the bible book of Genesis chapter 1 verse 2 and Genesis chapter 2 verse 7 as seen below with Hebrew inserts:

170

Yashu'a (Jesus) said: "Thou shalt love the Most High Heavenly Father, thy Sustainer with all thy heart, and with all thy soul, and with all thy mind. Thou shalt love thy neighbour as thyself."

Mind Gardening in the Creative Garden of Will (Your Mind) to Grow a Living Water Mentality!

CHILDREN OF THE MOST HIGH:
PRISTINE YOUTH AND FAMILY SOLUTIONS, LLC.
SONS AND DAUGHTERS OF THE MOST HIGH PUBLISHERS ®

Oh, Gracious Most High Heavenly father, Holy is your name,
Your Will Be Done Now and Forever!

The KJV bible book of Genesis chapter 1 verse 2 with Hebrew inserts:

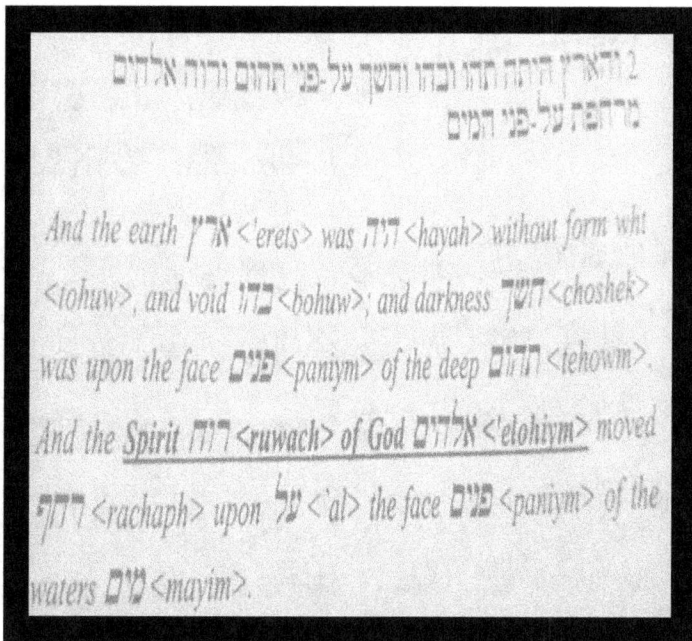

2 והארץ היתה תהו ובהו וחשך על-פני תהום ורוח אלהים
מרחפת על-פני המים.

And the earth אֶרֶץ <'erets> was הָיָה <hayah> without form wht <tohuw>, and void בֹּהוּ <bohuw>; and darkness חֹשֶׁךְ <choshek> was upon the face פָּנִים <paniym> of the deep תְּהוֹם <tehowm>. And the Spirit רוּחַ <ruwach> of God אֱלֹהִים <'elohiym> moved רָחַף <rachaph> upon עַל <'al> the face פָּנִים <paniym> of the waters מַיִם <mayim>.

171

Yashu'a (Jesus) said: "Thou shalt love the Most High Heavenly Father, thy Sustainer with all thy heart, and with all thy soul, and with all thy mind. Thou shalt love thy neighbour as thyself."

Mind Gardening in the Creative Garden of Will (Your Mind) to Grow a Living Water Mentality!

Oh, Gracious Most High Heavenly father, Holy is your name,
Your Will Be Done Now and Forever!

The KJV bible book of Genesis chapter 2 verse 7 with Hebrew inserts:

ויצר יהוה אלהים את-האדם עפר מן-האדמה ויפח באפי
נשמת חיים ויהי האדם לנפש היה

And the LORD יְהוָה <Yehovah> God אֱלֹהִים <'elohiym> formed יָצַר <yatsar> man אָדָם <'adam> of the dust עָפָר <'aphar> of Nm <min> the ground אֲדָמָה <'adamah>, and breathed נפח <naphach> into his nostrils אַף <'aph> the breath נְשָׁמָה <neshamah> of life חַי <chay>; and man אָדָם <'adam> became a living חַי <chay> soul נֶפֶשׁ <nephesh>.

172

Yashu'a (Jesus) said: "Thou shalt love the Most High Heavenly Father, thy Sustainer with all thy heart, and with all thy soul, and with all thy mind. Thou shalt love thy neighbour as thyself."

Mind Gardening in the Creative Garden of Will (Your Mind) to Grow a Living Water Mentality!

CHILDREN OF THE MOST HIGH:
PRISTINE YOUTH AND FAMILY SOLUTIONS, LLC.
SONS AND DAUGHTERS OF THE MOST HIGH PUBLISHERS ®

Oh, Gracious Most High Heavenly father, Holy is your name,
Your Will Be Done Now and Forever!

In the KJV bible book of Genesis chapter 1 verse 2; it states: "And the earth was without form, and void; and darkness was upon the face of the deep. And the Spirit of God moved upon the face of the waters." In the KJV bible book of Genesis chapter 2 verse 7; it states: "And **the Lord God** formed man of the dust of the ground, and **breathed into his nostrils the breath of life**; and man **became a living soul**." So, according to the previous verses, the connection occurred when the **Yahayyu, Yehovah (LORD) Elohiym (God) breathed the Khay or Hayy (Neshamaw Khayyeem** נשמה חיים **- Divine Breath of Life**) into the nostrils of Adam (man) and Adam became a **Nephesh Khay** which in the Aramic (Hebrew) language, **Nephesh is "Spirit"**.

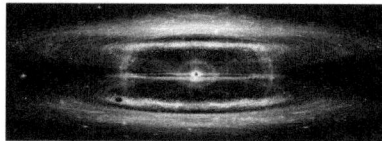

173

Yashu'a (Jesus) said: "Thou shalt love the Most High Heavenly Father, thy Sustainer with all thy heart, and with all thy soul, and with all thy mind. Thou shalt love thy neighbour as thyself."

Mind Gardening in the Creative Garden of Will (Your Mind) to Grow a Living Water Mentality!

CHILDREN OF THE MOST HIGH:
PRISTINE YOUTH AND FAMILY SOLUTIONS, LLC.
SONS AND DAUGHTERS OF THE MOST HIGH PUBLISHERS ®

Oh, Gracious Most High Heavenly father, Holy is your name,
Your Will Be Done Now and Forever!

According to the Online American Heritage Dictionary (2020), **trillionaire** is defined as: "**trill·lion·aire - (trĭll′yə-nâr′, trĭll′yə-nâr′).** *n.* A person whose wealth amounts to at least a trillion dollars, pounds, or the equivalent in other currency. So, according to the Children of the Most High: Pristine Youth and Family Solutions, LLC., <u>**A Spiritual Trillionaire is a being who utilizes all of their Neshamaw Khayyeem (נשמה חיים - Divine Breath of Life) - to be 100% mentally, spiritually, emotionally and physically devout and obedient to the Most High Heavenly Father with Unshakable True-Faith and Divine-Love for the Most High Heavenly Father only; and one who loves the Messiah Yashu'a (Jesus) and have accepted the Messiah Yashu'a (Jesus) as their personal Savior!**</u>

Yashu'a (Jesus) said: "Thou shalt love the Most High Heavenly Father, thy Sustainer with all thy heart, and with all thy soul, and with all thy mind. Thou shalt love thy neighbour as thyself."

Mind Gardening in the Creative Garden of Will (Your Mind) to Grow a Living Water Mentality!

CHILDREN OF THE MOST HIGH:
PRISTINE YOUTH AND FAMILY SOLUTIONS, LLC.
SONS AND DAUGHTERS OF THE MOST HIGH PUBLISHERS ®

Oh, Gracious Most High Heavenly father, Holy is your name, Your Will Be Done Now and Forever!

<u>A Spiritual Trillionaire also: only obeys the commandments of the Most High, only has positive intentions and only is an obedient vessel of the Most High Heavenly Father's "Will" being done through them by way of their True Vine "Yashu'a" (Jesus) good works. This makes our hearts pure so that the Most High Heavenly Father's "Will", will be done on earth as it is in heaven. This way of thinking, loving and doing removes all mental, spiritual and emotional potential barriers that a person may knowingly or unknowingly have; which allows our hearts to be prepared for the Most High to divide the disagreeable from agreeable in our hearts! The Most High is the Watcher of what is in the heart!</u>

175

Yashu'a (Jesus) said: "Thou shalt love the Most High Heavenly Father, thy Sustainer with all thy heart, and with all thy soul, and with all thy mind. Thou shalt love thy neighbour as thyself."

Mind Gardening in the Creative Garden of Will (Your Mind) to Grow a Living Water Mentality!

CHILDREN OF THE MOST HIGH:
PRISTINE YOUTH AND FAMILY SOLUTIONS, LLC.
SONS AND DAUGHTERS OF THE MOST HIGH PUBLISHERS ®

*Oh, Gracious Most High Heavenly father, Holy is your name,
Your Will Be Done Now and Forever!*

According the Messiah Yashu'a (Jesus), through obedience to the Most High, and by accepting him as our Savior; this leads to receiving eternal life after we take our last breath! This is why the Messiah Yashu'a (Jesus) said in the "KJV bible book of Mark chapter 8 verse 36; it states: **"For what shall it profit a man** (the word for **"man"** in this verse is the KJV bible Greek Strong's Concordance #444 word ἄνθρωπος **Anthropos, pronounced as: ä'n-thrō-pos**), which means **a human being, whether male or female generically, to include all human individuals.**), if he (or she) shall gain <u>the whole</u> (the KJV bible Greek Strong's Concordance word for the phrase: **"the whole"** is: ὅλος **Hólos, Hol'-os; which means "whole" or "all") world, and lose his own soul?"**

Yashu'a (Jesus) said: "Thou shalt love the Most High Heavenly Father, thy Sustainer with all thy heart, and with all thy soul, and with all thy mind. Thou shalt love thy neighbour as thyself."

Mind Gardening in the Creative Garden of Will (Your Mind) to Grow a Living Water Mentality!

CHILDREN OF THE MOST HIGH:
PRISTINE YOUTH AND FAMILY SOLUTIONS, LLC.
SONS AND DAUGHTERS OF THE MOST HIGH PUBLISHERS ®

Oh, Gracious Most High Heavenly father, Holy is your name,
Your Will Be Done Now and Forever!

So, according the Messiah Yashu'a (Jesus), all of the wealth of the world cannot afford to buy 1 human soul which makes becoming a **Spiritual Trillionaire *invaluable* (of inestimable value; priceless)**. Thus, by becoming a **P.A.S.S.I.O.N.A.T.E. P.A.T.H.F.I.N.D.E.R.** (Positive, Attitude, Smiling, Seeker, Improving, Optimistically, Now, Actively, Thriving, Efficiently, - Persevering, Agreeably, Thankful, Happy, Faithful, Inspired, Noble, Devoted, Empowered, Resiliency) on the path through the Messiah Yashu'a (Jesus) to get back to the Most High, a person has an opportunity to acquire, maintain and sustain positive spiritual health and positive spiritual wealth! According to Dr. Leaf, "when health invades your body, your mind and spirit are next (Leah, 2009, p.139)."

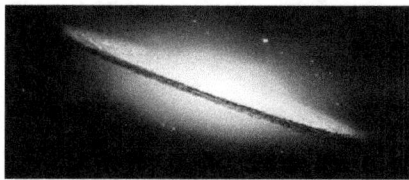

177

Yashu'a (Jesus) said: "Thou shalt love the Most High Heavenly Father, thy Sustainer with all thy heart, and with all thy soul, and with all thy mind. Thou shalt love thy neighbour as thyself."

Mind Gardening in the Creative Garden of Will (Your Mind) to Grow a Living Water Mentality!

CHILDREN OF THE MOST HIGH:
PRISTINE YOUTH AND FAMILY SOLUTIONS, LLC.
SONS AND DAUGHTERS OF THE MOST HIGH PUBLISHERS ®

Oh, Gracious Most High Heavenly father, Holy is your name,
Your Will Be Done Now and Forever!

Is it possible to become a Spiritual Trillionaire? Some may say: "it is **impossible** to become a Spiritual Trillionaire," right? The Children of the Most High: Pristine Youth and Family Solutions, LLC. merely ask; does the word: **Im-possible** spell **I'm-possible**? In the KJV bible book of Matthew Chapter 19 verse 26 the Messiah Yashu'a (Jesus) said: "**With men this is impossible, with God, all things are possible**." According to the KJV bible, is money evil? Or is the love of money evil? In the KJV bible book of 1st Timothy chapter 6 verse 10, it states: "For ***the love of money*** is the root of all evil: which while some coveted after, they have erred from the faith, and pierced themselves through with many sorrows."

178

Yashu'a (Jesus) said: "Thou shalt love the Most High Heavenly Father, thy Sustainer with all thy heart, and with all thy soul, and with all thy mind. Thou shalt love thy neighbour as thyself."

Mind Gardening in the Creative Garden of Will (Your Mind) to Grow a Living Water Mentality!

CHILDREN OF THE MOST HIGH:
PRISTINE YOUTH AND FAMILY SOLUTIONS, LLC.
SONS AND DAUGHTERS OF THE MOST HIGH PUBLISHERS ®

*Oh, Gracious Most High Heavenly father, Holy is your name,
Your Will Be Done Now and Forever!*

So, instead of loving money, consider what Mr. Gibran said: "**I love you, my brothers and sisters, whoever you are. You and I are all children of one faith, for the diverse paths of religion are fingers of the loving** hand of one Supreme Being, a hand extended to all offering completeness of spirit to all, eager to receive all, (Gibran, 1964, p.14)."

179

Yashu'a (Jesus) said: "Thou shalt love the Most High Heavenly Father, thy Sustainer with all thy heart, and with all thy soul, and with all thy mind. Thou shalt love thy neighbour as thyself."

Mind Gardening in the Creative Garden of Will (Your Mind) to Grow a Living Water Mentality!

CHILDREN OF THE MOST HIGH:
PRISTINE YOUTH AND FAMILY SOLUTIONS, LLC.
SONS AND DAUGHTERS OF THE MOST HIGH PUBLISHERS ®

Oh, Gracious Most High Heavenly father, Holy is your name,
Your Will Be Done Now and Forever!

Why does becoming a Spiritual Trillionaire matter?

Becoming a Spiritual Trillionaire may or may not matter to some people depending on what they value the most. However, becoming a Spiritual Trillionaire would only matter to the children of the Most High who want to **utilize all of their Neshamaw Khayyeem (נשמה חיים - Divine Breath of Life) - to be 100% mentally, spiritually, emotionally and physically devout and obedient to the Most High Heavenly Father with Unshakable True-Faith and Divine-Love for the Most High Heavenly Father only; and who loves the Messiah Yashu'a (Jesus) and has accepted the Messiah Yashu'a (Jesus) as their personal Savior, and all who are loving and are peacemakers at heart!**

180

Yashu'a (Jesus) said: "Thou shalt love the Most High Heavenly Father, thy Sustainer with all thy heart, and with all thy soul, and with all thy mind. Thou shalt love thy neighbour as thyself."

Mind Gardening in the Creative Garden of Will (Your Mind) to Grow a Living Water Mentality!

CHILDREN OF THE MOST HIGH:
PRISTINE YOUTH AND FAMILY SOLUTIONS, LLC.
SONS AND DAUGHTERS OF THE MOST HIGH PUBLISHERS ®

Oh, Gracious Most High Heavenly father, Holy is your name,
Your Will Be Done Now and Forever!

Also, becoming a Spiritual Trillionaire would only matter to the children of the Most High who only obeys the commandments of the Most High, only has positive intentions and only is an obedient vessel of the Most High's "Will" being done through them through their True Vine "Yashu'a" (Jesus) good works. **How can a person receive the holy spirit? And is this a mandatory step to becoming a Spiritual Trillionaire?** A child of the Most High must first become aware of what they value the most. If a child of the Most High values spiritual growth aspiration, according to the bible, a person must be born again.

181

Yashu'a (Jesus) said: "Thou shalt love the Most High Heavenly Father, thy Sustainer with all thy heart, and with all thy soul, and with all thy mind. Thou shalt love thy neighbour as thyself."

Mind Gardening in the Creative Garden of Will (Your Mind) to Grow a Living Water Mentality!

CHILDREN OF THE MOST HIGH:
PRISTINE YOUTH AND FAMILY SOLUTIONS, LLC.
SONS AND DAUGHTERS OF THE MOST HIGH PUBLISHERS ®

Oh, Gracious Most High Heavenly father, Holy is your name,
Your Will Be Done Now and Forever!

In the KJV bible book of John chapter 3 verses 3-9; Yashu'a (Jesus) said: "Verily, verily, I say unto thee, except a man **[person]** be born again, he **[a person]** cannot see the kingdom of God. "Nicodemus saith unto him, how can a man **[person]** be born when he **[a person]** is old? can he **[a person]** enter the second time into his mother's womb, and be born? Yashu'a said: "Verily, verily, I say unto thee, except a man [person] be born of water and of the Spirit, [a person] cannot enter into the kingdom of God. That which is born of the flesh is flesh; and that which is born of the Spirit is spirit. Marvel not that I said unto thee, Ye must be born again. The wind bloweth where it listeth, and thou hearest the sound thereof, but canst not tell whence it cometh, and whither it goeth: so is every one that is born of the Spirit."

Yashu'a (Jesus) said: "Thou shalt love the Most High Heavenly Father, thy Sustainer with all thy heart, and with all thy soul, and with all thy mind. Thou shalt love thy neighbour as thyself."

Mind Gardening in the Creative Garden of Will (Your Mind) to Grow a Living Water Mentality!

CHILDREN OF THE MOST HIGH:
PRISTINE YOUTH AND FAMILY SOLUTIONS, LLC.
SONS AND DAUGHTERS OF THE MOST HIGH PUBLISHERS

Oh, Gracious Most High Heavenly father, Holy is your name,
Your Will Be Done Now and Forever!

In the KJV bible book of Romans chapter 10 verses 9-10; it states: "That if thou shalt confess with thy mouth the Lord Jesus, and shalt believe in thine heart that God hath raised him from the dead, thou shalt be saved. For with the heart **[of a person]** believeth unto righteousness; and with the mouth confession is made unto salvation." Receiving the holy spirit is a mandatory step to becoming a Spiritual Trillionaire. The aforementioned verses gives' a person some insight into being born again. However, there is a plethora of additional lifelong works that a person has to do on themselves as they grow spiritually. Meaning, you have to rid yourself of everything that you think is right so that the holy spirit can access your temple (body).

183

Yashu'a (Jesus) said: "Thou shalt love the Most High Heavenly Father, thy Sustainer with all thy heart, and with all thy soul, and with all thy mind. Thou shalt love thy neighbour as thyself."

Mind Gardening in the Creative Garden of Will (Your Mind) to Grow a Living Water Mentality!

CHILDREN OF THE MOST HIGH:
PRISTINE YOUTH AND FAMILY SOLUTIONS, LLC.
SONS AND DAUGHTERS OF THE MOST HIGH PUBLISHERS ®

Oh, Gracious Most High Heavenly father, Holy is your name,
Your Will Be Done Now and Forever!

In the KJV bible book of 1st Corinthians chapter 6 verses 19-20; it states: "What? know ye not that your body is the temple of the Holy Ghost which is in you, which ye have of God, and ye are not your own? For ye are bought with a price: therefore, glorify God in your body, and in your spirit, which are God's."
In the KJV bible book of 1st Corinthians chapter 3 verses 16-17; it states: "Know ye not that ye are the temple of God, and that the Spirit of God dwelleth in you? If any [person] defile the temple of God, [that person] shall God destroy; for the temple of God is holy, which temple ye are."

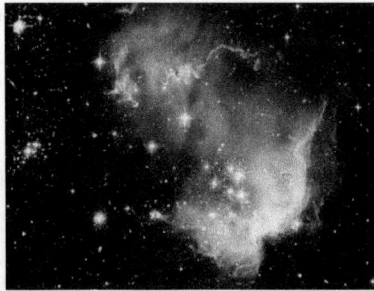

184

Yashu'a (Jesus) said: "Thou shalt love the Most High Heavenly Father, thy Sustainer with all thy heart, and with all thy soul, and with all thy mind. Thou shalt love thy neighbour as thyself."

Mind Gardening in the Creative Garden of Will (Your Mind) to Grow a Living Water Mentality!

CHILDREN OF THE MOST HIGH:
PRISTINE YOUTH AND FAMILY SOLUTIONS, LLC.
SONS AND DAUGHTERS OF THE MOST HIGH PUBLISHERS ®

Oh, Gracious Most High Heavenly father, Holy is your name,
Your Will Be Done Now and Forever!

So, the holy spirit can only come into a clean temple (body). The holy spirit can only stay in a comfortable, purified temple (body). This means, a person who is contemplating rather or not they are ready to receive the holy spirit has to be willing to commit themselves to moment to moment work of eradicating negative habits, negative thinking, negative speaking, negative intentions, negative aspirations, negative actions, and unhealthy eating. If a person does not eradicate themselves of the above-mentioned negative attributes, **<u>a holy (pure) spirit (pneuma, nephesh) cannot dwell inside an impure mind, impure heart and impure body</u>**.

185

Yashu'a (Jesus) said: "Thou shalt love the Most High Heavenly Father, thy Sustainer with all thy heart, and with all thy soul, and with all thy mind. Thou shalt love thy neighbour as thyself."

Mind Gardening in the Creative Garden of Will (Your Mind) to Grow a Living Water Mentality!

CHILDREN OF THE MOST HIGH:
PRISTINE YOUTH AND FAMILY SOLUTIONS, LLC.
SONS AND DAUGHTERS OF THE MOST HIGH PUBLISHERS ®

Oh, Gracious Most High Heavenly father, Holy is your name,
Your Will Be Done Now and Forever!

Acquiring, maintaining and sustaining positive spiritual health and positive spiritual wealth requires active discipline exhibited moment to moment on a daily basis. It is a serious commitment of **discipline** that is required in order to keep your temple (body) purified mentally, spiritually, emotionally and physically. The Online American Heritage Dictionary (2020) defines **discipline** as: **"1. Training expected to produce a specific character or pattern of behavior, especially training that produces moral or mental improvement: was raised in the strictest discipline. 2. b. Controlled behavior resulting from disciplinary training; self-control."**

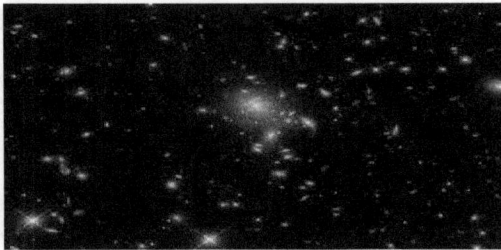

186

Yashu'a (Jesus) said: "Thou shalt love the Most High Heavenly Father, thy Sustainer with all thy heart, and with all thy soul, and with all thy mind. Thou shalt love thy neighbour as thyself."

Mind Gardening in the Creative Garden of Will (Your Mind) to Grow a Living Water Mentality!

CHILDREN OF THE MOST HIGH:
PRISTINE YOUTH AND FAMILY SOLUTIONS, LLC.
SONS AND DAUGHTERS OF THE MOST HIGH PUBLISHERS ®

*Oh, Gracious Most High Heavenly father, Holy is your name,
Your Will Be Done Now and Forever!*

The Children of the Most High Pristine Youth and Family Solutions, LLC. defines **discipline** as: **"doing what you need to do when it needs to be done whether you feel like doing it or not.**" Some people may make the mistake of thinking that they can just cleanse their mind and spirit without cleansing their body (temple) from unhealthy eating and unhealthy drinking. Many people may make statements like: "In my heart, I'm good and that's all that matters." "As long as I have God in my heart, that's all that matters." If that were the case, the Most High would put the truth in our hearts instead of in books and scriptures.

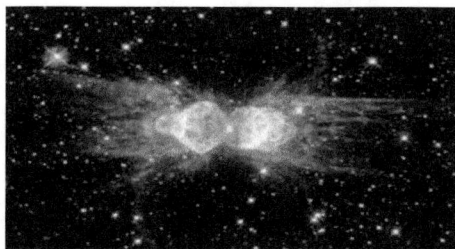

187

Yashu'a (Jesus) said: "Thou shalt love the Most High Heavenly Father, thy Sustainer with all thy heart, and with all thy soul, and with all thy mind. Thou shalt love thy neighbour as thyself."

Mind Gardening in the Creative Garden of Will (Your Mind) to Grow a Living Water Mentality!

CHILDREN OF THE MOST HIGH:
PRISTINE YOUTH AND FAMILY SOLUTIONS, LLC.
SONS AND DAUGHTERS OF THE MOST HIGH PUBLISHERS ®

*Oh, Gracious Most High Heavenly father, Holy is your name,
Your Will Be Done Now and Forever!*

Why would the Most High put the truth in a book like the Torah, Bible or other scriptures or a book like the one you are reading right now, when the Most High could have just put the information in our hearts? Because there is a part of becoming a Spiritual Trillionaire that is physical, that requires great discipline in order to not give into **the temptations of the 9 Deadly Venoms of the Desires of the dragon, that old serpent called the devil and satan that deceived the whole world**.

188

Yashu'a (Jesus) said: "Thou shalt love the Most High Heavenly Father, thy Sustainer with all thy heart, and with all thy soul, and with all thy mind. Thou shalt love thy neighbour as thyself."

Mind Gardening in the Creative Garden of Will (Your Mind) to Grow a Living Water Mentality!

CHILDREN OF THE MOST HIGH:
PRISTINE YOUTH AND FAMILY SOLUTIONS, LLC.
SONS AND DAUGHTERS OF THE MOST HIGH PUBLISHERS ®

Oh, Gracious Most High Heavenly father, Holy is your name,
Your Will Be Done Now and Forever!

The great discipline to not give into the temptations of the 9 Deadly Venoms is essential to overall potential spiritual growth success because the temptations cannot work on the soul, they can only work on the body. The body interprets the temptations for the soul. **For example:** As it relates to lusts, sometimes, the temptation is put on television through images of nudity in effort **to plant the thought in the mind** for the soul to interpret as lusts.

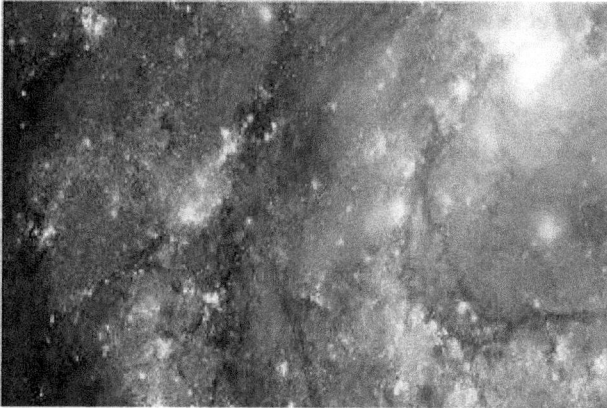

189

Yashu'a (Jesus) said: *"Thou shalt love the Most High Heavenly Father, thy Sustainer with all thy heart, and with all thy soul, and with all thy mind. Thou shalt love thy neighbour as thyself."*

Mind Gardening in the Creative Garden of Will (Your Mind) to Grow a Living Water Mentality!

CHILDREN OF THE MOST HIGH:
PRISTINE YOUTH AND FAMILY SOLUTIONS, LLC.
SONS AND DAUGHTERS OF THE MOST HIGH PUBLISHERS ®

Oh, Gracious Most High Heavenly father, Holy is your name,
Your Will Be Done Now and Forever!

So, when a person receives the holy spirit, he or she transforms from a son or daughter of human beings to a child of the Most High and the holy spirit will reeducate your soul over time and substantiate what you learn as the Most High's truth through evidence, reasoning and experience. Essentially, a person would have to make what the Children of the Most High: Pristine Youth and Family Solutions, LLC. refer to as a: **"True Vine "Yashu'a (Jesus) Conscious and Conscientious (C.A.C.) decision"** that will allow their mind to guide their brain to a Spiritual Trillionaire way of thinking.

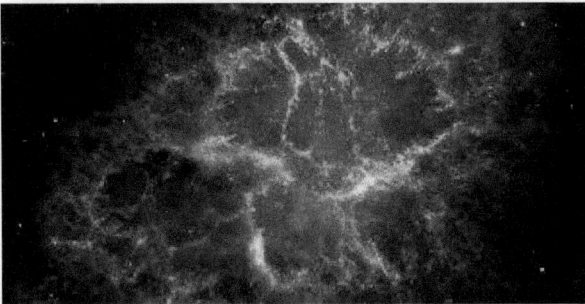

190

Yashu'a (Jesus) said: "Thou shalt love the Most High Heavenly Father, thy Sustainer with all thy heart, and with all thy soul, and with all thy mind. Thou shalt love thy neighbour as thyself."

Mind Gardening in the Creative Garden of Will (Your Mind) to Grow a Living Water Mentality!

CHILDREN OF THE MOST HIGH:
PRISTINE YOUTH AND FAMILY SOLUTIONS, LLC.
SONS AND DAUGHTERS OF THE MOST HIGH PUBLISHERS

*Oh, Gracious Most High Heavenly father, Holy is your name,
Your Will Be Done Now and Forever!*

This decision process is also referred to by the Children of the Most High: Pristine Youth and Family Solutions, LLC. as: **"Choices, Actions, Consequences and Repercussions (C.A.C.A.R) through Potential Diversification and Overstanding**." Dr. Leah refers to this process as: "The Brain Does the Bidding of the Mind, Leah, 2013, p.32)."

191

Yashu'a (Jesus) said: "Thou shalt love the Most High Heavenly Father, thy Sustainer with all thy heart, and with all thy soul, and with all thy mind. Thou shalt love thy neighbour as thyself."

Mind Gardening in the Creative Garden of Will (Your Mind) to Grow a Living Water Mentality!

CHILDREN OF THE MOST HIGH:
PRISTINE YOUTH AND FAMILY SOLUTIONS, LLC.
SONS AND DAUGHTERS OF THE MOST HIGH PUBLISHERS ®

Oh, Gracious Most High Heavenly father, Holy is your name,
Your Will Be Done Now and Forever!

The 9 Essential Elements in a Human Being that influences and empowers a person's overall well-being as it relates to **mind gardening in the creative garden of will (your mind) to grow a Living Water Mentality** on the **path to becoming a Spiritual Trillionaire**; are:

1. Spirit (KJV bible book of Genesis chapter 2 verse 7).
2. Mind (KJV bible book of Mathew chapter 22 verses 37-38).
3. Body (KJV bible book of Genesis chapter 2 verse 7).
4. Soul (KJV bible book of Genesis chapter 2 verse 7).
5. Plasma in you or Plasmatic You (KJV bible book of Leviticus chapter 17 verses 13-14, Life is in the blood).
6. Etheric (ether) you, is a person's genetic spiritual link to their Ancestors, the Ancient Ones and the Old Ones. (KJV bible book of Psalms chapter 82 verses 6-7).
7. Physical Heart (KJV bible book of Proverbs chapter 3 verses 5-6).
8. Spiritual Heart (KJV bible book of Revelation chapter 3 verse 20).
9. Spark of Life – Lifeforce of all living things (KJV bible book of John chapter 1 verses 1-5).

Yashu'a (Jesus) said: "Thou shalt love the Most High Heavenly Father, thy Sustainer with all thy heart, and with all thy soul, and with all thy mind. Thou shalt love thy neighbour as thyself."

Mind Gardening in the Creative Garden of Will (Your Mind) to Grow a Living Water Mentality!

CHILDREN OF THE MOST HIGH:
PRISTINE YOUTH AND FAMILY SOLUTIONS, LLC.
SONS AND DAUGHTERS OF THE MOST HIGH PUBLISHERS ®

*Oh, Gracious Most High Heavenly father, Holy is your name,
Your Will Be Done Now and Forever!*

As it relates to mind gardening in the creative garden of will (your mind) to grow a Living Water Mentality, the 9 True Vine Yashu'a (Jesus) Essential Habits of Healing the physical body are:

1. Daily intake of healthy food. In the KJV bible book of Exodus chapter 23 verse 25; it states: "And ye shall serve the LORD your God, and he shall bless thy bread, and thy water; and I will take sickness away from the midst of thee."

2. Daily intake of plenty healthy water. In the KJV bible book of John chapter 4 verse 14; it states: "But whosoever drinketh of the water that I shall give him shall never thirst; but the water that I shall give him shall be in him a well of water springing up into everlasting life."

193

Yashu'a (Jesus) said: "Thou shalt love the Most High Heavenly Father, thy Sustainer with all thy heart, and with all thy soul, and with all thy mind. Thou shalt love thy neighbour as thyself."

Mind Gardening in the Creative Garden of Will (Your Mind) to Grow a Living Water Mentality!

CHILDREN OF THE MOST HIGH:
PRISTINE YOUTH AND FAMILY SOLUTIONS, LLC.
SONS AND DAUGHTERS OF THE MOST HIGH PUBLISHERS ®

Oh, Gracious Most High Heavenly father, Holy is your name,
Your Will Be Done Now and Forever!

3. Daily Physical Health Self-Care – doing medical physician approved physical exercising (if possible). In the KJV bible book of 3rd John chapter 1 verse 2; states: "Beloved, I wish above all things that thou mayest prosper and be in health, even as thy soul prospereth."

4. Daily true-prayer supplication. In the KJV bible book of Philippians chapter 4 verse 6; it states: "Be careful for nothing; but in everything by prayer and supplication with thanksgiving let your requests be made known unto God."

194

Yashu'a (Jesus) said: "Thou shalt love the Most High Heavenly Father, thy Sustainer with all thy heart, and with all thy soul, and with all thy mind. Thou shalt love thy neighbour as thyself."

Mind Gardening in the Creative Garden of Will (Your Mind) to Grow a Living Water Mentality!

CHILDREN OF THE MOST HIGH:
PRISTINE YOUTH AND FAMILY SOLUTIONS, LLC.
SONS AND DAUGHTERS OF THE MOST HIGH PUBLISHERS ®

Oh, Gracious Most High Heavenly father, Holy is your name,
Your Will Be Done Now and Forever!

5. Daily meditation, healthy breathing and healthy and sober relaxation. In the KJV bible book of Psalms chapter 1 verse 2; it states: "But his delight [is] in the law of the LORD; and in his law doth he meditates day and night."

6. Daily high-quality sufficient amounts of sleep. In the KJV bible book of Psalms chapter 127 verse 2; it states: "[It is] vain for you to rise up early, to sit up late, to eat the bread of sorrows: [for] so he giveth his beloved sleep."

195

Yashu'a (Jesus) said: "Thou shalt love the Most High Heavenly Father, thy Sustainer with all thy heart, and with all thy soul, and with all thy mind. Thou shalt love thy neighbour as thyself."

Mind Gardening in the Creative Garden of Will (Your Mind) to Grow a Living Water Mentality!

CHILDREN OF THE MOST HIGH:
PRISTINE YOUTH AND FAMILY SOLUTIONS, LLC.
SONS AND DAUGHTERS OF THE MOST HIGH PUBLISHERS ®

Oh, Gracious Most High Heavenly father, Holy is your name,
Your Will Be Done Now and Forever!

7. Daily loving and obeying the Messiah Yashu'a (Jesus). In the KJV bible book of John chapter 14 verse 15; Yashu'a (Jesus) said: "If ye love me, keep my commandments."

8. Daily having and practicing True-Faith in the Most High Heavenly Father. In the KJV bible book of Mark chapter 11 verse 22; it states: "And Yashu'a (Jesus) answering saith unto them, "Have faith in God."

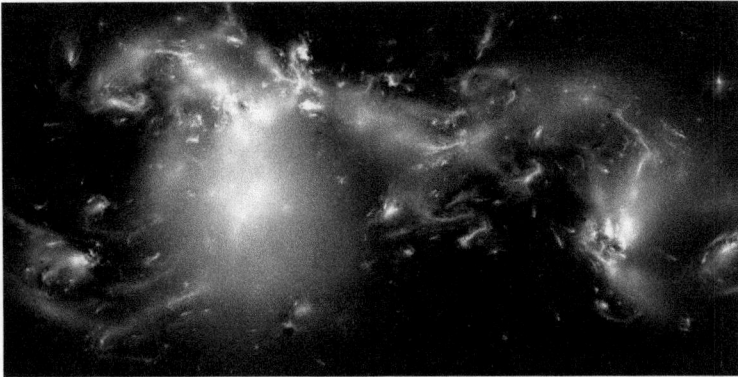

196

Yashu'a (Jesus) said: "Thou shalt love the Most High Heavenly Father, thy Sustainer with all thy heart, and with all thy soul, and with all thy mind. Thou shalt love thy neighbour as thyself."

Mind Gardening in the Creative Garden of Will (Your Mind) to Grow a Living Water Mentality!

CHILDREN OF THE MOST HIGH:
PRISTINE YOUTH AND FAMILY SOLUTIONS, LLC.
SONS AND DAUGHTERS OF THE MOST HIGH PUBLISHERS ®

*Oh, Gracious Most High Heavenly father, Holy is your name,
Your Will Be Done Now and Forever!*

9. Daily having and expressing divine love for the Most High Heavenly Father, loving and obeying the Most High Heavenly Father with all of your heart, with all your spirit, with all of your soul, and with all of your mind. In the KJV bible book of Matthew chapter 22 verse 37; Yashu'a (Jesus) said unto him: "Thou shalt love the Lord thy God with all thy heart, and with all thy soul, and with all thy mind."

197

Yashu'a (Jesus) said: "Thou shalt love the Most High Heavenly Father, thy Sustainer with all thy heart, and with all thy soul, and with all thy mind. Thou shalt love thy neighbour as thyself."

Mind Gardening in the Creative Garden of Will (Your Mind) to Grow a Living Water Mentality!

CHILDREN OF THE MOST HIGH:
PRISTINE YOUTH AND FAMILY SOLUTIONS, LLC.
SONS AND DAUGHTERS OF THE MOST HIGH PUBLISHERS ®

Oh, Gracious Most High Heavenly father, Holy is your name,
Your Will Be Done Now and Forever!

The **9 True Vine Yashu'a (Jesus) Work Ethics** as it relates **to mind gardening in the creative garden of will (your mind) to grow a Living Water Mentality** are:

1. **Responsible** – In the KJV bible book of Romans chapter 14 verse 12; it states: "So then every one of us shall give account of himself [or herself] to God."

2. **Active Listener** – In the KJV bible book of James chapter 1 verse 19; it states: "Wherefore, my beloved brethren [or sisters], let every man [woman and child] be swift to hear, slow to speak, slow to wrath."

198

Yashu'a (Jesus) said: "Thou shalt love the Most High Heavenly Father, thy Sustainer with all thy heart, and with all thy soul, and with all thy mind. Thou shalt love thy neighbour as thyself."

CHILDREN OF THE MOST HIGH:
PRISTINE YOUTH AND FAMILY SOLUTIONS, LLC.
SONS AND DAUGHTERS OF THE MOST HIGH PUBLISHERS ®

Oh, Gracious Most High Heavenly father, Holy is your name, Your Will Be Done Now and Forever!

3. **Trustworthy** – In the KJV bible book of Proverbs chapter 3 verses 5-6; it states: "Trust in the LORD with all thine heart; and lean not unto thine own understanding. In all thy ways acknowledge him, and he shall direct thy **paths**." In the KJV bible book of Matthew chapter 10 verse 13; it states: The Messiah Yashu'a (Jesus) said: "And if the house be worthy, let your peace come upon it: but if it be not worthy, let your peace return to you." In the KJV bible book of Matthew chapter 10 verses 37-38; the Messiah Yashu'a (Jesus) said: "He [or She] that loveth father or mother more than me is not worthy of me: and he [or She] that loveth son or daughter more than me is not worthy of me. And he [or she] that taketh not his cross, and followeth after me, is not worthy of me."

Yashu'a (Jesus) said: "Thou shalt love the Most High Heavenly Father, thy Sustainer with all thy heart, and with all thy soul, and with all thy mind. Thou shalt love thy neighbour as thyself."

Mind Gardening in the Creative Garden of Will (Your Mind) to Grow a Living Water Mentality!

CHILDREN OF THE MOST HIGH:
PRISTINE YOUTH AND FAMILY SOLUTIONS, LLC.
SONS AND DAUGHTERS OF THE MOST HIGH PUBLISHERS ®

*Oh, Gracious Most High Heavenly father, Holy is your name,
Your Will Be Done Now and Forever!*

4. <u>**Respectful**</u> – In the KJV bible book of Psalms chapter 119 verse 6; it states: "Then shall I not be ashamed, when I have respect unto all thy commandments." In the KJV bible book of Psalms chapter 119 verse 15; it states: "I will meditate in thy precepts, and have respect unto thy ways." In the KJV bible book of Psalms chapter 119 verse 117; it states: "Hold thou me up, and I shall be safe: and I will have respect unto thy statutes continually."

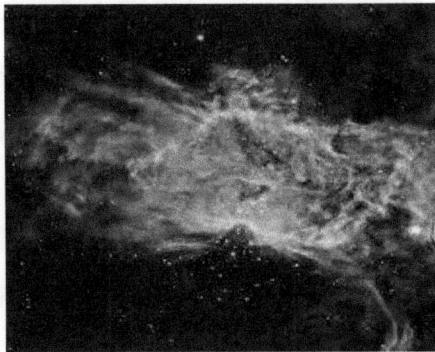

200

Yashu'a (Jesus) said: "Thou shalt love the Most High Heavenly Father, thy Sustainer with all thy heart, and with all thy soul, and with all thy mind. Thou shalt love thy neighbour as thyself."

Mind Gardening in the Creative Garden of Will (Your Mind) to Grow a Living Water Mentality!

CHILDREN OF THE MOST HIGH:
PRISTINE YOUTH AND FAMILY SOLUTIONS, LLC.
SONS AND DAUGHTERS OF THE MOST HIGH PUBLISHERS ®

Oh, Gracious Most High Heavenly father, Holy is your name,
Your Will Be Done Now and Forever!

5. **Dependable** – In the KJV bible book of 2nd Samuel chapter 22 verse 3; it states: "The God of my rock; in him will I trust [and depend upon]: he is my shield, and the horn of my salvation, my high tower, and my refuge, my savior; thou savest me from violence." In the KJV bible book of Revelation chapter 21 verse 23; it states: "And the city had no need of the sun, neither of the moon, to shine in it: for the glory of God did lighten it, and the Lamb is the light thereof."

6. **Positive Attitude** – In the KJV bible book of Psalms chapter 45 verse 7; it states: "Thou lovest righteousness, and hatest wickedness: therefore God, thy God, hath anointed thee with the oil of gladness above thy fellows."

Yashu'a (Jesus) said: "Thou shalt love the Most High Heavenly Father, thy Sustainer with all thy heart, and with all thy soul, and with all thy mind. Thou shalt love thy neighbour as thyself."

Mind Gardening in the Creative Garden of Will (Your Mind) to Grow a Living Water Mentality!

CHILDREN OF THE MOST HIGH:
PRISTINE YOUTH AND FAMILY SOLUTIONS, LLC.
SONS AND DAUGHTERS OF THE MOST HIGH PUBLISHERS ®

Oh, Gracious Most High Heavenly father, Holy is your name,
Your Will Be Done Now and Forever!

7. **<u>Positive Behavior</u>** – In the KJV bible book of Philippians chapter 4 verse 8; it states: "Finally, brethren, whatsoever things are true, whatsoever things [are] honest, whatsoever things [are] just, whatsoever things [are] pure, whatsoever things [are] lovely, whatsoever things [are] of good report; if [there be] any virtue, and if [there be] any praise, think on these things."

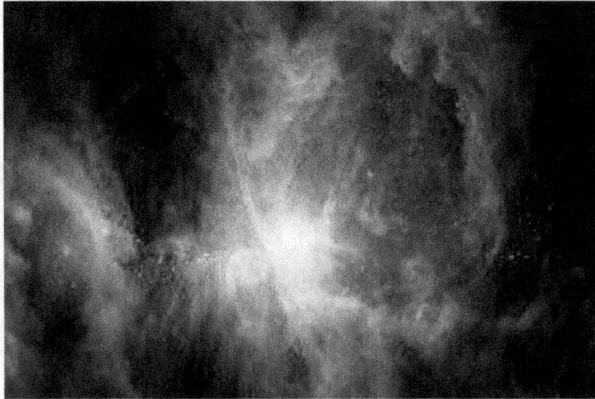

202

Yashu'a (Jesus) said: "Thou shalt love the Most High Heavenly Father, thy Sustainer with all thy heart, and with all thy soul, and with all thy mind. Thou shalt love thy neighbour as thyself."

Mind Gardening in the Creative Garden of Will (Your Mind) to Grow a Living Water Mentality!

CHILDREN OF THE MOST HIGH:
PRISTINE YOUTH AND FAMILY SOLUTIONS, LLC.
SONS AND DAUGHTERS OF THE MOST HIGH PUBLISHERS ®

*Oh, Gracious Most High Heavenly father, Holy is your name,
Your Will Be Done Now and Forever!*

8. **Impactful** – In the KJV bible book of Proverbs chapter 13 verse 20; it states: "He that walketh with wise [men] shall be wise: but a companion of fools shall be destroyed."

9. **Team Player** – In the KJV bible book of Ecclesiastes chapter 4 verses 9-10; it states: "Two [are] better than one; because they have a good reward for their labor. For if they fall, the one will lift up his fellow: but woe to him [or her] [that is] alone when he [or she] falleth; for [he hath] [or she hath] not another to help him [or her] up, (Hughes, 2019)."

203

Yashu'a (Jesus) said: "Thou shalt love the Most High Heavenly Father, thy Sustainer with all thy heart, and with all thy soul, and with all thy mind. Thou shalt love thy neighbour as thyself."

Mind Gardening in the Creative Garden of Will (Your Mind) to Grow a Living Water Mentality!

CHILDREN OF THE MOST HIGH:
PRISTINE YOUTH AND FAMILY SOLUTIONS, LLC.
SONS AND DAUGHTERS OF THE MOST HIGH PUBLISHERS ®

*Oh, Gracious Most High Heavenly father, Holy is your name,
Your Will Be Done Now and Forever!*

Therefore; having a **total, unshakable foundation** of **trust in the Most High Heavenly Father, and loving the Most High Heavenly Father with all of your heart, all of your mind, all of your spirit, and all of your soul**; are the **essential elements** of **the True Vine (Yashu'a, Jesus) Trust-Mind** of a **Spiritual Trillionaire!**

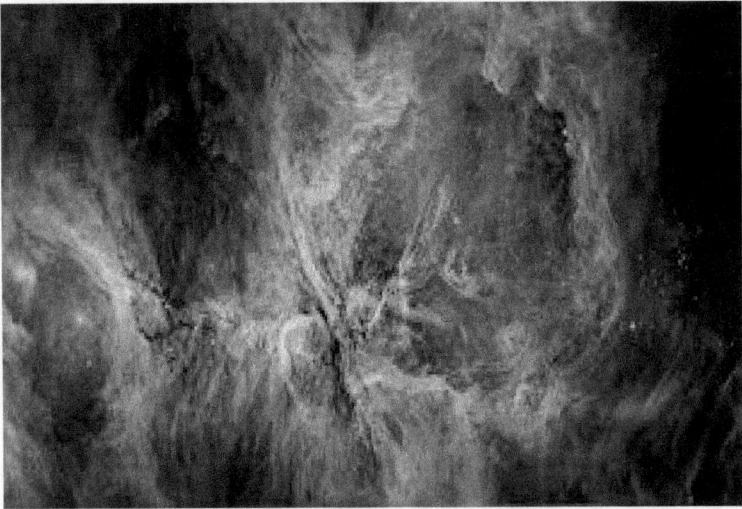

204

Yashu'a (Jesus) said: "Thou shalt love the Most High Heavenly Father, thy Sustainer with all thy heart, and with all thy soul, and with all thy mind. Thou shalt love thy neighbour as thyself."

Mind Gardening in the Creative Garden of Will (Your Mind) to Grow a Living Water Mentality!

CHILDREN OF THE MOST HIGH:
PRISTINE YOUTH AND FAMILY SOLUTIONS, LLC.
SONS AND DAUGHTERS OF THE MOST HIGH PUBLISHERS ®

*Oh, Gracious Most High Heavenly father, Holy is your name,
Your Will Be Done Now and Forever!*

Chapter 12 Mind Meditation on the Most High!

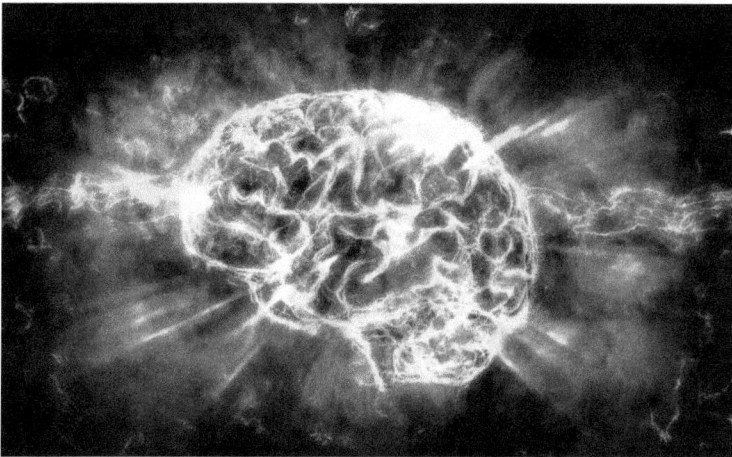

What does the word "ALL" mean the KJV bible book of Matthew chapter 22 verse 37? In the KJV bible book of Matthew chapter 22 verse 37; the Messiah Yashu'a (Jesus) said: "Thou shalt love the Lord thy God with all thy heart, and with all thy soul, and with all thy mind."

205

Yashu'a (Jesus) said: "Thou shalt love the Most High Heavenly Father, thy Sustainer with all thy heart, and with all thy soul, and with all thy mind. Thou shalt love thy neighbour as thyself."

Mind Gardening in the Creative Garden of Will (Your Mind) to Grow a Living Water Mentality!

CHILDREN OF THE MOST HIGH:
PRISTINE YOUTH AND FAMILY SOLUTIONS, LLC.
SONS AND DAUGHTERS OF THE MOST HIGH PUBLISHERS ®

*Oh, Gracious Most High Heavenly father, Holy is your name,
Your Will Be Done Now and Forever!*

According to the KJV bible Greek Strong's Concordance "**#3650 ὅλος Holos (Hol'-os)** is the word for "**all**" in the aforementioned verse. **ὅλος Holos** means: **all, whole, completely.**" Thereby, **meditating on the Most High Heavenly One as "ALL" through total attention and intentional concentration on the Most High Heavenly One as "ALL" through divine love for the Most High,** with all thy heart, and with all thy soul, and with all thy mind! "**Meditate** upon these things; give thyself wholly to them; that thy profiting may appear to all." In the KJV bible Greek Strong's Concordance "**#3191 μελετάω Meletaō (Me-le-tä'-o)** is the word for "**Meditate**". **μελετάω Meletaō** means: **to care for, attend to carefully, practice, to meditate, to devise, contrive; be diligent in practicing meditation, revolve in the mind: imagine, (pre-)meditate.**"

206

Yashu'a (Jesus) said: "Thou shalt love the Most High Heavenly Father, thy Sustainer with all thy heart, and with all thy soul, and with all thy mind. Thou shalt love thy neighbour as thyself."

Mind Gardening in the Creative Garden of Will (Your Mind) to Grow a Living Water Mentality!

CHILDREN OF THE MOST HIGH:
PRISTINE YOUTH AND FAMILY SOLUTIONS, LLC.
SONS AND DAUGHTERS OF THE MOST HIGH PUBLISHERS ®

Oh, Gracious Most High Heavenly father, Holy is your name,
Your Will Be Done Now and Forever!

According to the American Heritage Online Dictionary (2020), **Meditate** means: **"To train, calm, or empty the mind, often by achieving an altered state, as by focusing on a single object."** **"To engage in focused thought on scriptural passages or on particular doctrines or mysteries of a religion, or spirituality. To engage in devotional contemplation, especially prayer. To think or reflect, especially in a calm and deliberate manner. To engage in meditation regarding (a religious mystery, for example). To plan in the mind; intend."**

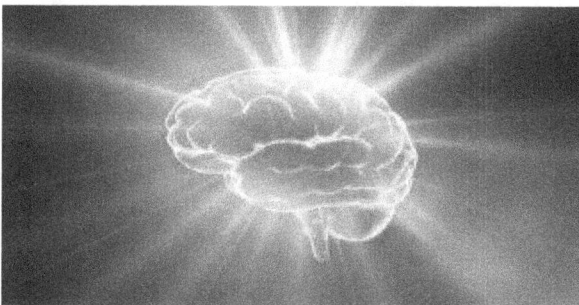

207

Yashu'a (Jesus) said: "Thou shalt love the Most High Heavenly Father, thy Sustainer with all thy heart, and with all thy soul, and with all thy mind. Thou shalt love thy neighbour as thyself."

Mind Gardening in the Creative Garden of Will (Your Mind) to Grow a Living Water Mentality!

CHILDREN OF THE MOST HIGH:
PRISTINE YOUTH AND FAMILY SOLUTIONS, LLC.
SONS AND DAUGHTERS OF THE MOST HIGH PUBLISHERS ®

*Oh, Gracious Most High Heavenly father, Holy is your name,
Your Will Be Done Now and Forever!*

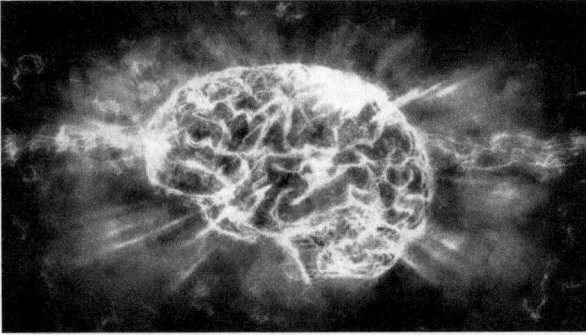

So, the children of the Most High Heavenly Father must practice loving the Most High Heavenly One with all of **our finite mind**, while remembering that the boundless universes are creations of **infinite mind**.

208

Yashu'a (Jesus) said: "Thou shalt love the Most High Heavenly Father, thy Sustainer with all thy heart, and with all thy soul, and with all thy mind. Thou shalt love thy neighbour as thyself."

Mind Gardening in the Creative Garden of Will (Your Mind) to Grow a Living Water Mentality!

CHILDREN OF THE MOST HIGH:
PRISTINE YOUTH AND FAMILY SOLUTIONS, LLC.
SONS AND DAUGHTERS OF THE MOST HIGH PUBLISHERS ®

*Oh, Gracious Most High Heavenly father, Holy is your name,
Your Will Be Done Now and Forever!*

When the Messiah yashu'a (Jesus) says: "Love the Most High Heavenly Father with all thy heart, and with all thy soul, and with all thy mind!" **All thy mind in its aspect of being, projects; in the creative garden of will (your mind), toward its aspect of becoming, in the process of growing a Living Water Mentality.**

209

Yashu'a (Jesus) said: "Thou shalt love the Most High Heavenly Father, thy Sustainer with all thy heart, and with all thy soul, and with all thy mind. Thou shalt love thy neighbour as thyself."

Mind Gardening in the Creative Garden of Will (Your Mind) to Grow a Living Water Mentality!

CHILDREN OF THE MOST HIGH:
PRISTINE YOUTH AND FAMILY SOLUTIONS, LLC.
SONS AND DAUGHTERS OF THE MOST HIGH PUBLISHERS ®

*Oh, Gracious Most High Heavenly father, Holy is your name,
Your Will Be Done Now and Forever!*

The KJV bible Greek Strong's Concordance word for "**heart**" in the KJV bible book of Matthew chapter 22 verse 37 is "**#2588 καρδία Kardia (Kar-dee'-ah)** for the **innermost aspect of thoughts (mind) feelings (heart). καρδία Kardia (Kar-dee'-ah)** means: **the heart, that organ in the body which is the center of the circulation of the blood, and hence was regarded as the seat of physical life, the innermost aspect of thoughts (mind) feelings (heart), denotes the center of all physical and spiritual life, the soul or mind, as it is the fountain and seat of the thoughts, passions, desires, appetites, affections, purposes, endeavors of the understanding, the faculty and seat of the intelligence of the will and character**."

210

Yashu'a (Jesus) said: "Thou shalt love the Most High Heavenly Father, thy Sustainer with all thy heart, and with all thy soul, and with all thy mind. Thou shalt love thy neighbour as thyself."

Mind Gardening in the Creative Garden of Will (Your Mind) to Grow a Living Water Mentality!

CHILDREN OF THE MOST HIGH:
PRISTINE YOUTH AND FAMILY SOLUTIONS, LLC.
SONS AND DAUGHTERS OF THE MOST HIGH PUBLISHERS ®

*Oh, Gracious Most High Heavenly father, Holy is your name,
Your Will Be Done Now and Forever!*

Therefore, all of our divine love for the Most High must grow from **voluntary** to **involuntary** with all thy heart, and with all thy soul, and all thy mind. The American Heritage Online Dictionary (2020) defines **voluntary** as: "**Done or undertaken of one's own free will: Acting or done willingly and without constraint or expectation of reward: Capable of making choices; having the faculty of will. Involuntary** is defined as: **Acting or done automatically without one's will; not subject to control of the volition. Volition** is defined as: **the act of making a conscious choice or decision. The power or faculty of choosing; the will.**" **Evolutionary** is defined as: **A gradual process in which something changes into a different and usually more complex or better form.**"

211

Yashu'a (Jesus) said: "Thou shalt love the Most High Heavenly Father, thy Sustainer with all thy heart, and with all thy soul, and with all thy mind. Thou shalt love thy neighbour as thyself."

Mind Gardening in the Creative Garden of Will (Your Mind) to Grow a Living Water Mentality!

CHILDREN OF THE MOST HIGH:
PRISTINE YOUTH AND FAMILY SOLUTIONS, LLC.
SONS AND DAUGHTERS OF THE MOST HIGH PUBLISHERS ®

Oh, Gracious Most High Heavenly father, Holy is your name,
Your Will Be Done Now and Forever!

The **involuntary stage of creation** of **divine love** for the Most High is an outpouring of **divine energy**, just as **the evolutionary stage is the beginning of experiencing** God's (אֱלֹהִים **Elohiym**) **A**ll **W**ise **A**bundant **R**ight Exact **(A.W.A.R.E) knowledge.** As it relates to καρδία **Kardia (Kar-dee'-ah (the heart)** as the **faculty and seat of the intelligence of the will and character**.

212

Yashu'a (Jesus) said: "Thou shalt love the Most High Heavenly Father, thy Sustainer with all thy heart, and with all thy soul, and with all thy mind. Thou shalt love thy neighbour as thyself."

Mind Gardening in the Creative Garden of Will (Your Mind) to Grow a Living Water Mentality!

CHILDREN OF THE MOST HIGH:
PRISTINE YOUTH AND FAMILY SOLUTIONS, LLC.
SONS AND DAUGHTERS OF THE MOST HIGH PUBLISHERS ®

Oh, Gracious Most High Heavenly father, Holy is your name,
Your Will Be Done Now and Forever!

The **9 True Vine "Yashu'a" (Jesus) Fruits of the Spirit of Positive Character-Building Essentials** as it relates to **mind gardening in the creative garden of will (your mind) to grow a Living Water Mentality** are:

1: <u>Love</u> – ἀγάπη Agápē, ag-ah'-pay; from KJV Bible Strong's Greek # G25; which means: love, i.e. affection or benevolence; specially (plural) a love-feast: — (feast of) charity(-ably), dear, love. Affection, good will, love, benevolence, brotherly love, love feasts. In KJV bible book of Galatians chapter 5 verse 22; it states: "But the fruit of the Spirit is **love**, joy, peace, longsuffering, gentleness, goodness, faith."

213

Yashu'a (Jesus) said: "Thou shalt love the Most High Heavenly Father, thy Sustainer with all thy heart, and with all thy soul, and with all thy mind. Thou shalt love thy neighbour as thyself."

Mind Gardening in the Creative Garden of Will (Your Mind) to Grow a Living Water Mentality!

CHILDREN OF THE MOST HIGH:
PRISTINE YOUTH AND FAMILY SOLUTIONS, LLC.
SONS AND DAUGHTERS OF THE MOST HIGH PUBLISHERS ®

*Oh, Gracious Most High Heavenly father, Holy is your name,
Your Will Be Done Now and Forever!*

The True Vine Yashu'a (Jesus) Fruit of the Spirit of Positive Character-Building Essential of "Love" through true-faith in the Most High Heavenly Father to overcome and resist the 5th of the 9 Deadly Venoms of the Desires of the great dragon, that old serpent called the devil and satan which deceiveth the whole world known as "Lust" by expressing divine love for the most High Heavenly Father, loving the Messiah Yashu'a to overcoming the longing for something that is forbidden (**Love – ἀγάπη Agápē**) according to the commandments of the Most High.

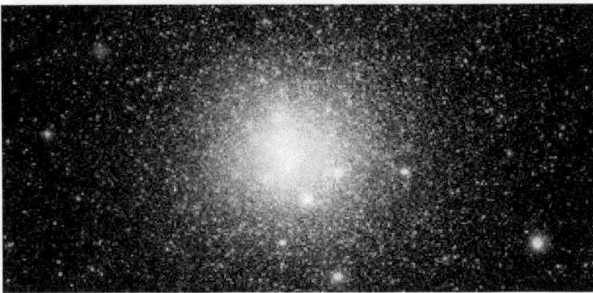

214

Yashu'a (Jesus) said: "Thou shalt love the Most High Heavenly Father, thy Sustainer with all thy heart, and with all thy soul, and with all thy mind. Thou shalt love thy neighbour as thyself."

Mind Gardening in the Creative Garden of Will (Your Mind) to Grow a Living Water Mentality!

CHILDREN OF THE MOST HIGH:
PRISTINE YOUTH AND FAMILY SOLUTIONS, LLC.
SONS AND DAUGHTERS OF THE MOST HIGH PUBLISHERS ®

Oh, Gracious Most High Heavenly father, Holy is your name,
Your Will Be Done Now and Forever!

2: Joy – χαρά **Chará, Khar-ah'**; from KJV Bible Strong's Greek #**G5463**; which means: cheerfulness, i.e. calm delight:— gladness, × greatly, (X be exceeding) joy(-ful, -fully, -fulness, -ous). Joy, gladness, the joy received from you, the cause or occasion of joy, of persons who are one's joy. In KJV bible book of Galatians chapter 5 verse 22; it states: "But the fruit of the Spirit is love, **joy**, peace, longsuffering, gentleness, goodness, faith." According to **"The will to Kill"**: **Making sense of senseless murder** (2018), over 90% of all **Heinous Murder**s were committed by people who were not joyful, but were very angry or enraged. The **True Vine Yashu'a (Jesus) Fruit of the Spirit of Positive Character-Building Essential of "Joy"** through true-faith in the Most High Heavenly Father to overcome and resist the **8th of the 9 Deadly Venoms of the Desires of the great dragon, that old serpent called the devil**

Yashu'a (Jesus) said: "Thou shalt love the Most High Heavenly Father, thy Sustainer with all thy heart, and with all thy soul, and with all thy mind. Thou shalt love thy neighbour as thyself."

Mind Gardening in the Creative Garden of Will (Your Mind) to Grow a Living Water Mentality!

CHILDREN OF THE MOST HIGH:
PRISTINE YOUTH AND FAMILY SOLUTIONS, LLC.
SONS AND DAUGHTERS OF THE MOST HIGH PUBLISHERS ®

*Oh, Gracious Most High Heavenly father, Holy is your name,
Your Will Be Done Now and Forever!*

and satan which deceiveth the whole world known as "**Heinous Murder**" by learning and practicing being happy inside, **cheerful**, **calm** and **delightful (Joy – χαρά Chará, Khar-ah')** every day (Hughes, 2019). **3: Peace – εἰρήνη Eirḗnē, i-ray'-nay**; from KJV Bible Strong's Greek **#1515** probably from a primary verb εἴρω eírō (to join); which means: peace (literally or figuratively); by implication, prosperity: one, peace, quietness, rest, + set at one again. A state of national tranquility, exemption from the rage and havoc of war, peace between individuals, i.e. harmony, concord, security, safety, prosperity, felicity, (because peace and harmony make and keep things safe and prosperous); of the Messiah's peace, the way that leads to peace (salvation), the blessed state of **devout and upright** men after death.

Yashu'a (Jesus) said: "Thou shalt love the Most High Heavenly Father, thy Sustainer with all thy heart, and with all thy soul, and with all thy mind. Thou shalt love thy neighbour as thyself."

Mind Gardening in the Creative Garden of Will (Your Mind) to Grow a Living Water Mentality!

CHILDREN OF THE MOST HIGH:
PRISTINE YOUTH AND FAMILY SOLUTIONS, LLC.
SONS AND DAUGHTERS OF THE MOST HIGH PUBLISHERS ®

Oh, Gracious Most High Heavenly father, Holy is your name, Your Will Be Done Now and Forever!

In KJV bible book of Galatians chapter 5 verse 22; it states: "But the fruit of the Spirit is love, joy, **peace**, longsuffering, gentleness, goodness, faith." The **True Vine Yashu'a (Jesus) Fruit of the Spirit of Positive Character-Building Essential of** "Peace" through true-faith in the Most High Heavenly Father to overcome and resist the **7th of the 9 Deadly Venoms of the Desires of the great dragon, that old serpent called the devil and satan which deceiveth the whole world** known as "**Lying**" by learning and practicing being **peaceful, devout and upright (Peace – εἰρήνη Eirēnē). 4:** <u>Longsuffering</u> – μακροθυμία **Makrothymía,** **Mak-roth-oo-mee'-ah;** longanimity, which means: (objectively) forbearance or (subjectively) fortitude, patience, endurance, constancy, steadfastness, perseverance, longsuffering, slowness in avenging wrongs.

Yashu'a (Jesus) said: "Thou shalt love the Most High Heavenly Father, thy Sustainer with all thy heart, and with all thy soul, and with all thy mind. Thou shalt love thy neighbour as thyself."

Mind Gardening in the Creative Garden of Will (Your Mind) to Grow a Living Water Mentality!

CHILDREN OF THE MOST HIGH:
PRISTINE YOUTH AND FAMILY SOLUTIONS, LLC.
SONS AND DAUGHTERS OF THE MOST HIGH PUBLISHERS ®

*Oh, Gracious Most High Heavenly father, Holy is your name,
Your Will Be Done Now and Forever!*

In KJV bible book of Galatians chapter 5 verse 22; it states: "But the fruit of the Spirit is love, joy, peace, **longsuffering**, gentleness, goodness, faith." The **True Vine Yashu'a (Jesus) Fruit of the Spirit of Positive Character-Building Essential of "longsuffering"** through true-faith in the Most High Heavenly Father to overcome and resist the **2nd of the 9 Deadly Venoms of the Desires of the great dragon, that old serpent called the devil and satan which deceiveth the whole world** known as "**Wrath**" by learning and practicing **longsuffering μακροθυμία makrothymía** which overcomes **Wrath**. Wrath is a negative unhealthy energy in action through <u>e</u>-motion or <u>e</u>nergy in <u>m</u>otion ($E=mc$). When a person gives into wrath, for those moments, they are literally out of their positive mind and are controlled by emotions.

Yashu'a (Jesus) said: "Thou shalt love the Most High Heavenly Father, thy Sustainer with all thy heart, and with all thy soul, and with all thy mind. Thou shalt love thy neighbour as thyself."

Mind Gardening in the Creative Garden of Will (Your Mind) to Grow a Living Water Mentality!

CHILDREN OF THE MOST HIGH:
PRISTINE YOUTH AND FAMILY SOLUTIONS, LLC.
SONS AND DAUGHTERS OF THE MOST HIGH PUBLISHERS ®

Oh, Gracious Most High Heavenly father, Holy is your name, Your Will Be Done Now and Forever!

Energy in motion equals emotions (E=mc²) which can become dangerous when they are in motion. These are the identical emotions that are the roots for hate, war, lust, greed, envy, pride and fear. **5: "Gentleness – Chrēstotēs χρηστότης** KJV Bible Strong's Concordance#5544 which means: khray-stot'-ace; from G5543; **usefulness**, i.e. morally, excellence (in character or demeanor):—gentleness, good(-ness), kindness. Overcomes being **Slothful**. In KJV bible book of Galatians chapter 5 verse 22; it states: "But the fruit of the Spirit is love, joy, peace, longsuffering, **gentleness**, goodness, faith." So, a person who has **accepted the Lord Jesus Christ (Yashu'a Ha Mashiakh – Jesus the Messiah or Yehoshu'a – Yahayyu is Salvation or Yahayyu Saves) as their Savior, is in the Body of Christ** and can access **the True Vine Yashu'a (Jesus) Fruits of the Spirit Positive Character-Building Essentials of "Gentleness –**

219

Yashu'a (Jesus) said: "Thou shalt love the Most High Heavenly Father, thy Sustainer with all thy heart, and with all thy soul, and with all thy mind. Thou shalt love thy neighbour as thyself."

Mind Gardening in the Creative Garden of Will (Your Mind) to Grow a Living Water Mentality!

CHILDREN OF THE MOST HIGH:
PRISTINE YOUTH AND FAMILY SOLUTIONS, LLC.
SONS AND DAUGHTERS OF THE MOST HIGH PUBLISHERS ®

Oh, Gracious Most High Heavenly father, Holy is your name,
Your Will Be Done Now and Forever!

Chrēstotēs (χρηστότης) through true-faith in the Most High Heavenly Father to overcome and resist the **1 of 9 Deadly Venoms of the Desires of the great dragon, that old serpent called the devil and satan which deceiveth the whole world** known as "**Slothfulness**" by being kind to all life and positively useful every day. **6: <u>Goodness</u>** - ἀγαθωσύνη **Agathōsýnē**, ag-ath-o-soo'-nay; from KJV Bible Strong's Greek #G18; which means: goodness, uprightness of heart and life, kindness, i.e. virtue or beneficence. In KJV bible book of Galatians chapter 5 verse 22; it states: "But the fruit of the Spirit is love, joy, peace, longsuffering, gentleness, **goodness**, faith." The **True Vine Yashu'a (Jesus) Fruit of the Spirit of Positive Character-Building Essential** of "**Goodness**" through true-faith in the Most High Heavenly Father to overcome and resist the **9th of the 9 Deadly Venoms of the Desires of the great dragon, that**

Yashu'a (Jesus) said: "Thou shalt love the Most High Heavenly Father, thy Sustainer with all thy heart, and with all thy soul, and with all thy mind. Thou shalt love thy neighbour as thyself."

*Oh, Gracious Most High Heavenly father, Holy is your name,
Your Will Be Done Now and Forever!*

old serpent called the devil and satan which deceiveth the whole world known as **"Wickedness"** by learning and practicing goodness, uprightness of heart and life, kindness, and the virtue of beneficence (**Goodness - ἀγαθωσύνη Agathōsýnē**) every day. 7: <u>Faith</u> - **πίστις Pístis**, pis'-tis; from KJV Bible Strong's Greek #<u>**G3982**</u>; which means: persuasion, i.e. credence; moral conviction (of religious truth, or the truthfulness of God or a religious teacher), especially reliance upon Christ for salvation; abstractly, constancy in such profession; by extension, the system of religious (Gospel) truth itself: —assurance, belief, believe, faith, fidelity. In KJV bible book of Galatians chapter 5 verse 22; it states: "But the fruit of the Spirit is love, joy, peace, longsuffering, gentleness, goodness, **faith**."

221

Yashu'a (Jesus) said: "Thou shalt love the Most High Heavenly Father, thy Sustainer with all thy heart, and with all thy soul, and with all thy mind. Thou shalt love thy neighbour as thyself."

Mind Gardening in the Creative Garden of Will (Your Mind) to Grow a Living Water Mentality!

CHILDREN OF THE MOST HIGH:
PRISTINE YOUTH AND FAMILY SOLUTIONS, LLC.
SONS AND DAUGHTERS OF THE MOST HIGH PUBLISHERS ®

*Oh, Gracious Most High Heavenly father, Holy is your name,
Your Will Be Done Now and Forever!*

The **True Vine Yashu'a (Jesus) Fruit of the Spirit of Positive Character-Building Essential** of "Faith" through true-faith in the Most High Heavenly Father to overcome and resist the **6th of the 9 Deadly Venoms of the Desires of the great dragon, that old serpent called the devil and satan which deceiveth the whole world** known as "Hopeless-Fear- Disobedience" by learning and practicing **true-faith (Faith - πίστις Pístis)** in the Most High heavenly Father through the Messiah Yashu'a (Jesus). "**Hopeless Fear Disobedience**" are rooted in a lack of faith in the Most High Heavenly Father. Real fear is the lack of true-faith in the Most High Heavenly Father. **8: <u>Meekness</u>** - πραότης **praiótēs**, prah-ot'-ace; which means: gentleness, mildness by implication, humility. In KJV bible book of Galatians chapter 5 verse 23; it states: "**Meekness**, temperance: against such there is no law."

222

Yashu'a (Jesus) said: "Thou shalt love the Most High Heavenly Father, thy Sustainer with all thy heart, and with all thy soul, and with all thy mind. Thou shalt love thy neighbour as thyself."

Mind Gardening in the Creative Garden of Will (Your Mind) to Grow a Living Water Mentality!

CHILDREN OF THE MOST HIGH:
PRISTINE YOUTH AND FAMILY SOLUTIONS, LLC.
SONS AND DAUGHTERS OF THE MOST HIGH PUBLISHERS ®

Oh, Gracious Most High Heavenly father, Holy is your name,
Your Will Be Done Now and Forever!

The **True Vine Yashu'a (Jesus) Fruit of the Spirit of Positive Character-Building Essential** of "Meekness" through true-faith in the Most High Heavenly Father to overcome and resist the **3rd of the 9 Deadly Venoms of the Desires of the great dragon, that old serpent called the devil and satan which deceiveth the whole world** known as "**Pride**" by learning and practicing **Meekness - πρᾳότης praiótēs true-faith (Faith - πίστις Pístis)** which overcomes pride. **9: Temperance ἐγκράτεια Enkráteia**, eng-krat'-i-ah; from KJV Bible Strong's Greek **#G1468**; which means: self-control (especially continence): temperance. Self-control (the virtue of one who masters his or her desires and passions, esp. his sensual appetites). In KJV bible book of Galatians chapter 5 verse 23; it states: "Meekness, **temperance**: against such there is no law."

Yashu'a (Jesus) said: "Thou shalt love the Most High Heavenly Father, thy Sustainer with all thy heart, and with all thy soul, and with all thy mind. Thou shalt love thy neighbour as thyself."

Mind Gardening in the Creative Garden of Will (Your Mind) to Grow a Living Water Mentality!

CHILDREN OF THE MOST HIGH:
PRISTINE YOUTH AND FAMILY SOLUTIONS, LLC.
SONS AND DAUGHTERS OF THE MOST HIGH PUBLISHERS ®

Oh, Gracious Most High Heavenly father, Holy is your name,
Your Will Be Done Now and Forever!

The **True Vine Yashu'a (Jesus) Fruit of the Spirit of Positive Character-Building Essential** of "**Temperance**" through true-faith in the Most High Heavenly Father to overcome and resist the **4th of the 9 Deadly Venoms of the Desires of the great dragon, that old serpent called the devil and satan which deceiveth the whole world** known as "**Greed**" by learning and practicing self-control which is the virtue of one who masters his or her desires and passions every day, (Hughes, 2019). Therefore, **daily Mind Meditation on the Most High** is essential to **mind gardening in the creative garden of will (your mind) to grow a Living Water Mentality!**

224

Yashu'a (Jesus) said: "Thou shalt love the Most High Heavenly Father, thy Sustainer with all thy heart, and with all thy soul, and with all thy mind. Thou shalt love thy neighbour as thyself."

Mind Gardening in the Creative Garden of Will (Your Mind) to Grow a Living Water Mentality!

CHILDREN OF THE MOST HIGH:
PRISTINE YOUTH AND FAMILY SOLUTIONS, LLC.
SONS AND DAUGHTERS OF THE MOST HIGH PUBLISHERS ®

Oh, Gracious Most High Heavenly father, Holy is your name,
Your Will Be Done Now and Forever!

Chapter 13: The Past and Future Don't Exist in the NOW-Mind!

225

Yashu'a (Jesus) said: "Thou shalt love the Most High Heavenly Father, thy Sustainer with all thy heart, and with all thy soul, and with all thy mind. Thou shalt love thy neighbour as thyself."

Mind Gardening in the Creative Garden of Will (Your Mind) to Grow a Living Water Mentality!

CHILDREN OF THE MOST HIGH:
PRISTINE YOUTH AND FAMILY SOLUTIONS, LLC.
SONS AND DAUGHTERS OF THE MOST HIGH PUBLISHERS ®

Oh, Gracious Most High Heavenly father, Holy is your name,
Your Will Be Done Now and Forever!

In the KJV bible book of John chapter 4 verse 23; the Messiah Yashu'a (Jesus) said: "**But the hour cometh, and <u>now</u> is, when the true worshippers shall worship the Father in spirit and in truth: for the Father seeketh such to worship him.**" The KJV bible Greek Strong's Concordance "**#3568 νῦν Nyn (Nü'n, Noon) is the word for "now". νῦν Nyn means: at this time, the present, now.**" The American Heritage Online Dictionary (2020), defines **now** as: "**At the present time, at once; immediately, the present time or moment; of the present time; current.**" In the KJV bible book of 1st John chapter 2 verse 8; it states: "Again, a new commandment I write unto you, which thing is true in him and in you: because the darkness is **past**, and the true light **now** shineth." The KJV bible Greek Strong's Concordance "**#3855 παράγω Paragō (Par-ag'-o) is the word for "past". παράγω Paragō means: pass by,**

Yashu'a (Jesus) said: "Thou shalt love the Most High Heavenly Father, thy Sustainer with all thy heart, and with all thy soul, and with all thy mind. Thou shalt love thy neighbour as thyself."

Mind Gardening in the Creative Garden of Will (Your Mind) to Grow a Living Water Mentality!

CHILDREN OF THE MOST HIGH:
PRISTINE YOUTH AND FAMILY SOLUTIONS, LLC.
SONS AND DAUGHTERS OF THE MOST HIGH PUBLISHERS ®

*Oh, Gracious Most High Heavenly father, Holy is your name,
Your Will Be Done Now and Forever!*

to lead past, lead by, to lead aside, mislead, to lead away, to lead to, to lead forth, bring forward, to pass by, go past, to depart, **go away**; **metaphorically- disappear**. In the KJV bible book of revelation chapter 9 verse 12; it states: "One woe is **past**; and, behold, there come two woes more hereafter." The KJV bible Greek Strong's Concordance "**#565 ἀπέρχομαι Apérchomai, (Ap-erkh'-om-ahee**) is the word for "**past**". ἀπέρχομαι **Apérchomai** means: **to go away**, depart, to go away in order to follow any one, go after him, to follow his party, follow him as a leader, of departing evils and sufferings, **of good things taken away from one**, literally or figuratively:—come, depart, go (aside, away, back, out, ways), **pass away, be past**."

227

Yashu'a (Jesus) said: "Thou shalt love the Most High Heavenly Father, thy Sustainer with all thy heart, and with all thy soul, and with all thy mind. Thou shalt love thy neighbour as thyself."

Mind Gardening in the Creative Garden of Will (Your Mind) to Grow a Living Water Mentality!

CHILDREN OF THE MOST HIGH:
PRISTINE YOUTH AND FAMILY SOLUTIONS, LLC.
SONS AND DAUGHTERS OF THE MOST HIGH PUBLISHERS ®

Oh, Gracious Most High Heavenly father, Holy is your name, Your Will Be Done Now and Forever!

The American Heritage Online Dictionary (2020), defines **past** as: **no longer current; gone by; over. The time before the present. Future** is defined as: **the indefinite time yet to come, that is to be or to come; of or existing in later time.**" In the KJV bible book of 1st Peter chapter 4 verse 1; it states: "Forasmuch then as **Christ** hath suffered for us in the flesh, arm yourselves likewise with the **same mind**: for he that hath suffered in the flesh hath ceased from sin." The KJV bible Greek Strong's Concordance "**#1771 ἔννοια Ennoia** is the word for "**mind**" in this verse. **ἔννοια Ennoia (En'-noy-ah)** means: **thoughtfulness, moral understanding, intent, mind. The act of thinking, consideration, meditation, a thought, notion, conception mind, understanding, will, manner of feeling, and thinking.**"

228

Yashu'a (Jesus) said: "Thou shalt love the Most High Heavenly Father, thy Sustainer with all thy heart, and with all thy soul, and with all thy mind. Thou shalt love thy neighbour as thyself."

Mind Gardening in the Creative Garden of Will (Your Mind) to Grow a Living Water Mentality!

CHILDREN OF THE MOST HIGH:
PRISTINE YOUTH AND FAMILY SOLUTIONS, LLC.
SONS AND DAUGHTERS OF THE MOST HIGH PUBLISHERS ®

Oh, Gracious Most High Heavenly father, Holy is your name,
Your Will Be Done Now and Forever!

So, the **NOW-M.I.N.D.** (**M**aking **I**ntentional **N**oble **D**ecisions) is **the present time or moment <u>Mind of intentional moral overstanding in A.C.T.I.O.N.</u>** (Activated, Conscious, Timely, Intentions, Obligated, Now)! Through **Mind Gardening in the Creative Garden of Will (your mind) to Grow a Living Water Mentality**; this **creates a** change of thinking, a change of behavior, a change of habits which can only occur in the **NOW-Mind (in the present "<u>mind</u>" ἔννοια Ennoia (<u>En'-noy-ah</u>)**, which is reinforced through moment to moment or daily repetition over time through **the 9 True Vine "Yashu'a, Jesus" Work Ethics Habits of Success** in <u>**A.C.T.I.O.N.**</u> (Activated, Conscious, Timely, Intentions, Obligated, Now)!

229

Yashu'a (Jesus) said: "Thou shalt love the Most High Heavenly Father, thy Sustainer with all thy heart, and with all thy soul, and with all thy mind. Thou shalt love thy neighbour as thyself."

Mind Gardening in the Creative Garden of Will (Your Mind) to Grow a Living Water Mentality!

CHILDREN OF THE MOST HIGH:
PRISTINE YOUTH AND FAMILY SOLUTIONS, LLC.
SONS AND DAUGHTERS OF THE MOST HIGH PUBLISHERS ®

Oh, Gracious Most High Heavenly father, Holy is your name,
Your Will Be Done Now and Forever!

The **Creative Garden of Will (your mind) to Grow a Living Water Mentality 9 True Vine Yashu'a (Jesus) Work Ethics Habits of Success** are:

1. **<u>Responsible</u>** – In the KJV bible book of Romans chapter 14 verse 12; it states: "So then every one of us shall give account of himself [or herself] to God."

2. **<u>Active Listener</u>** – In the KJV bible book of James chapter 1 verse 19; it states: "Wherefore, my beloved brethren [or sisters], let every man [woman and child] be swift to hear, slow to speak, slow to wrath."

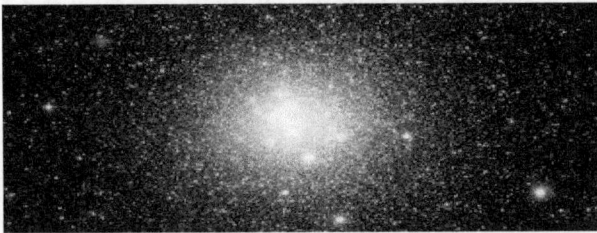

230

Yashu'a (Jesus) said: "Thou shalt love the Most High Heavenly Father, thy Sustainer with all thy heart, and with all thy soul, and with all thy mind. Thou shalt love thy neighbour as thyself."

Mind Gardening in the Creative Garden of Will (Your Mind) to Grow a Living Water Mentality!

CHILDREN OF THE MOST HIGH: PRISTINE YOUTH AND FAMILY SOLUTIONS, LLC. SONS AND DAUGHTERS OF THE MOST HIGH PUBLISHERS ®

Oh, Gracious Most High Heavenly father, Holy is your name, Your Will Be Done Now and Forever!

3. **Trustworthy** – In the KJV bible book of Proverbs chapter 3 verses 5-6; it states: "Trust in the LORD with all thine heart; and lean not unto thine own understanding. In all thy ways acknowledge him, and he shall direct thy **paths**." In the KJV bible book of Matthew chapter 10 verse 13; it states: The Messiah Yashu'a (Jesus) said: "And if the house be worthy, let your peace come upon it: but if it be not worthy, let your peace return to you." In the KJV bible book of Matthew chapter 10 verses 37-38; the Messiah Yashu'a (Jesus) said: "He [or She] that loveth father or mother more than me is not worthy of me: and he [or She] that loveth son or daughter more than me is not worthy of me. And he [or she] that taketh not his cross, and followeth after me, is not worthy of me."

231

Yashu'a (Jesus) said: "Thou shalt love the Most High Heavenly Father, thy Sustainer with all thy heart, and with all thy soul, and with all thy mind. Thou shalt love thy neighbour as thyself."

Mind Gardening in the Creative Garden of Will (Your Mind) to Grow a Living Water Mentality!

CHILDREN OF THE MOST HIGH:
PRISTINE YOUTH AND FAMILY SOLUTIONS, LLC.
SONS AND DAUGHTERS OF THE MOST HIGH PUBLISHERS ®

*Oh, Gracious Most High Heavenly father, Holy is your name,
Your Will Be Done Now and Forever!*

4. <u>**Respectful**</u> – In the KJV bible book of Psalms chapter 119 verse 6; it states: "Then shall I not be ashamed, when I have respect unto all thy commandments." In the KJV bible book of Psalms chapter 119 verse 15; it states: "I will meditate in thy precepts, and have respect unto thy ways." In the KJV bible book of Psalms chapter 119 verse 117; it states: "Hold thou me up, and I shall be safe: and I will have respect unto thy statutes continually."

232

Yashu'a (Jesus) said: "Thou shalt love the Most High Heavenly Father, thy Sustainer with all thy heart, and with all thy soul, and with all thy mind. Thou shalt love thy neighbour as thyself."

Mind Gardening in the Creative Garden of Will (Your Mind) to Grow a Living Water Mentality!

CHILDREN OF THE MOST HIGH:
PRISTINE YOUTH AND FAMILY SOLUTIONS, LLC.
SONS AND DAUGHTERS OF THE MOST HIGH PUBLISHERS ®

Oh, Gracious Most High Heavenly father, Holy is your name,
Your Will Be Done Now and Forever!

5. **Dependable** – In the KJV bible book of 2nd Samuel chapter 22 verse 3; it states: "The God of my rock; in him will I trust [and depend upon]: he is my shield, and the horn of my salvation, my high tower, and my refuge, my savior; thou savest me from violence." In the KJV bible book of Revelation chapter 21 verse 23; it states: "And the city had no need of the sun, neither of the moon, to shine in it: for the glory of God did lighten it, and the Lamb is the light thereof."

6. **Positive Attitude** – In the KJV bible book of Psalms chapter 45 verse 7; it states: "Thou lovest righteousness, and hatest wickedness: therefore God, thy God, hath anointed thee with the oil of gladness above thy fellows."

Yashu'a (Jesus) said: "Thou shalt love the Most High Heavenly Father, thy Sustainer with all thy heart, and with all thy soul, and with all thy mind. Thou shalt love thy neighbour as thyself."

Mind Gardening in the Creative Garden of Will (Your Mind) to Grow a Living Water Mentality!

CHILDREN OF THE MOST HIGH:
PRISTINE YOUTH AND FAMILY SOLUTIONS, LLC.
SONS AND DAUGHTERS OF THE MOST HIGH PUBLISHERS ®

Oh, Gracious Most High Heavenly father, Holy is your name,
Your Will Be Done Now and Forever!

7. **<u>Positive Behavior</u>** – In the KJV bible book of Philippians chapter 4 verse 8; it states: "Finally, brethren, whatsoever things are true, whatsoever things [are] honest, whatsoever things [are] just, whatsoever things [are] pure, whatsoever things [are] lovely, whatsoever things [are] of good report; if [there be] any virtue, and if [there be] any praise, think on these things."

8. **<u>Impactful</u>** – In the KJV bible book of Proverbs chapter 13 verse 20; it states: "He that walketh with wise [men] shall be wise: but a companion of fools shall be destroyed."

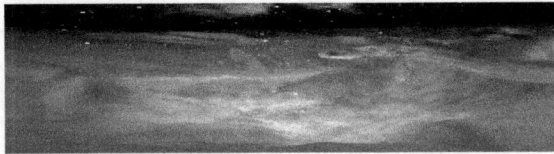

234

Yashu'a (Jesus) said: "Thou shalt love the Most High Heavenly Father, thy Sustainer with all thy heart, and with all thy soul, and with all thy mind. Thou shalt love thy neighbour as thyself."

Mind Gardening in the Creative Garden of Will (Your Mind) to Grow a Living Water Mentality!

CHILDREN OF THE MOST HIGH:
PRISTINE YOUTH AND FAMILY SOLUTIONS, LLC.
SONS AND DAUGHTERS OF THE MOST HIGH PUBLISHERS ®

Oh, Gracious Most High Heavenly father, Holy is your name,
Your Will Be Done Now and Forever!

9. <u>**Team Player**</u> – In the KJV bible book of Ecclesiastes chapter 4 verses 9-10; it states: "Two [are] better than one; because they have a good reward for their labor. For if they fall, the one will lift up his fellow: but woe to him [or her] [that is] alone when he [or she] falleth; for [he hath] [or she hath] not another to help him [or her] up."

Since the **past** and **future** don't **exist** in the **NOW-Mind**; putting the **9 True Vine "Yashu'a, Jesus" Work Ethics** in action from moment to moment each will assist the children of the Most High with being successful in **Mind Gardening in the Creative Garden of Will (Your Mind) to Grow a Living Water Mentality!**

235

Yashu'a (Jesus) said: "Thou shalt love the Most High Heavenly Father, thy Sustainer with all thy heart, and with all thy soul, and with all thy mind. Thou shalt love thy neighbour as thyself."

Mind Gardening in the Creative Garden of Will (Your Mind) to Grow a Living Water Mentality!

Oh, Gracious Most High Heavenly father, Holy is your name, Your Will Be Done Now and Forever!

Chapter 14: Sun of Righteousness
Thought Rhythm of Sound Wisdom Mentality!

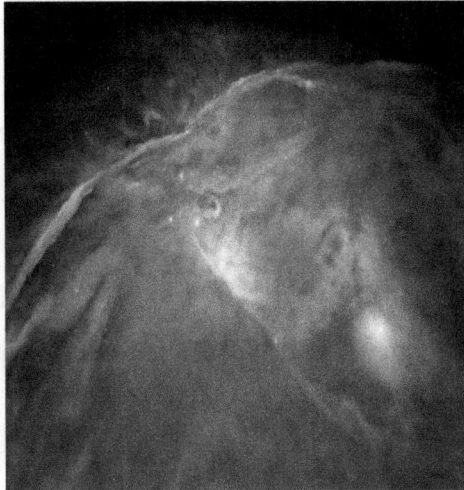

In the KJV bible book of Malachi chapter 4 verse 2; it states: "But unto you that fear my name shall the **Sun of righteousness** arise with healing in his wings; and ye shall go forth, and grow up as calves of the stall."

Yashu'a (Jesus) said: "Thou shalt love the Most High Heavenly Father, thy Sustainer with all thy heart, and with all thy soul, and with all thy mind. Thou shalt love thy neighbour as thyself."

Mind Gardening in the Creative Garden of Will (Your Mind) to Grow a Living Water Mentality!

CHILDREN OF THE MOST HIGH:
PRISTINE YOUTH AND FAMILY SOLUTIONS, LLC.
SONS AND DAUGHTERS OF THE MOST HIGH PUBLISHERS ®

*Oh, Gracious Most High Heavenly father, Holy is your name,
Your Will Be Done Now and Forever!*

The Messiah Yashu'a (Jesus) said: "Take therefore no thought for the morrow: for the morrow shall take thought for the things of itself. Sufficient unto the day is the evil thereof, KJV Matthew 6:34." "He layeth up **sound wisdom** for the righteous: he is a buckler to them that walk uprightly, KJV Proverbs 2:7."

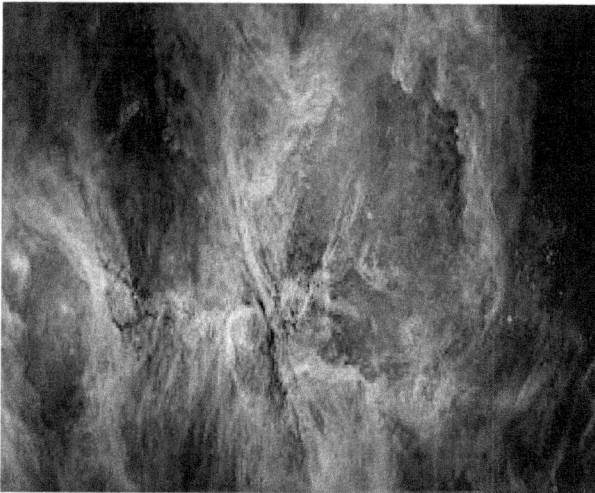

237

Yashu'a (Jesus) said: "Thou shalt love the Most High Heavenly Father, thy Sustainer with all thy heart, and with all thy soul, and with all thy mind. Thou shalt love thy neighbour as thyself."

Mind Gardening in the Creative Garden of Will (Your Mind) to Grow a Living Water Mentality!

CHILDREN OF THE MOST HIGH:
PRISTINE YOUTH AND FAMILY SOLUTIONS, LLC.
SONS AND DAUGHTERS OF THE MOST HIGH PUBLISHERS ®

Oh, Gracious Most High Heavenly father, Holy is your name, Your Will Be Done Now and Forever!

What does the Title: "Sun of Righteousness Thought Rhythm of Sound Wisdom Mentality" mean?

According to the KJV bible Hebrew Strong's Concordance "#8121 שֶׁמֶשׁ Shemesh (Sheh'-mesh)** is the word for "sun".

שֶׁמֶשׁ **Shemesh** literally means **the sun** (KJV Malachi 4:2).

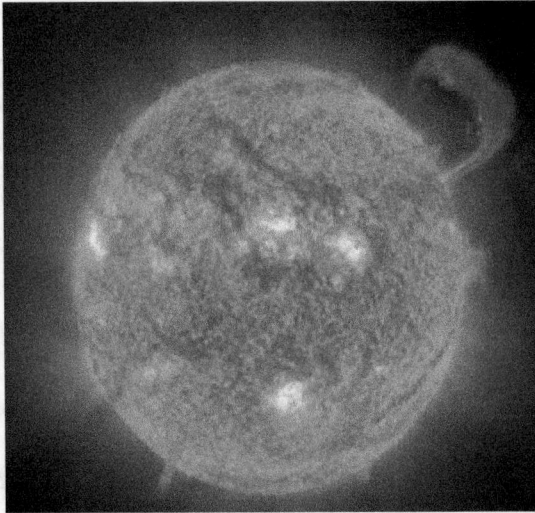

Yashu'a (Jesus) said: "Thou shalt love the Most High Heavenly Father, thy Sustainer with all thy heart, and with all thy soul, and with all thy mind. Thou shalt love thy neighbour as thyself."

Mind Gardening in the Creative Garden of Will (Your Mind) to Grow a Living Water Mentality!

CHILDREN OF THE MOST HIGH:
PRISTINE YOUTH AND FAMILY SOLUTIONS, LLC.
SONS AND DAUGHTERS OF THE MOST HIGH PUBLISHERS ®

*Oh, Gracious Most High Heavenly father, Holy is your name,
Your Will Be Done Now and Forever!*

The KJV bible Hebrew Strong's Concordance "#6666 צְדָקָה Tsedaqah (Tsed-aw-kaw') is the word for "**Righteousness**". צְדָקָה Tsedaqah means: **rightness, morally (virtue), justice, righteousness, righteousness (in government), of judge, ruler, king of law, righteousness (of God's attribute), righteousness (in a case or cause), truthfulness, righteousness (as ethically right), righteousness (as vindicated), justification, salvation, of God, prosperity (of people), and righteous acts.**" The KJV bible Greek Strong's Concordance "#3309 μεριμνάω Merimnaō (Mer-im-nah'-o) is the word for "**thought**". μεριμνάω Merimnaō means: **to be anxious; to be troubled with cares, to care for, look out for (a thing), to seek to promote one's interests, caring or providing for.**"

239

Yashu'a (Jesus) said: "Thou shalt love the Most High Heavenly Father, thy Sustainer with all thy heart, and with all thy soul, and with all thy mind. Thou shalt love thy neighbour as thyself."

Mind Gardening in the Creative Garden of Will (Your Mind) to Grow a Living Water Mentality!

Oh, Gracious Most High Heavenly father, Holy is your name,
Your Will Be Done Now and Forever!

The KJV bible Hebrew Strong's Concordance "#8454 תּוּשִׁיָּה Tuwshiyah (Too-shee-yaw') for the words "**sound wisdom**".

תּוּשִׁיָּה **Tuwshiyah** means: **wisdom, sound knowledge, success, sound or efficient wisdom, abiding success, sound or efficient wisdom, abiding success (of the effect of sound wisdom), (intellectual) understanding, (sound) wisdom, working.**" The American Heritage Online Dictionary (2020), defines **rhythm** as: **movement or variation characterized by the regular recurrence or alternation of different quantities or conditions.**"

240

Yashu'a (Jesus) said: "Thou shalt love the Most High Heavenly Father, thy Sustainer with all thy heart, and with all thy soul, and with all thy mind. Thou shalt love thy neighbour as thyself."

Mind Gardening in the Creative Garden of Will (Your Mind) to Grow a Living Water Mentality!

CHILDREN OF THE MOST HIGH:
PRISTINE YOUTH AND FAMILY SOLUTIONS, LLC.
SONS AND DAUGHTERS OF THE MOST HIGH PUBLISHERS ®

Oh, Gracious Most High Heavenly father, Holy is your name, Your Will Be Done Now and Forever!

Does Yashu'a (Jesus) have his own book in the bible? In the KJV bible book of Revelation chapter 1 verses 1-3; it states: <u>**"The Revelation of Jesus Christ, which God (θεός Theos) gave unto him,**</u> to shew unto his servants' things which must shortly come to pass; and <u>**he sent and signified *it* by his angel**</u> unto his servant John." Who bare record of the word of God, and of the testimony of Jesus Christ, and of all things that he saw. "Blessed *is* he [or she] that readeth, and they that hear the words of this prophecy, and keep those things which are written therein: <u>**for the time *is* at hand**</u>." Therefore; according to the KJV book of Revelation chapter 1 verse 1; the KJV book of Revelation is <u>**"The Revelation of Jesus Christ, which God gave unto him."**</u>

Yashu'a (Jesus) said: "Thou shalt love the Most High Heavenly Father, thy Sustainer with all thy heart, and with all thy soul, and with all thy mind. Thou shalt love thy neighbour as thyself."

Mind Gardening in the Creative Garden of Will (Your Mind) to Grow a Living Water Mentality!

CHILDREN OF THE MOST HIGH:
PRISTINE YOUTH AND FAMILY SOLUTIONS, LLC.
SONS AND DAUGHTERS OF THE MOST HIGH PUBLISHERS ®

Oh, Gracious Most High Heavenly father, Holy is your name,
Your Will Be Done Now and Forever!

So, in response to the question, **YES**, **according the word of God** (*θεός* Theos), **God** (*θεός* Theos) **gave the book of Revelation to the Messiah Yashu'a (Jesus)**; to shew unto his servants' things which must shortly come to pass; and **he sent and signified *it* by his angel** unto his servant John." Who bare record of the word of God, and of the testimony of Jesus Christ, and of all things that he saw." The aforementioned verse also mentioned that the Messiah Yashu'a (Jesus) will send **his angel** or if the **Messiah Yashu'a (Jesus)** made the statement in the first person, it would be "**My Angel**" instead of being said in the second person as "**His Angel**." What does the phrase "**My Angel**" mean in the Messiah Yashu'a (Jesus) **Galilean** or **Judean tongue (language)**? In the **Galilean** or **Judean language**, the phrase "**My Angel**" means "**Malachi**" *ᑎᎩᚷ-Ꮖᚅ, מלאכי* which corresponds with the KJV

Yashu'a (Jesus) said: "Thou shalt love the Most High Heavenly Father, thy Sustainer with all thy heart, and with all thy soul, and with all thy mind. Thou shalt love thy neighbour as thyself."

Mind Gardening in the Creative Garden of Will (Your Mind) to Grow a Living Water Mentality!

CHILDREN OF THE MOST HIGH:
PRISTINE YOUTH AND FAMILY SOLUTIONS, LLC.
SONS AND DAUGHTERS OF THE MOST HIGH PUBLISHERS ®

Oh, Gracious Most High Heavenly father, Holy is your name,
Your Will Be Done Now and Forever!

Bible Hebrew Strong's Concordance#**4397**, Aramic (Hebrew) word "מַלְאָךְ **Mal'awk**, which means **angel**, **king**, **priest**, **messenger** and **Galilean Ashuric/Syriac (Arabic)** word **Malaakehe** (according to the Arabic Lanes Dictionary (2003), means "**Angelic-Being**").

243

Yashu'a (Jesus) said: "Thou shalt love the Most High Heavenly Father, thy Sustainer with all thy heart, and with all thy soul, and with all thy mind. Thou shalt love thy neighbour as thyself."

Mind Gardening in the Creative Garden of Will (Your Mind) to Grow a Living Water Mentality!

CHILDREN OF THE MOST HIGH:
PRISTINE YOUTH AND FAMILY SOLUTIONS, LLC.
SONS AND DAUGHTERS OF THE MOST HIGH PUBLISHERS ®

Oh, Gracious Most High Heavenly father, Holy is your name,
Your Will Be Done Now and Forever!

מַלְאָךְ m. (from the root לָאַךְ to depute which see).

(1) *one sent, a messenger*, whether from a private person, Job 1:14, or of a king, 1 Sa. 16:19; 19:11, 14, 20; 1 Ki. 19:2, etc. (Syr. ܡܠܐܟܐ, Arab. ملاك id.)

(2) *a messenger of God*, i. e.—(a) *an angel*, Ex. 23:20; 33:2; 2 Sam. 24:16; Job 33:23 (see לִיץ); Zec. 1:9, seq.; 2:2, 7; 4:1, seq.; more fully יְיָ מַלְאָךְ Gen. 16:7; 21:17; 22:11, 15; Num. 22:22, seqq.; Jud. 6:11, seqq.; Cf. De Angelologia V. T., De Wettii Bibl. Dogm. § 171, seqq. edit. 2.—(b) *a prophet*, Hag. 1:13; Mal. 3:1.—(c) *a priest*, Ecc. 5:5; Mal.

1:1: Malachi 2:6; Malachi 2:7; Malachi 3:1; Malachi 4:1;"

Malachi 4:2; Malachi 4:3; Malachi 4:1; Malachi 4:2:

Malachi 4:3, Malachi 4:4, Malachi 4:5, Malachi 4:6."

244

Yashu'a (Jesus) said: "Thou shalt love the Most High
Heavenly Father, thy Sustainer with all thy heart, and
with all thy soul, and with all thy mind. Thou shalt love
thy neighbour as thyself."

Mind Gardening in the Creative Garden of Will (Your Mind) to Grow a Living Water Mentality!

*Oh, Gracious Most High Heavenly father, Holy is your name,
Your Will Be Done Now and Forever!*

In the KJV bible book of Exodus chapter 23 verses 23-24; it states: "For mine **Angel** (the KJV bible Hebrew Strong's Concordance#**4397**, **Aramic (Hebrew)** word "מַלְאָךְ **Mal'awk**, which means **angel, king, priest, messenger**) shall go before thee, and bring thee in unto the Amorites, and the Hittites, and the Perizzites, and the Canaanites, the Hivites, and the Jebusites: and I will cut them off. **Thou shalt not bow down to their gods, nor serve them, nor do after their works**: but thou shalt utterly overthrow them, and quite **break down their images**." In the KJV bible book of Haggai chapter 1 verse 13; it states: "Then spake Haggai the LORD'S **messenger** (the KJV bible Hebrew Strong's Concordance#**4397**, **Aramic (Hebrew)** word מַלְאָךְ **Mal'awk**, which means **angel, king, priest, messenger; in the Galilean Ashuric/Syriac (Arabic) is** known as **Al Khidr** (الـخـضـر) "**The Green One**" in

245

Yashu'a (Jesus) said: "Thou shalt love the Most High Heavenly Father, thy Sustainer with all thy heart, and with all thy soul, and with all thy mind. Thou shalt love thy neighbour as thyself."

Mind Gardening in the Creative Garden of Will (Your Mind) to Grow a Living Water Mentality!

CHILDREN OF THE MOST HIGH:
PRISTINE YOUTH AND FAMILY SOLUTIONS, LLC.
SONS AND DAUGHTERS OF THE MOST HIGH PUBLISHERS ®

Oh, Gracious Most High Heavenly father, Holy is your name,
Your Will Be Done Now and Forever!

reference to sustaining and healing; For example: healthy green vegetation is healthy or **the first 4 letters of the word healthy, spell the word heal; Malachi is also the name Malachite, a dark green mineral carbonate of copper)** in the LORD'S **message** (the KJV bible Hebrew Strong's Concordance **"#4397, Aramic (Hebrew)** word (מַלְאָכוּת **MAL-AK-OOTH, Mal'akuwth,** means **message)** unto the people, saying, I am with you, saith the LORD." In the KJV bible book of Genesis chapter 14 verse 13; it states: "And **Melchizedek** (is the KJV bible Hebrew Strong's Concordance**#4442, Aramic (Hebrew)** word "מַלְכִּי־צֶדֶק **Malkiy-Tsedeq (Mal·ke·tseh'·dek),** means **justice, righteousness)** king of **Salem (Salem** is the KJV bible Hebrew Strong's Concordance**#8004** word "שָׁלֵם **Sha-Lomé, Sha-Lom, Shâlêm, Shaw-lame, and means Peace."

246
Yashu'a (Jesus) said: "Thou shalt love the Most High Heavenly Father, thy Sustainer with all thy heart, and with all thy soul, and with all thy mind. Thou shalt love thy neighbour as thyself."

Mind Gardening in the Creative Garden of Will (Your Mind) to Grow a Living Water Mentality!

CHILDREN OF THE MOST HIGH:
PRISTINE YOUTH AND FAMILY SOLUTIONS, LLC.
SONS AND DAUGHTERS OF THE MOST HIGH PUBLISHERS ®

Oh, Gracious Most High Heavenly father, Holy is your name,
Your Will Be Done Now and Forever!

In the KJV bible book of Matthew chapter 5 verse 9; the Messiah Yashu'a said: "Blessed are the peacemakers: for they shall be called the children of God"), brought forth bread and wine: and he *was* the priest of the Most High God." In the KJV bible book of Malachi chapter 4 verse 2; it states: "But unto you that fear my name shall the **Sun of righteousness** (the KJV bible Hebrew Strong's Concordance**#8121**, is the **Aramic (Hebrew)** word for "**Sun**" שֶׁמֶשׁ **Shemesh** pronounced **Sheh'·mesh**, and the word for "**Righteousness**" is **Tsĕdaqah** שֶׁמֶשׁ pronounced **Tsed·ä·kä'**) arise with healing in his wings; and ye shall go forth, and grow up as calves of the stall.

247

Yashu'a (Jesus) said: "Thou shalt love the Most High Heavenly Father, thy Sustainer with all thy heart, and with all thy soul, and with all thy mind. Thou shalt love thy neighbour as thyself."

CHILDREN OF THE MOST HIGH:
PRISTINE YOUTH AND FAMILY SOLUTIONS, LLC.
SONS AND DAUGHTERS OF THE MOST HIGH PUBLISHERS ®

Oh, Gracious Most High Heavenly father, Holy is your name,
Your Will Be Done Now and Forever!

The Word **Tsedeq** (צדיק) Or **Sodoq** (צדיק) Meaning *"Justice Or Righteousness"* Is Spelled Zodoq When Translated. In The Ashuric/Syriac (Arabic) The Word **Zodoq** Is **Sodoq** (صدق) From The Root Word **Sadaqa** (صدق) Meaning *"Righteous."* The Koran Uses Different Forms Of The Word Sodoq Such As **El Saddiqiyn, El Saddiquwn** (الصدقون And الصدقين) Meaning *"The Righteous"*, In Plural (*Koran 4:69*) And **Musaddiqiyn** (مصدقين) Meaning *"Ones Who Are Of Righteous"* (*Koran 57:18*). The Word **Saddiyq** (صديق) Was Also Used For Joseph (*Koran 12:46*), ENOCH (ADAFA) Who Was Known As Idris (*Koran 19:56*), And Abraham (*Koran 19:41*).

248

Yashu'a (Jesus) said: "Thou shalt love the Most High Heavenly Father, thy Sustainer with all thy heart, and with all thy soul, and with all thy mind. Thou shalt love thy neighbour as thyself."

Mind Gardening in the Creative Garden of Will (Your Mind) to Grow a Living Water Mentality!

CHILDREN OF THE MOST HIGH:
PRISTINE YOUTH AND FAMILY SOLUTIONS, LLC.
SONS AND DAUGHTERS OF THE MOST HIGH PUBLISHERS ®

Oh, Gracious Most High Heavenly father, Holy is your name,
Your Will Be Done Now and Forever!

In the KJV bible book of Daniel chapter 12 verse 1; it states: "And at that time shall **Michael** (the KJV bible Hebrew Strong's Concordance**#4317**, is the **Aramic (Hebrew)** word for "**Michael**" is מִיכָאֵל **Miyka'el, pronounced as "Me·Kä·Al" which means "who dares to be like the Most High Heavenly Father (ELYOWN עֶלְיוֹן EL אֵל), or "Who is like God"**) stand up, the great prince which standeth for the children of thy people: and there shall be a time of trouble, such as never was since there was a nation even to that same time: and at that time thy people shall be delivered, every one that shall be found written in the book."

249

Yashu'a (Jesus) said: "Thou shalt love the Most High Heavenly Father, thy Sustainer with all thy heart, and with all thy soul, and with all thy mind. Thou shalt love thy neighbour as thyself."

CHILDREN OF THE MOST HIGH:
PRISTINE YOUTH AND FAMILY SOLUTIONS, LLC.
SONS AND DAUGHTERS OF THE MOST HIGH PUBLISHERS ®

Oh, Gracious Most High Heavenly father, Holy is your name,
Your Will Be Done Now and Forever!

In the KJV bible book of Revelation chapter 12 verses 7-9; it states: "And there was war in heaven: **Michael and his angels** (ἄγγελος **Angelos, meaning Messengers** according to the **KJV bible Greek Strong's Concordance#32**) fought against the **dragon**; and **the dragon fought and his angels** (ἄγγελος **Angelos, meaning Messengers**, according to the KJV bible Greek **Strong's Concordance#32**, And prevailed not; neither was their place found any more in heaven. And the **great dragon** was cast out, that **old serpent**, **called the Devil, and Satan**, which deceiveth the whole world: he was cast out into the earth, and his **angels** (ἄγγελος **Angelos, meaning Messengers**) were cast out with him."

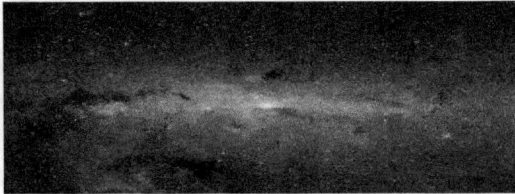

250

Yashu'a (Jesus) said: "Thou shalt love the Most High Heavenly Father, thy Sustainer with all thy heart, and with all thy soul, and with all thy mind. Thou shalt love thy neighbour as thyself."

Mind Gardening in the Creative Garden of Will (Your Mind) to Grow a Living Water Mentality!

CHILDREN OF THE MOST HIGH:
PRISTINE YOUTH AND FAMILY SOLUTIONS, LLC.
SONS AND DAUGHTERS OF THE MOST HIGH PUBLISHERS ®

*Oh, Gracious Most High Heavenly father, Holy is your name,
Your Will Be Done Now and Forever!*

In the KJV bible book of Hebrews chapter 7 verses 1-4; it states: "For this **Melchisedec** (Μελχισέδεκ Melchisedek), **king of Salem** (Σαλήμ Salēm from the KJV bible Hebrew Strong's Concordance#8004 word "שָׁלֵם Sha-Lomé, Sha-Lom, Shâlêm, Shaw-lame, and means **Peace**), **Priest of the Most High God**, who met Abraham returning from the slaughter of the kings, and blessed him; to whom also Abraham gave a tenth part of all; first being by interpretation **King of Righteousness**, and after that also **King of Salem**, which is, **King of Peace**; **without father, without mother, without descent, having neither beginning of days, nor end of life; but made like unto the Son of God; abideth a priest continually**. Now consider how great this man *was*, unto whom even the patriarch Abraham gave the tenth of the spoils."

Yashu'a (Jesus) said: "Thou shalt love the Most High Heavenly Father, thy Sustainer with all thy heart, and with all thy soul, and with all thy mind. Thou shalt love thy neighbour as thyself."

Mind Gardening in the Creative Garden of Will (Your Mind) to Grow a Living Water Mentality!

CHILDREN OF THE MOST HIGH:
PRISTINE YOUTH AND FAMILY SOLUTIONS, LLC.
SONS AND DAUGHTERS OF THE MOST HIGH PUBLISHERS ®

Oh, Gracious Most High Heavenly father, Holy is your name, Your Will Be Done Now and Forever!

Is Yashua's (Jesus) Melchizedek? In the KJV bible book of Hebrews chapter 5 verses 5-10; it states: "So, also Christ glorified not himself to be made a high priest; but he that said unto him, thou art my Son, today have I begotten thee. As he saith also in another place, **Thou art a priest for ever after the order of Melchisedec. Who in the days of his flesh, when he had offered up prayers and supplications with strong crying and tears unto him that was able to save him from death, and was heard in that he feared**; Though he were a Son, yet learned he obedience by the things which he suffered; and being made perfect, **he became the author of eternal salvation unto all them that obey him**; Called of God an high priest after the order of Melchisedec."

Yashu'a (Jesus) said: "Thou shalt love the Most High Heavenly Father, thy Sustainer with all thy heart, and with all thy soul, and with all thy mind. Thou shalt love thy neighbour as thyself."

Mind Gardening in the Creative Garden of Will (Your Mind) to Grow a Living Water Mentality!

CHILDREN OF THE MOST HIGH:
PRISTINE YOUTH AND FAMILY SOLUTIONS, LLC.
SONS AND DAUGHTERS OF THE MOST HIGH PUBLISHERS ®

*Oh, Gracious Most High Heavenly father, Holy is your name,
Your Will Be Done Now and Forever!*

So, from the aforementioned verses; the **Messiah** Yashu'a (Jesus) **is after the Order of Melchizedek, and is not the Angelic-Being** "מַלְכִּי־צֶדֶק **Malkiy-Tsedeq (Malachi, Al Khidr, or Melchizedek, or the Sun of Righteousness) which are various titles of the same Arch Angelic-Being** מִיכָאֵל **Miyka'el (Michael).**

So, what is the Sun of Righteousness Thought Rhythm of Sound Wisdom Mentality? The **Sun of Righteousness Thought Rhythm of Sound Wisdom Mentality** is the **God's** (אֱלֹהִים **Elohiym**) **A**ll **W**ise **A**bundant **R**ight Exact (**A.W.A.R.E**) knowledge that is essential for **Mind Gardening in the Creative Garden of Will (Your Mind) to Grow a Living Water Mentality!**

253

Yashu'a (Jesus) said: "Thou shalt love the Most High Heavenly Father, thy Sustainer with all thy heart, and with all thy soul, and with all thy mind. Thou shalt love thy neighbour as thyself."

CHILDREN OF THE MOST HIGH:
PRISTINE YOUTH AND FAMILY SOLUTIONS, LLC.
SONS AND DAUGHTERS OF THE MOST HIGH PUBLISHERS ®

*Oh, Gracious Most High Heavenly father, Holy is your name,
Your Will Be Done Now and Forever!*

Chapter 15: Love and Hate Mental States!

What is the Mission and the Vision of the Children of the Most High; Pristine Youth and Family Solutions, LLC?

The Mission is: To inspire and empower all children of the Most High to pristinely make the world a safe and healthy place for all members of humanity. **The Vision is**: To create a world that is ruled by Love and the "**Will**" of the Most High, void of negative emotions, greed, lusts and love of money. According to the KJV bible book of Matthew chapter 19 verse 26, the Messiah Yashu'a (Jesus) said unto them, "With men this is impossible; but with God all things are possible." According to the KJV bible book of Philippians chapter 4 verse 13; it states: "I can do all things through Christ which strengthened me."

254

Yashu'a (Jesus) said: "Thou shalt love the Most High Heavenly Father, thy Sustainer with all thy heart, and with all thy soul, and with all thy mind. Thou shalt love thy neighbour as thyself."

Mind Gardening in the Creative Garden of Will (Your Mind) to Grow a Living Water Mentality!

CHILDREN OF THE MOST HIGH:
PRISTINE YOUTH AND FAMILY SOLUTIONS, LLC.
SONS AND DAUGHTERS OF THE MOST HIGH PUBLISHERS ®

*Oh, Gracious Most High Heavenly father, Holy is your name,
Your Will Be Done Now and Forever!*

In the KJV bible book of Matthew chapter 6 verses 19-24; the Messiah Yashu'a (Jesus) said: "Lay not up for yourselves treasures upon earth, where moth and rust doth corrupt, and where thieves break through and steal: But lay up for yourselves treasures in heaven, where neither moth nor rust doth corrupt, and where thieves do not break through nor steal: For where your treasure is, there will your heart be also. The light of the body is the eye: if therefore thine eye be single; thy whole body shall be full of light. But if thine eye be evil; thy whole body shall be full of darkness. If therefore the light that is in thee be darkness, how great is that darkness! No man can serve two masters: for either he will hate the one, and love the other; or else he will hold to the one, and despise the other. Ye cannot serve God and mammon."

255

*Yashu'a (Jesus) said: "Thou shalt love the Most High
Heavenly Father, thy Sustainer with all thy heart, and
with all thy soul, and with all thy mind. Thou shalt love
thy neighbour as thyself."*

Mind Gardening in the Creative Garden of Will (Your Mind) to Grow a Living Water Mentality!

CHILDREN OF THE MOST HIGH:
PRISTINE YOUTH AND FAMILY SOLUTIONS, LLC.
SONS AND DAUGHTERS OF THE MOST HIGH PUBLISHERS ®

Oh, Gracious Most High Heavenly father, Holy is your name,
Your Will Be Done Now and Forever!

Explain the aforementioned KJV bible Matthew chapter 6 verses 19 through 24? These words spoken by the Messiah Yashu'a (Jesus) in these verses **are the foundation** of **Mind Gardening in the Creative Garden of Will (Your Mind) to Grow a Living Water Mentality**, if **truly overstood** by the **sincere-hearted, child of the Most High who is a seeker child of the Most High Doctrine (Truth)!** The **Children of the Most High: Pristine Youth and Family Solutions, LLC.** define **"overstood"** as acquired through **overstanding**. **"Overstanding is mastering the comprehension of what is understood or what many may not have an understanding of."**

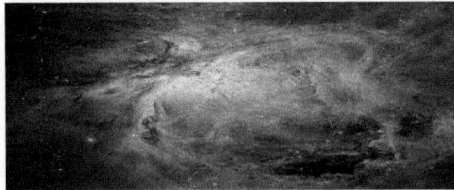

256

Yashu'a (Jesus) said: "Thou shalt love the Most High Heavenly Father, thy Sustainer with all thy heart, and with all thy soul, and with all thy mind. Thou shalt love thy neighbour as thyself."

Mind Gardening in the Creative Garden of Will (Your Mind) to Grow a Living Water Mentality!

CHILDREN OF THE MOST HIGH:
PRISTINE YOUTH AND FAMILY SOLUTIONS, LLC.
SONS AND DAUGHTERS OF THE MOST HIGH PUBLISHERS ®

Oh, Gracious Most High Heavenly father, Holy is your name,
Your Will Be Done Now and Forever!

The **Rabboni (Master) Yashu'a (Jesus)** said: "Lay not up for yourselves treasures upon earth, where moth and rust doth corrupt, and where thieves break through and steal, But lay up for yourselves treasures in heaven, where neither moth nor rust doth corrupt, and where thieves do not break through nor steal: For where your treasure is, there will your heart be also, KJV Matthew 6:19-21." The KJV bible Greek Strong's Concordance "#2344 Θησαυρός Thēsauros **(Thay-sow-ros)** for the word "**treasures**". Θησαυρός Thēsauros means: **treasures, the place in which good and precious things are collected and laid up, a casket, coffer, or other receptacle, in which valuables are kept, wealth (literally or figuratively): treasure.**" The KJV bible Greek Strong's Concordance "#2588 καρδία Kardia (Kar-dee'-ah) is the word for "**heart**".

Yashu'a (Jesus) said: "Thou shalt love the Most High Heavenly Father, thy Sustainer with all thy heart, and with all thy soul, and with all thy mind. Thou shalt love thy neighbour as thyself."

Mind Gardening in the Creative Garden of Will (Your Mind) to Grow a Living Water Mentality!

CHILDREN OF THE MOST HIGH:
PRISTINE YOUTH AND FAMILY SOLUTIONS, LLC.
SONS AND DAUGHTERS OF THE MOST HIGH PUBLISHERS ®

*Oh, Gracious Most High Heavenly father, Holy is your name,
Your Will Be Done Now and Forever!*

"καρδία Kardia means: **the heart**, the heart (feelings), the mind (thoughts), the organ in the body which is the center of the circulation of the blood, and hence was regarded as the seat of physical life, denotes the center of all physical and spiritual life, the vigor and sense of physical life, the center and seat of spiritual life, the soul or mind, as it is the fountain and seat of the thoughts, passions, desires, appetites, affections, purposes, endeavors of the understanding, <u>the faculty and seat of the intelligence of the will and character</u> <u>of the soul so far as it is affected and stirred in a bad way or good</u>, <u>or of the soul as the seat of the sensibilities, affections, emotions, desires, appetites, passions of the middle or central or inmost part of anything, even though inanimate</u>."

258

Yashu'a (Jesus) said: "Thou shalt love the Most High Heavenly Father, thy Sustainer with all thy heart, and with all thy soul, and with all thy mind. Thou shalt love thy neighbour as thyself."

Mind Gardening in the Creative Garden of Will (Your Mind) to Grow a Living Water Mentality!

CHILDREN OF THE MOST HIGH:
PRISTINE YOUTH AND FAMILY SOLUTIONS, LLC.
SONS AND DAUGHTERS OF THE MOST HIGH PUBLISHERS ®

Oh, Gracious Most High Heavenly father, Holy is your name,
Your Will Be Done Now and Forever!

The **Rabboni (Master) Yashu'a (Jesus)** said: "The light (λύχνος **Lychnos (Lookh'-nos) – lamp, candle, light**) of the body (σῶμα **Sōma (So'-mah) – the living body**) is the eye (ὀφθαλμός **Ophthalmos (Of-thal-mos) - the eye of the mind, the faculty of knowing**): if therefore thine eye be single, thy whole body (σῶμα **Sōma – the living body**) shall be full of light (λύχνος **Lychnos – lamp, candle, light**). But if thine eye be evil (πονηρός **Ponēros (Pon-ay-ros) - hurtful, evil, (morally) culpable, derelict, vicious, facinorous; mischief, malice, or (plural) guilt; the devil, or (plural) sinners: — bad, grievous, harm, lewd, malicious, wicked(-ness)**, thy whole body shall be full of darkness. If therefore the light that is in thee be darkness, how great is that darkness (σκοτεινός **Skoteinos (Skot-i-nos') - full of darkness, covered with darkness** from the **root word "σκότος Skótos, Skot'-os"** - of **ignorance respecting "divine things and**

Yashu'a (Jesus) said: "Thou shalt love the Most High
Heavenly Father, thy Sustainer with all thy heart, and
with all thy soul, and with all thy mind. Thou shalt love
thy neighbour as thyself."

Mind Gardening in the Creative Garden of Will (Your Mind) to Grow a Living Water Mentality!

CHILDREN OF THE MOST HIGH:
PRISTINE YOUTH AND FAMILY SOLUTIONS, LLC.
SONS AND DAUGHTERS OF THE MOST HIGH PUBLISHERS ®

Oh, Gracious Most High Heavenly father, Holy is your name,
Your Will Be Done Now and Forever!

human duties, and the accompanying ungodliness and immorality, together with their consequent misery in hell, persons in whom darkness becomes visible and holds sway)! No man (οὐδείς Oudeis (Oo-dice') – no one, nothing, no male or female human being) can serve two masters (κύριος Kyrios (Koo'-ree-os) – master, lord, the Messiah): for either he will hate (μισέω Miseō (Mis-eh'-o) – hate, hatred, to hate, pursue with hatred, detest) the one, and love (ἀγαπάω Agapaō (Ag-ap-ah'-o) - to love (in a social or moral sense) the other; or else he will hold to the one, and despise the other. Ye cannot serve God and mammon (μαμωνᾶς Mamōnas (Mam-mo-nas') - wealth, personified); avarice (deified), KJV Matthew 6:24."

260

Yashu'a (Jesus) said: "Thou shalt love the Most High Heavenly Father, thy Sustainer with all thy heart, and with all thy soul, and with all thy mind. Thou shalt love thy neighbour as thyself."

Mind Gardening in the Creative Garden of Will (Your Mind) to Grow a Living Water Mentality!

Oh, Gracious Most High Heavenly father, Holy is your name, Your Will Be Done Now and Forever!

So, as it relates to not laying up your treasures on earth, but; rather lay up your treasures in heaven; the children of the Most High **must not** utilize our limited time of being alive on this realm (earth) **valuing most, the things money can buy**. Rather, the children of the Most High **must** utilize our limited time of being alive on this realm (earth) **valuing the most, what money cannot buy**! If we, the children of the Most High **value most the things that money cannot buy, our mind's eye** (ὀφθαλμός Ophthalmos (Of-thal-mos) - **the eye of the mind, the faculty of knowing**): will be single (ἁπλοῦς Haplous (Hap-looce'); means: **simple, sound (to have sound health, be well** (in body); **to be uncorrupt (true in doctrine**): —be safe and sound, (be) whole(-some); **whole, single (figuratively, clear)**, and our whole body (σῶμα Sōma (So'-mah) – **the living body)** shall be full of light (λύχνος Lychnos (Lookh'-nos) – **lamp, candle, light).**"

261

Yashu'a (Jesus) said: "Thou shalt love the Most High Heavenly Father, thy Sustainer with all thy heart, and with all thy soul, and with all thy mind. Thou shalt love thy neighbour as thyself."

Mind Gardening in the Creative Garden of Will (Your Mind) to Grow a Living Water Mentality!

CHILDREN OF THE MOST HIGH:
PRISTINE YOUTH AND FAMILY SOLUTIONS, LLC.
SONS AND DAUGHTERS OF THE MOST HIGH PUBLISHERS ®

Oh, Gracious Most High Heavenly father, Holy is your name, Your Will Be Done Now and Forever!

However; **if we value most the things money can buy**, thine eye be evil (πονηρός Ponēros (Pon-ay-ros) - **hurtful, evil, (morally) culpable, derelict, vicious, facinorous; mischief, malice, or (plural) guilt; the devil, or (plural) sinners: — bad, grievous, harm, lewd, malicious, wicked(-ness)**, thy whole body shall be full of darkness. If therefore the light that is in thee be darkness, how great is that darkness (σκοτεινός Skoteinos (Skot-i-nos') - **full of darkness, covered with darkness** from the **root word** "σκότος Skótos, Skot'-os" - of **ignorance respecting "divine things and human duties, and the accompanying ungodliness and immorality, together with their consequent misery in hell, persons in whom darkness becomes visible and holds sway**)!

262

Yashu'a (Jesus) said: "Thou shalt love the Most High Heavenly Father, thy Sustainer with all thy heart, and with all thy soul, and with all thy mind. Thou shalt love thy neighbour as thyself."

Mind Gardening in the Creative Garden of Will (Your Mind) to Grow a Living Water Mentality!

CHILDREN OF THE MOST HIGH:
PRISTINE YOUTH AND FAMILY SOLUTIONS, LLC.
SONS AND DAUGHTERS OF THE MOST HIGH PUBLISHERS ®

Oh, Gracious Most High Heavenly father, Holy is your name,
Your Will Be Done Now and Forever!

The **Hate Mental State** values all of the things money can buy, and is the root foundation of evil thoughts (**seeds**) in the **Reprobate Mind or Deceptive Mind!** The **Hate Mental State** also can exist **in Mind Gardening in the Creative Garden of Will (Your Mind) to Grow** <u>evil thoughts (seeds)</u> in the **Deceptive Mind** that <u>produces every imagination of the wicked thoughts</u>, and **only** fills the hearts with evil continually! In the KJV bible book of Genesis chapter 3 verse 15; it states: "And I will put **enmity (אֵיבָה 'Eybah (Ay-baw') - hostility:—enmity (Deep-seated, hatred)** between thee and the woman, and between thy seed and her seed; it shall bruise thy head, and thou shalt bruise his heel." It is the **Hate Mental State** that is the foundation of **all racial enmity (אֵיבָה 'Eybah (Ay-baw') - hostility: —enmity (Deep-seated, hatred)** that exists!

Yashu'a (Jesus) said: "Thou shalt love the Most High Heavenly Father, thy Sustainer with all thy heart, and with all thy soul, and with all thy mind. Thou shalt love thy neighbour as thyself."

Mind Gardening in the Creative Garden of Will (Your Mind) to Grow a Living Water Mentality!

CHILDREN OF THE MOST HIGH:
PRISTINE YOUTH AND FAMILY SOLUTIONS, LLC.
SONS AND DAUGHTERS OF THE MOST HIGH PUBLISHERS ®

*Oh, Gracious Most High Heavenly father, Holy is your name,
Your Will Be Done Now and Forever!*

The **Love Mental State** values most; loving the Most High Heavenly Father with all of your heart, all of your soul, all of your spirit, all of your might, and all of your mind; and loving the **Messiah Yashu'a (Jesus)**! The **Love Mental State** values Most, the **positive aspects** of **existence** (**exist-and see**) that money cannot buy, and is the root foundation of positive thoughts (**seeds**) of the **9 True Vine** (Yashu'a, Jesus) **Elements of Healthy Living!**

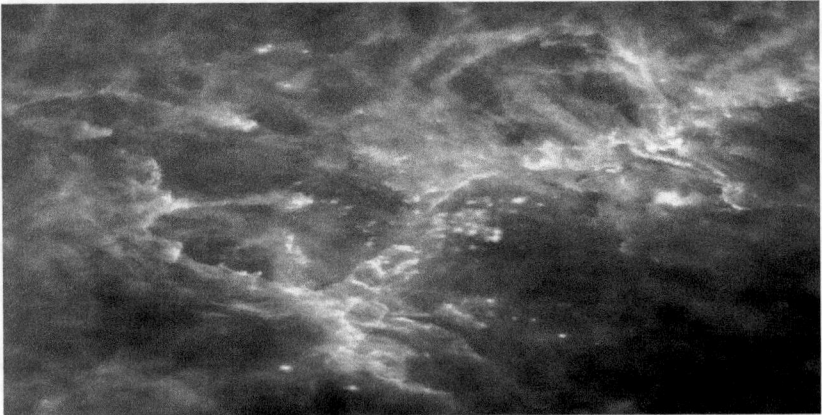

264

*Yashu'a (Jesus) said: "Thou shalt love the Most High
Heavenly Father, thy Sustainer with all thy heart, and
with all thy soul, and with all thy mind. Thou shalt love
thy neighbour as thyself."*

Mind Gardening in the Creative Garden of Will (Your Mind) to Grow a Living Water Mentality!

CHILDREN OF THE MOST HIGH:
PRISTINE YOUTH AND FAMILY SOLUTIONS, LLC.
SONS AND DAUGHTERS OF THE MOST HIGH PUBLISHERS ®

Oh, Gracious Most High Heavenly father, Holy is your name,
Your Will Be Done Now and Forever!

The **9 True Vine** (Yashu'a, Jesus) **Elements of Healthy Living** are:

1. **<u>A Resilient - Sound Mind</u>** – In the KJV bible book of 2nd Timothy chapter 1 verse 7; it states: "For God hath not given us the spirit of fear; but of power, and of love, and of a sound mind." In the KJV bible book of Hebrews chapter 8 verse 10; it states: "For this is the covenant that I will make with the house of Israel after those days, saith the Lord; I will put my laws into their mind, and write them in their hearts: and I will be to them a God, and they shall be to me a people."

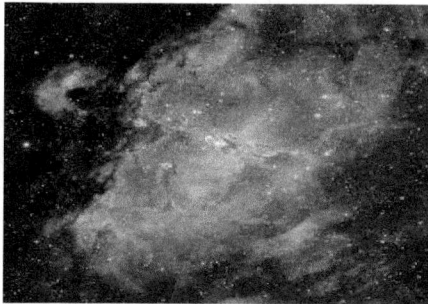

265

Yashu'a (Jesus) said: "Thou shalt love the Most High Heavenly Father, thy Sustainer with all thy heart, and with all thy soul, and with all thy mind. Thou shalt love thy neighbour as thyself."

Mind Gardening in the Creative Garden of Will (Your Mind) to Grow a Living Water Mentality!

CHILDREN OF THE MOST HIGH:
PRISTINE YOUTH AND FAMILY SOLUTIONS, LLC.
SONS AND DAUGHTERS OF THE MOST HIGH PUBLISHERS ®

*Oh, Gracious Most High Heavenly father, Holy is your name,
Your Will Be Done Now and Forever!*

2. <u>**A Clean Soul**</u> – In the KJV bible book of Mark chapter 7 verses 20-23; the Messiah Yashu'a (Jesus) said: "That which cometh out of the man, that defileth the man [or person]. For from within, out of the heart of men, proceed evil thoughts, adulteries, fornications, murders, thefts, covetousness, wickedness, deceit, lasciviousness, an evil eye, blasphemy, pride, foolishness: All these evil things come from within, and defile the man [or person]."

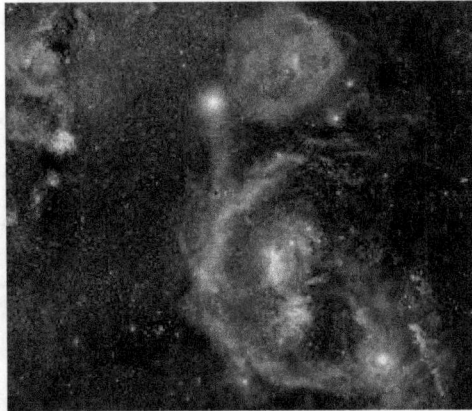

266

Yashu'a (Jesus) said: "Thou shalt love the Most High Heavenly Father, thy Sustainer with all thy heart, and with all thy soul, and with all thy mind. Thou shalt love thy neighbour as thyself."

Mind Gardening in the Creative Garden of Will (Your Mind) to Grow a Living Water Mentality!

CHILDREN OF THE MOST HIGH:
PRISTINE YOUTH AND FAMILY SOLUTIONS, LLC.
SONS AND DAUGHTERS OF THE MOST HIGH PUBLISHERS ®

Oh, Gracious Most High Heavenly father, Holy is your name,
Your Will Be Done Now and Forever!

3. <u>**A Holy Spirit**</u> – In the KJV bible book of Luke chapter 11 verse 13; the Messiah Yashu'a (Jesus) said: "If ye then, being evil, know how to give good gifts unto your children: how much more shall your heavenly Father give the Holy Spirit to them that ask him?" In the KJV bible book of Isaiah chapter 11 verse 2; it states: "And the spirit of the LORD shall rest upon him, the spirit of wisdom and understanding, the spirit of counsel and might, the spirit of knowledge and of the fear of the LORD."

4. <u>**A Clear Conscious**</u> – In the KJV bible book of 1st John chapter 1 verse 9; it states: "If we confess our sins, he is faithful and just to forgive us our sins, and to cleanse us from all unrighteousness."

Yashu'a (Jesus) said: "Thou shalt love the Most High Heavenly Father, thy Sustainer with all thy heart, and with all thy soul, and with all thy mind. Thou shalt love thy neighbour as thyself."

CHILDREN OF THE MOST HIGH:
PRISTINE YOUTH AND FAMILY SOLUTIONS, LLC.
SONS AND DAUGHTERS OF THE MOST HIGH PUBLISHERS ®

*Oh, Gracious Most High Heavenly father, Holy is your name,
Your Will Be Done Now and Forever!*

5. **A Clean Heart** – In the KJV bible book of Psalms chapter 51 verse 10; it states: "Create in me a clean heart, O God; and renew a right spirit within me." In the KJV bible book of Deuteronomy chapter 6 verses 4-7; it states: "Hear, O Israel: The LORD our God is one LORD: And thou shalt love the LORD thy God with all thine heart, and with all thy soul, and with all thy might. And these words, which I command thee this day, shall be in thine heart: And thou shalt teach them diligently unto thy children, and shalt talk of them when thou sittest in thine house, and when thou walkest by the way, and when thou liest down, and when thou risest up."

268

Yashu'a (Jesus) said: "Thou shalt love the Most High Heavenly Father, thy Sustainer with all thy heart, and with all thy soul, and with all thy mind. Thou shalt love thy neighbour as thyself."

Mind Gardening in the Creative Garden of Will (Your Mind) to Grow a Living Water Mentality!

CHILDREN OF THE MOST HIGH:
PRISTINE YOUTH AND FAMILY SOLUTIONS, LLC.
SONS AND DAUGHTERS OF THE MOST HIGH PUBLISHERS ®

Oh, Gracious Most High Heavenly father, Holy is your name,
Your Will Be Done Now and Forever!

6. **A Caring Person** – In the KJV bible book of John chapter 13 verses 34-35 Yashu'a (Jesus) said: "A new commandment I give unto you, that ye love one another; as I have loved you, that ye also love one another. By this shall all men [women and children] know that ye are my disciples, if ye have love one to another."

7. **An Honest Personality** – In the KJV bible book of James chapter 4 verse 8; it states: "Draw nigh to God, and he will draw nigh to you. Cleanse your hands, ye sinners; and purify your hearts, ye double minded."

269

Yashu'a (Jesus) said: "Thou shalt love the Most High Heavenly Father, thy Sustainer with all thy heart, and with all thy soul, and with all thy mind. Thou shalt love thy neighbour as thyself."

Mind Gardening in the Creative Garden of Will (Your Mind) to Grow a Living Water Mentality!

CHILDREN OF THE MOST HIGH:
PRISTINE YOUTH AND FAMILY SOLUTIONS, LLC.
SONS AND DAUGHTERS OF THE MOST HIGH PUBLISHERS ®

Oh, Gracious Most High Heavenly father, Holy is your name,
Your Will Be Done Now and Forever!

8. **A Being who is Loving** – In the KJV bible book of 1ˢᵗ John chapter 4 verse 8; it states: "He that loveth not knoweth not God; for God is love." In the KJV bible book of John chapter 13 verses 34-35; the Messiah Yashu'a (Jesus) said: "A new commandment I give unto you, that ye love one another; as I have loved you, that ye also love one another. By this shall all men [women and children] know that ye are my disciples, if ye have love one to another."

270

Yashu'a (Jesus) said: "Thou shalt love the Most High Heavenly Father, thy Sustainer with all thy heart, and with all thy soul, and with all thy mind. Thou shalt love thy neighbour as thyself."

Mind Gardening in the Creative Garden of Will (Your Mind) to Grow a Living Water Mentality!

Oh, Gracious Most High Heavenly father, Holy is your name, Your Will Be Done Now and Forever!

9. **A Clean Healthy Body** in a Sound Environment that receives daily high dosages of quality sleep. In the KJV bible book of John chapter 15 verse 3; the Messiah Yashu'a (Jesus) said: "Now ye are clean through the word which I have spoken unto you." In the KJV bible book of Matthew chapter 6 verse 22; the Messiah Yashu'a (Jesus) said: "The light of the body is the eye: if therefore thine eye be single; thy whole body shall be full of light."

The **Love Mental State 9 True Vine** (Yashu'a, Jesus) **Elements of Healthy Living** are the root foundation **in Mind Gardening in the Creative Garden of Will (Your Mind) to Grow a Living Water Mentality!**

271

Yashu'a (Jesus) said: "Thou shalt love the Most High Heavenly Father, thy Sustainer with all thy heart, and with all thy soul, and with all thy mind. Thou shalt love thy neighbour as thyself."

CHILDREN OF THE MOST HIGH:
PRISTINE YOUTH AND FAMILY SOLUTIONS, LLC.
SONS AND DAUGHTERS OF THE MOST HIGH PUBLISHERS ®

Oh, Gracious Most High Heavenly father, Holy is your name,
Your Will Be Done Now and Forever!

Chapter 16: "The Amen" Mentality!

CHILDREN OF THE MOST HIGH:
PRISTINE YOUTH AND FAMILY SOLUTIONS, LLC.
SONS AND DAUGHTERS OF THE MOST HIGH PUBLISHERS ®

In the KJV bible book of Revelation chapter 3 verse 14; **the Messiah Yashu'a (Jesus)** said: "And unto the angel of the church of the Laodiceans write; These things saith the Amen, the faithful and true witness, the beginning of the creation of God."

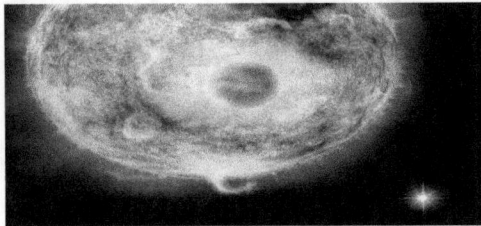

272

Yashu'a (Jesus) said: "Thou shalt love the Most High Heavenly Father, thy Sustainer with all thy heart, and with all thy soul, and with all thy mind. Thou shalt love thy neighbour as thyself."

Mind Gardening in the Creative Garden of Will (Your Mind) to Grow a Living Water Mentality!

*Oh, Gracious Most High Heavenly father, Holy is your name,
Your Will Be Done Now and Forever!*

According to the KJV bible Greek Strong's Concordance **#281** ἀμήν Amēn (**Am-ane'** (**O Am-ane'**- "**THE AMOM**" which is the **Greek** word **Pis-tos for "faithful"**) is word for "**The Amen**". ἀμήν Amēn means: **faithful, verily, verily, amen, truly, of a truth**; of Hebrew origin (**H543**); אָמֵן **'âmên, Aw-mane'**; from **H539; sure; faithfulness**; adverb, **truly**: —Amen, **so be it, truth**. Root Word (Etymology) From אָמַן (**H539**) From root word אָמַן **'âman, Aw-man'**; אָמַן (H539) **be faithful, reliable, to stand firm, to trust, to be certain, morally to be true or certain**. These things **Τάδε hode** saith **λέγω legō the Amen Ἀμήν Amēn the faithful πιστός Pistos** and **καί kai** true **ἀληθινός alēthinos** witness **μάρτυς martys** the **beginning** ἀρχή **archē of the creation κτίσις ktisis of God** θεός **Theos**; was in the beginning of creation and witnessed the creation of the **Hebrew God** called: **YHWH, Elohiym, Adonai, Thehos, Hashem, El, Elowah, Yah, El Shadi, Yahweh, Yehova, Yahuwa, and Jehovah**."

273

Yashu'a (Jesus) said: "Thou shalt love the Most High Heavenly Father, thy Sustainer with all thy heart, and with all thy soul, and with all thy mind. Thou shalt love thy neighbour as thyself."

Mind Gardening in the Creative Garden of Will (Your Mind) to Grow a Living Water Mentality!

CHILDREN OF THE MOST HIGH:
PRISTINE YOUTH AND FAMILY SOLUTIONS, LLC.
SONS AND DAUGHTERS OF THE MOST HIGH PUBLISHERS ®

Oh, Gracious Most High Heavenly father, Holy is your name, Your Will Be Done Now and Forever!

Let us examine the other aforementioned verse key words in Revelation chapter 3 verse 14:

- **KJV Strong's Concordance "#3144: "Witness"** μάρτυς **(Mar'-toos)** – means: **martys, a witness**.

- **KJV Strong's Concordance "#746: "Beginning"** ἀρχή **Archē (Ar-khay')** – means: **beginning, origin, the person or thing that commences, the first person or thing in a series, the leader."**

- **KJV Strong's Concordance "#2937: "Creation"** κτίσις Ktisis – means: creature, creation, building, of individual things, beings, a creature, a creation, from κτίζω ktízō (ktid'-zo) – meaning to create, Creator, make; from the Greek word κτάομαι ktáomai (ktah'-om-ahee); meaning: to get, i.e. acquire (by any means; own):—obtain, possess, provide, purchase. to acquire, get, or procure a thing for one's self, to possess <u>to marry a wife.</u>

- **KJV Strong's Concordance "#2316: "God"** θεός Theós, (Theh'-os), meaning: a god or goddess, a general name of deities or divinities."

Yashu'a (Jesus) said: "Thou shalt love the Most High Heavenly Father, thy Sustainer with all thy heart, and with all thy soul, and with all thy mind. Thou shalt love thy neighbour as thyself."

Mind Gardening in the Creative Garden of Will (Your Mind) to Grow a Living Water Mentality!

*Oh, Gracious Most High Heavenly father, Holy is your name,
Your Will Be Done Now and Forever!*

Also, in the KJV book of revelation chapter 3 verse 14, **the definite article**: (**The**) is in front of "**The Amen**", O Am-ane'- "**THE AMOM**", **who** existed thousands of years in **Ancient Africa** as "**AMUN**" (**Yet I am the LORD thy God from the land of Egypt**, and thou shalt know no god but me: for there is no **saviour** (**Yashu'a, יְשַׁע Yasha**) beside me, KJV Hosea 13:9)."

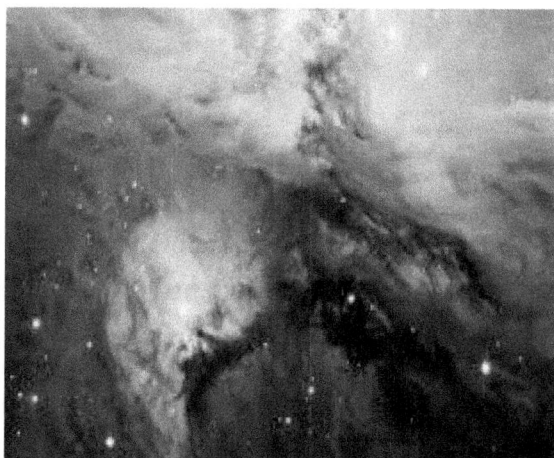

275

Yashu'a (Jesus) said: "Thou shalt love the Most High Heavenly Father, thy Sustainer with all thy heart, and with all thy soul, and with all thy mind. Thou shalt love thy neighbour as thyself."

Mind Gardening in the Creative Garden of Will (Your Mind) to Grow a Living Water Mentality!

*Oh, Gracious Most High Heavenly father, Holy is your name,
Your Will Be Done Now and Forever!*

So, "**The Amen**", O Am-ane'- "**THE AMOM**", **who** existed thousands of years in **Ancient Africa** as "**AMUN**" before the creation of the **Hebrew God YHWH as the Messiah Yashu'a (Jesus) himself** in the verse as: "the faithful and true witness, the beginning of the creation of God." This is why the KJV bible book of John chapter 1 verse 14 stated: "**And the Word was made flesh, and dwelt among us.**" **The Word** is λόγος **Logos (Log'-os)**, was made γίνομαι **ginomai** flesh σάρξ **sarx** and καί **kai** dwelt σκηνόω **skēnoō** among ἐν **en** us ἡμῖν **hemin**" which relates to the prophecy of the KJV book of Malachi chapter 4 verse 2, before the **light** ("**Sun**" is **Shemesh** צְדָקָה) as **Logos** λόγος is manifested in the flesh as **Yashu'a Ha-Mashiakh** translated as "**Jesus The Anointed**". This also why the **Messiah Yashu'a (Jesus)** said: "Verily (ἀμήν **Amēn**), verily (ἀμήν **Amēn**), I say unto you, Before Abraham was, I am, KJV John 8:58."

276

Yashu'a (Jesus) said: "Thou shalt love the Most High Heavenly Father, thy Sustainer with all thy heart, and with all thy soul, and with all thy mind. Thou shalt love thy neighbour as thyself."

Mind Gardening in the Creative Garden of Will (Your Mind) to Grow a Living Water Mentality!

CHILDREN OF THE MOST HIGH:
PRISTINE YOUTH AND FAMILY SOLUTIONS, LLC.
SONS AND DAUGHTERS OF THE MOST HIGH PUBLISHERS ®

Oh, Gracious Most High Heavenly father, Holy is your name,
Your Will Be Done Now and Forever!

אָמֵן—(1) verbal adj. *firm,* metaph. *faithful.*
(Arab. اَمِين, Syr. ܐܡܝܢ.) Compare Apoc. 3:14.
Neutr. *faithfulness, fidelity,* Isa. 65:16.

(2) adv. *truly, verily, Amen!* Jer. 28:6. אָמֵן
וְאָמֵן Ps. 41:14; 72:19; 89:53. Its proper place
is where one person confirms the words of another,
and expresses a wish for the issue of his vows or pre-
dictions: *fiat, ita sit;* "Amen, so be it;" LXX, well,
γένοιτο. 1 Ki. 1:36; Jer. 11:5; Nu. 5:22; Deu.
27:15, seq.; Neh. 5:13; 8:6; 1 Ch. 16:36.

277

Yashu'a (Jesus) said: "Thou shalt love the Most High
Heavenly Father, thy Sustainer with all thy heart, and
with all thy soul, and with all thy mind. Thou shalt love
thy neighbour as thyself."

Mind Gardening in the Creative Garden of Will (Your Mind) to Grow a Living Water Mentality!

CHILDREN OF THE MOST HIGH:
PRISTINE YOUTH AND FAMILY SOLUTIONS, LLC.
SONS AND DAUGHTERS OF THE MOST HIGH PUBLISHERS ®

*Oh, Gracious Most High Heavenly father, Holy is your name,
Your Will Be Done Now and Forever!*

In the KJV bible book of John chapter 3 verses 5-6; the **Messiah Yashu'a (Jesus)** said: "Verily (ἀμήν Amēn), verily (ἀμήν Amēn), I say unto thee, except a man be born of water and of the Spirit, he cannot enter into the kingdom of God. That which is born of the flesh is flesh; and that which is born of the Spirit is spirit (πνεῦμα Pneûma, Pnyoo'-mah-Spirit); a current of air, breath (blast) or a breeze**; by analogy or figuratively, **a spirit, vital principle, mental disposition, Christ's spirit, the Holy Spirit:—ghost, life, spirit(-ual, - ually), mind. John 6:63. the rational spirit, the power by which a human being feels, thinks, wills, decides.** The Messiah Yashu'a (Jesus) said: "It is the spirit that quickeneth; the flesh profiteth nothing: the words that I speak unto you, they are spirit, and they are life, KJV John 6:63."

278

Yashu'a (Jesus) said: "Thou shalt love the Most High Heavenly Father, thy Sustainer with all thy heart, and with all thy soul, and with all thy mind. Thou shalt love thy neighbour as thyself."

Mind Gardening in the Creative Garden of Will (Your Mind) to Grow a Living Water Mentality!

CHILDREN OF THE MOST HIGH:
PRISTINE YOUTH AND FAMILY SOLUTIONS, LLC.
SONS AND DAUGHTERS OF THE MOST HIGH PUBLISHERS ®

*Oh, Gracious Most High Heavenly father, Holy is your name,
Your Will Be Done Now and Forever!*

Therefore; "**The Amen" Mentality** in the eyesight of the Most High, is a **Faithful** and **True** (like the **Messiah Yashu'a, Jesus**) **mental disposition (the power or liberty to control, direct, or dispose, habitual inclination tendency) from Christ's spirit** that is essential for **Mind Gardening in the Creative Garden of Will (Your Mind) to Grow a Living Water Mentality!**

279

Yashu'a (Jesus) said: "Thou shalt love the Most High Heavenly Father, thy Sustainer with all thy heart, and with all thy soul, and with all thy mind. Thou shalt love thy neighbour as thyself."

Mind Gardening in the Creative Garden of Will (Your Mind) to Grow a Living Water Mentality!

CHILDREN OF THE MOST HIGH:
PRISTINE YOUTH AND FAMILY SOLUTIONS, LLC.
SONS AND DAUGHTERS OF THE MOST HIGH PUBLISHERS ®

Oh, Gracious Most High Heavenly father, Holy is your name, Your Will Be Done Now and Forever!

Chapter 17: True Vine (Yashu'a, Jesus) Mind Gardener – Mind Gardening Memorization Keys to Success!

In the KJV bible book of John chapter 20 verses 11-16; it states: "But Mary stood without at the sepulchre weeping: and as she wept, she stooped down, and looked into the sepulchre, And seeth two angels in white sitting, the one at the head, and the other at the feet, where the body of Jesus **had lain**. And they say unto her, Woman, why weepest thou? She saith unto them,

Yashu'a (Jesus) said: "Thou shalt love the Most High Heavenly Father, thy Sustainer with all thy heart, and with all thy soul, and with all thy mind. Thou shalt love thy neighbour as thyself."

Mind Gardening in the Creative Garden of Will (Your Mind) to Grow a Living Water Mentality!

CHILDREN OF THE MOST HIGH:
PRISTINE YOUTH AND FAMILY SOLUTIONS, LLC.
SONS AND DAUGHTERS OF THE MOST HIGH PUBLISHERS ®

Oh, Gracious Most High Heavenly father, Holy is your name,
Your Will Be Done Now and Forever!

"Because, they have taken away my Lord, and I know not where they have laid him. And when she had thus said, **she turned herself back, and saw Jesus standing, and knew not that it was Jesus**. Jesus saith unto her, Woman, why weepest thou? whom seekest thou?"

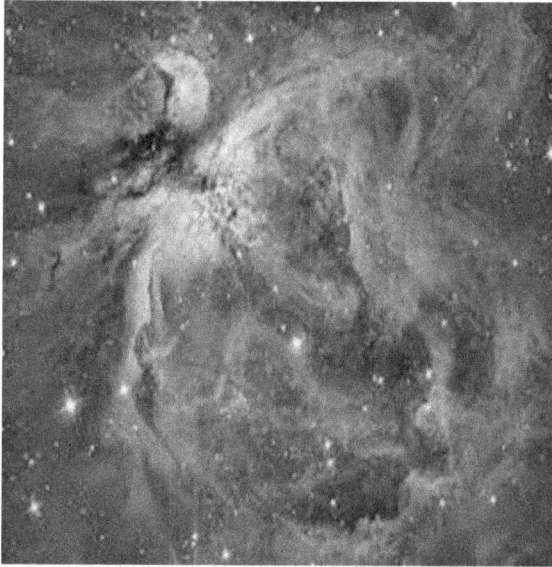

281

Yashu'a (Jesus) said: "Thou shalt love the Most High Heavenly Father, thy Sustainer with all thy heart, and with all thy soul, and with all thy mind. Thou shalt love thy neighbour as thyself."

Mind Gardening in the Creative Garden of Will (Your Mind) to Grow a Living Water Mentality!

CHILDREN OF THE MOST HIGH:
PRISTINE YOUTH AND FAMILY SOLUTIONS, LLC.
SONS AND DAUGHTERS OF THE MOST HIGH PUBLISHERS ®

*Oh, Gracious Most High Heavenly father, Holy is your name,
Your Will Be Done Now and Forever!*

"**She, supposing him to be the gardener**, saith unto him, Sir, if thou have borne him hence, tell me where thou hast laid him, and I will take him away. Jesus saith unto her, Mary. She turned herself, **and saith unto him**, **Rabboni**; (ῥαββουνί Rhabbouni (Rab-bon-ee') - of Aramaic origin (meaning Master) **which is to say**, **Master** (διδάσκαλος Didaskalos (Did-as'-kal-os) – meaning an instructor, doctor, master, teacher.)" In the previous verses, the **True Vine (Yashu'a, Jesus)** is acknowledged as: "**Master**" and **thought** (the process of **thinking**; or a product of **thinking** as **mental activity** in the **Mind**) to be the "**Gardner**". Thus, **introducing the Creative Garden of Will (Your Mind) to thoughts of**: "Mind Gardner", "True Vine (Yashu'a, Jesus) Master Gardner", and "True Vine (Yashu'a, Jesus) Mind Master Gardner" **to give birth to the idea in your mind** that is essential to **Grow the Living Water Mentality!**

282

Yashu'a (Jesus) said: "Thou shalt love the Most High Heavenly Father, thy Sustainer with all thy heart, and with all thy soul, and with all thy mind. Thou shalt love thy neighbour as thyself."

Mind Gardening in the Creative Garden of Will (Your Mind) to Grow a Living Water Mentality!

CHILDREN OF THE MOST HIGH:
PRISTINE YOUTH AND FAMILY SOLUTIONS, LLC.
SONS AND DAUGHTERS OF THE MOST HIGH PUBLISHERS ®

Oh, Gracious Most High Heavenly father, Holy is your name,
Your Will Be Done Now and Forever!

According to (Hughes, 2019); "The **1ˢᵗ of the 9X9 True Vine (Yashu'a, Jesus) B.A.-K.A.-R.E.** Sequential Order of Learning Habits of Success**, that introduces **the mind to thoughts that give birth to new ideas**; are **the 9 True Vine (Yashu'a, Jesus) Mind Gardening Memorization Keys to Success** that may help a person" to **grow a Living Water Mentality** are:

1. **G**lorify the Most High Heavenly Father through the Messiah Yashu'a (Jesus).

2. **A**pply the Most High's Scriptural Knowledge in all that you do.

3. **R**evere the Most High and have moral reverence for the Most High.

4. **D**ecrease so that the Messiah Yashu'a (Jesus) can increase within you.

Yashu'a (Jesus) said: "Thou shalt love the Most High Heavenly Father, thy Sustainer with all thy heart, and with all thy soul, and with all thy mind. Thou shalt love thy neighbour as thyself."

Mind Gardening in the Creative Garden of Will (Your Mind) to Grow a Living Water Mentality!

CHILDREN OF THE MOST HIGH:
PRISTINE YOUTH AND FAMILY SOLUTIONS, LLC.
SONS AND DAUGHTERS OF THE MOST HIGH PUBLISHERS ®

Oh, Gracious Most High Heavenly father, Holy is your name,
Your Will Be Done Now and Forever!

5. Except a person be born again, he or she cannot see the kingdom of the Most High.

6. Nourish yourself and others with the Most High's Scriptural Knowledge.

7. Inform yourself and others about the Most High's Scriptural Knowledge.

8. Narrow is the way that leads unto eternal life through the Messiah Yashu'a (Jesus).

9. Grace and truth came by way of the Messiah Yashu'a (Jesus).

284

Yashu'a (Jesus) said: "Thou shalt love the Most High Heavenly Father, thy Sustainer with all thy heart, and with all thy soul, and with all thy mind. Thou shalt love thy neighbour as thyself."

Mind Gardening in the Creative Garden of Will (Your Mind) to Grow a Living Water Mentality!

CHILDREN OF THE MOST HIGH:
PRISTINE YOUTH AND FAMILY SOLUTIONS, LLC.
SONS AND DAUGHTERS OF THE MOST HIGH PUBLISHERS ®

*Oh, Gracious Most High Heavenly father, Holy is your name,
Your Will Be Done Now and Forever!*

Explain how the 9 True Vine (Yashu'a, Jesus) Mind Gardening Memorization Keys to Success concept of <u>Gardening</u> relates to Mind Gardening and its relationship to the Most High, the True Vine (the Messiah Yashu'a, Jesus), the branches, obeying the laws of the Most High, mind, heart, and grace? The Most High Heavenly Father is the Creator of the Mind and on a macro level from the people on earth viewpoint, the Boundless Universes combined may be one of the Most High's Garden's. The Messiah Yashu'a (Jesus) is **the True Vine** as stated in the KJV bible book of John chapter 15 verse 1; he said: "I am the true vine, and my Father is the husbandman." The children of the Most High who accept the Messiah Yashu'a (Jesus) into their **hearts** as their savior, will be **the branches** as Yashu'a (Jesus) said in the KJV bible book of John chapter 15 verse 4; he said: (I am the vine, ye are the branches: He that abideth in me, and I in him, the same bringeth forth much fruit: for without me ye can do nothing)."

285

Yashu'a (Jesus) said: "Thou shalt love the Most High Heavenly Father, thy Sustainer with all thy heart, and with all thy soul, and with all thy mind. Thou shalt love thy neighbour as thyself."

Mind Gardening in the Creative Garden of Will (Your Mind) to Grow a Living Water Mentality!

CHILDREN OF THE MOST HIGH:
PRISTINE YOUTH AND FAMILY SOLUTIONS, LLC.
SONS AND DAUGHTERS OF THE MOST HIGH PUBLISHERS ®

Oh, Gracious Most High Heavenly father, Holy is your name,
Your Will Be Done Now and Forever!

Growth occurs over time by learning and obeying the laws of the Most High which initiates all thoughts through the activating of the **"Will"** of the Most High Heavenly Father in the minds of the children of the Most High. Once this occurs, Yashu'a (Jesus) makes them into **Mind Gardeners** who become practitioners of **Mind Gardening**! In the KJV bible book of Hebrews chapter 10 verse 16; it states: **"This is the covenant that I will make with them after those days, saith the Lord, I will put my laws into their hearts, and in their minds will I write them."** In the KJV bible book of Revelation chapter 22 verse 14; it states: "Blessed are they that do his commandments, that they may have right to the tree of life, and may enter in through the gates into the city."

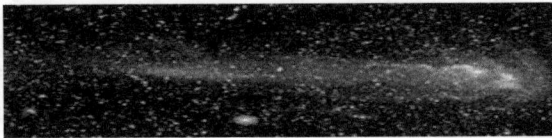

286

Yashu'a (Jesus) said: "Thou shalt love the Most High Heavenly Father, thy Sustainer with all thy heart, and with all thy soul, and with all thy mind. Thou shalt love thy neighbour as thyself."

Mind Gardening in the Creative Garden of Will (Your Mind) to Grow a Living Water Mentality!

CHILDREN OF THE MOST HIGH:
PRISTINE YOUTH AND FAMILY SOLUTIONS, LLC.
SONS AND DAUGHTERS OF THE MOST HIGH PUBLISHERS ®

Oh, Gracious Most High Heavenly father, Holy is your name,
Your Will Be Done Now and Forever!

As it relates to **Mind Gardening, what does the heart have to do with the mind**? As a necessary essential **Living Water Mentality** growth requirement, a person must have a clean or pure heart that is forgiven of all sins through repentance which is why the Messiah Yashu'a (Jesus) stands at the door of the **hearts** of people offering **grace, truth** (KJV bible book of John chapter 1 verse 17) and **eternal life**. The Messiah Yashu'a (Jesus) said in the KJV bible book of Revelation chapter 3 verse 20; he said: "Behold, I stand at the door, and knock: if any man [person] hear my voice, and open the door [of the **heart**], I will come in to him, and will sup with him [or her], and he [or she] with me."

287

Yashu'a (Jesus) said: "Thou shalt love the Most High Heavenly Father, thy Sustainer with all thy heart, and with all thy soul, and with all thy mind. Thou shalt love thy neighbour as thyself."

Mind Gardening in the Creative Garden of Will (Your Mind) to Grow a Living Water Mentality!

CHILDREN OF THE MOST HIGH:
PRISTINE YOUTH AND FAMILY SOLUTIONS, LLC.
SONS AND DAUGHTERS OF THE MOST HIGH PUBLISHERS ®

*Oh, Gracious Most High Heavenly father, Holy is your name,
Your Will Be Done Now and Forever!*

"The word "**Grace**" is the KJV bible Greek Strong's Concordance #5485 word: χάρις **charis (khar`-ece)**, which means graciousness (as gratifying), of manner or act (abstract or concrete; literal, figurative or spiritual; especially the divine influence upon the heart, and its reflection in the life; including gratitude): acceptable, benefit, favor, gift, grace(- ious), joy, liberality, pleasure, thank(-s, -worthy)." This is why the Messiah Yashu'a (Jesus) said in the KJV bible book of Matthew chapter 6 verse 21; he said: "For where your treasure is, there will your heart be also." **Therefore; allowing the Most High to divide the disagreeable from agreeable in our hearts is essential to growing a Living Water Mentality!**

288

Yashu'a (Jesus) said: "Thou shalt love the Most High Heavenly Father, thy Sustainer with all thy heart, and with all thy soul, and with all thy mind. Thou shalt love thy neighbour as thyself."

Mind Gardening in the Creative Garden of Will (Your Mind) to Grow a Living Water Mentality!

CHILDREN OF THE MOST HIGH:
PRISTINE YOUTH AND FAMILY SOLUTIONS, LLC.
SONS AND DAUGHTERS OF THE MOST HIGH PUBLISHERS ®

Oh, Gracious Most High Heavenly father, Holy is your name,
Your Will Be Done Now and Forever!

Explain the 9 True Vine Yashu'a (Jesus) Mind Gardening Memorization Keys to Success of <u>Gardening</u> as it relates to the Mind Gardening from the Original language of the Bible verses where they come from?

The 9 True Vine (Yashu'a, Jesus) Memorization Keys to Success acronyms of **<u>Gardening</u>** as it relates to the True Vine Yashu'a (Jesus) Mind Gardening from the original language that the Bible verses were revealed in is listed below:

1. Glorify – In the KJV bible book of Matthew chapter 5 verse 16; Yashu'a (Jesus) said: "Let your light so shine before men, that they may see your good works, and glorify your Father which is in heaven." In this verse, the word for "**glorify**", is the KJV bible Greek Strong's Concordance#1392 word: δοξάζω doxazo (**dox-ad`-zo**), which means to render (or esteem) glorious (in a wide application): (make) glorify(-ious), full of (have) glory, honor, magnify.

289

Yashu'a (Jesus) said: "Thou shalt love the Most High
Heavenly Father, thy Sustainer with all thy heart, and
with all thy soul, and with all thy mind. Thou shalt love
thy neighbour as thyself."

CHILDREN OF THE MOST HIGH:
PRISTINE YOUTH AND FAMILY SOLUTIONS, LLC.
SONS AND DAUGHTERS OF THE MOST HIGH PUBLISHERS ®

Oh, Gracious Most High Heavenly father, Holy is your name, Your Will Be Done Now and Forever!

2. <u>A</u>pply - In the KJV bible book of Psalms chapter 90 verse 12; it states: "So teach us to number our days, **that we may apply** our hearts unto wisdom." In this verse, the KJV bible Hebrew Strong's Concordance#935 word: בּוֹא **bow'** (bō), which is the word for the phrase "**that we may apply**" which means to apply, attain, get, follow."

3. <u>R</u>evere or <u>R</u>everence – In the KJV bible book of Proverbs chapter 1 verse 7; it states: "**The <u>fear</u> of the LORD is the beginning of knowledge: but fools** אֱוִיל **'eviyl** (the phrase: "**but fools**" is KJV bible Hebrew Strong's Concordance #191 word "**ev·ēl'**" meaning to be perverse, be foolish, foolish, of one who despises wisdom, of one who mocks when guilty, of one who is quarrelsome, of one who is licentious silly: fool(-ish). **despise wisdom and instruction**." In this verse, the word for "**fear**" is the KJV bible Hebrew Strong's Concordance #3374 word: יִרְאָה **yir'ah** (yir·ä'), which means to "**fear**", to respect, reverence, piety revered respect, having moral reverence."

Yashu'a (Jesus) said: "Thou shalt love the Most High Heavenly Father, thy Sustainer with all thy heart, and with all thy soul, and with all thy mind. Thou shalt love thy neighbour as thyself."

Oh, Gracious Most High Heavenly father, Holy is your name,
Your Will Be Done Now and Forever!

4. <u>D</u>ecrease – In the KJV bible book of John chapter 3 verse 30; it states: "He must increase, but I **must decrease**." In this verse, the word for the phrase "**must decrease**" is the KJV bible Greek Strong's Concordance **#1642** word: ἐλαττόω **elattoo (el-at-to`-o)**, which means to lessen, make lower to make less or inferior: in dignity, to be made less or inferior: in dignity; to decrease in authority or popularity."

5. <u>E</u>xcept – In the KJV bible book of John chapter 3 verse 3; Yashu'a (Jesus) said unto him: "Verily, verily, I say unto thee, **except** a man be born again, he cannot see the kingdom of God." In this verse, the word for "**except**" is the KJV bible Greek Strong's Concordance #3362 word: ἐὰν μή **ean mē (eh-an`-may)**, which means if not, unless, before, but, except.

291

Yashu'a (Jesus) said: "Thou shalt love the Most High Heavenly Father, thy Sustainer with all thy heart, and with all thy soul, and with all thy mind. Thou shalt love thy neighbour as thyself."

Mind Gardening in the Creative Garden of Will (Your Mind) to Grow a Living Water Mentality!

CHILDREN OF THE MOST HIGH:
PRISTINE YOUTH AND FAMILY SOLUTIONS, LLC.
SONS AND DAUGHTERS OF THE MOST HIGH PUBLISHERS ®

Oh, Gracious Most High Heavenly father, Holy is your name,
Your Will Be Done Now and Forever!

6. <u>N</u>ourish – In the KJV bible book of Genesis chapter 50 verse 21; it states: "Now therefore fear ye not: **I will nourish you**, and your little ones. And he comforted them, and spake kindly unto them." In this verse, the phrase for "**I will nourish you**" is the KJV bible Hebrew Strong's Concordance **#3557** word: כּוּל **kuwl** (kool), which means to maintain, sustain, provide sustenance."

7. <u>I</u>nform – In the KJV bible book of Deuteronomy chapter 17 verse 10; it states: "And thou shalt do according to the sentence, which they of that place which the LORD shall choose shall shew thee; and thou shalt observe to do **according to all that they <u>inform</u>** thee." In this verse, the phrase for "**according to all they inform**" is the KJV bible Hebrew Strong's Concordance **#3384** word: יָרָה **yarah** (yaw-raw`), which means to teach, direct, teach through, instruct, inform."

Yashu'a (Jesus) said: "Thou shalt love the Most High Heavenly Father, thy Sustainer with all thy heart, and with all thy soul, and with all thy mind. Thou shalt love thy neighbour as thyself."

Mind Gardening in the Creative Garden of Will (Your Mind) to Grow a Living Water Mentality!

CHILDREN OF THE MOST HIGH:
PRISTINE YOUTH AND FAMILY SOLUTIONS, LLC.
SONS AND DAUGHTERS OF THE MOST HIGH PUBLISHERS ®

Oh, Gracious Most High Heavenly father, Holy is your name,
Your Will Be Done Now and Forever!

8. Narrow – In the KJV bible book of Matthew chapter 7 verse 14; Yashu'a (Jesus) said: "Because strait is the gate, and narrow is the way, which leadeth unto life, and few there be that find it." In this verse, the word for "**narrow**" is the KJV bible Greek King James Strong Concordance#2346 word: θλίβω thlibō (thlee`-bo), which means thin, tight, small width, slim, slender, limited in extent, amount, or scope; restricted, narrow."

9. Grace – In the KJV bible book of Matthew chapter 1 verse 7; it stated: "For the law was given by Moses, but **grace** and truth came by Jesus Christ." In this verse, the word for "**grace**" is the KJV bible Greek King James Strong Concordance #5485 word: χάρις charis (khä'-rēs) means graciousness (as gratifying), of manner or act (abstract or concrete; literal, figurative or spiritual; especially the divine influence upon the heart, and its reflection in the life; including gratitude); acceptable, benefit, favor, gift, grace(- ious), joy, liberality, pleasure, thank(-s, -worthy)."

Therefore; the **True Vine (Yashu'a, Jesus) Mind Gardener – Mind Gardening Memorization Keys to Success** are essential for **Mind Gardening in the Creative Garden of Will (Your Mind) to Grow a Living Water Mentality!**

Yashu'a (Jesus) said: "Thou shalt love the Most High Heavenly Father, thy Sustainer with all thy heart, and with all thy soul, and with all thy mind. Thou shalt love thy neighbour as thyself."

Mind Gardening in the Creative Garden of Will (Your Mind) to Grow a Living Water Mentality!

CHILDREN OF THE MOST HIGH:
PRISTINE YOUTH AND FAMILY SOLUTIONS, LLC.
SONS AND DAUGHTERS OF THE MOST HIGH PUBLISHERS ®

Oh, Gracious Most High Heavenly father, Holy is your name, Your Will Be Done Now and Forever!

Chapter 18: Transfigure Your Thinking to Transform Your Mental Reality - True Vine (Yashu'a, Jesus) Master Gardener – Mental Transformation Principles!

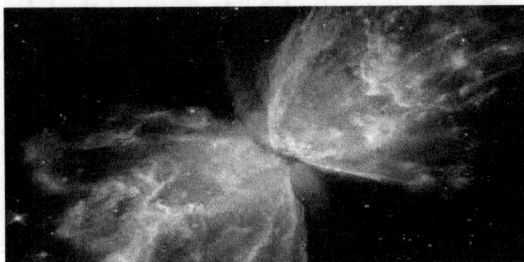

In the KJV bible book of John chapter 5 verse 30; the Messiah Yashu'a (Jesus) said: "I can of mine own self do nothing: as I hear, I judge: and my judgment is just; because I seek not mine own will, but the will of the Father which hath sent me." "Ye have heard how I said unto you, I go away, and come again unto you. If ye loved me, ye would rejoice, because I said, I go unto the Father: for my Father is greater than I, KJV John 14:28."

Yashu'a (Jesus) said: "Thou shalt love the Most High Heavenly Father, thy Sustainer with all thy heart, and with all thy soul, and with all thy mind. Thou shalt love thy neighbour as thyself."

Mind Gardening in the Creative Garden of Will (Your Mind) to Grow a Living Water Mentality!

CHILDREN OF THE MOST HIGH:
PRISTINE YOUTH AND FAMILY SOLUTIONS, LLC.
SONS AND DAUGHTERS OF THE MOST HIGH PUBLISHERS ®

*Oh, Gracious Most High Heavenly father, Holy is your name,
Your Will Be Done Now and Forever!*

In the KJV bible book of Matthew chapter 17 verse 2; it states: "And after six days **Jesus** taketh Peter, James, and John his brother, and bringeth them up into a high mountain apart, And **was transfigured before them**: and **his face did shine as the sun, and his raiment was white as the light**."

What does the aforementioned verse mean when it states that: "Jesus was transfigured before them: and his face did shine as the sun, and his raiment was white as the light? According to the KJV bible Greek Strong's Concordance "#3339 μεταμορφόω Metamorphoō (Met-am-or-fo'-o) for the word "**transfigured**". μεταμορφόω **Metamorphoō** means: **to change into another form, to transform (literally or figuratively, "metamorphose", change, transfigure, transform**."

Yashu'a (Jesus) said: "Thou shalt love the Most High Heavenly Father, thy Sustainer with all thy heart, and with all thy soul, and with all thy mind. Thou shalt love thy neighbour as thyself."

Mind Gardening in the Creative Garden of Will (Your Mind) to Grow a Living Water Mentality!

CHILDREN OF THE MOST HIGH:
PRISTINE YOUTH AND FAMILY SOLUTIONS, LLC.
SONS AND DAUGHTERS OF THE MOST HIGH PUBLISHERS ®

Oh, Gracious Most High Heavenly father, Holy is your name,
Your Will Be Done Now and Forever!

"**Christ appearance was changed and was** resplendent with divine brightness on the mount of **transfiguration.**" The American Heritage Online Dictionary (2020) defines **transfiguration** as: **A marked change** in form or appearance; a **metamorphosis. A change** that glorifies or exalts. **Transfigured** is defined as: **Changed the form or appearance of. Transfigure** is defined as: **to change the form or appearance of; transform.** **Transform** is defined as: **to change markedly the appearance or form of; to change the nature, function, or condition of; convert. Convert** is defined as: **to change (something) into another form, substance, state, or product**; transform: convert water into ice. **Adapt to a new or different purpose**: convert a forest into farmland. **Mental** is defined as: **executed or performed by the mind; existing in the mind. Reality** is defined as: **the quality or state of being actual or true.** The **totality of all things possessing actuality, existence, or essence.**"

Yashu'a (Jesus) said: "Thou shalt love the Most High Heavenly Father, thy Sustainer with all thy heart, and with all thy soul, and with all thy mind. Thou shalt love thy neighbour as thyself."

Mind Gardening in the Creative Garden of Will (Your Mind) to Grow a Living Water Mentality!

CHILDREN OF THE MOST HIGH:
PRISTINE YOUTH AND FAMILY SOLUTIONS, LLC.
SONS AND DAUGHTERS OF THE MOST HIGH PUBLISHERS ®

*Oh, Gracious Most High Heavenly father, Holy is your name,
Your Will Be Done Now and Forever!*

In the KJV bible book of John chapter 18 verses 5-8; it states: "They answered **him, Jesus** of Nazareth. Jesus saith unto them, I am he. And Judas also, which betrayed him, stood with them. **As soon then as he had said unto them**, I am he, **they went backward, and fell to the ground**. Then asked he them again, Whom seek ye? And they said, Jesus of Nazareth. Jesus answered, I have told you that I am he: if therefore ye seek me, let these go their way." In the KJV bible book of 2nd Corinthians chapter 11 verses 13-15; it states: "For such are false apostles, deceitful workers, **transforming** (μετασχηματίζω Metaschēmatizō (Met-askh-ay-mat-id'-zo) themselves into the apostles of Christ. And no marvel; for Satan himself is **transformed** μετασχηματίζω Metaschēmatizō (Met-askh-ay-mat-id'-zo) into an angel of light."

297

Yashu'a (Jesus) said: "Thou shalt love the Most High Heavenly Father, thy Sustainer with all thy heart, and with all thy soul, and with all thy mind. Thou shalt love thy neighbour as thyself."

Mind Gardening in the Creative Garden of Will (Your Mind) to Grow a Living Water Mentality!

CHILDREN OF THE MOST HIGH:
PRISTINE YOUTH AND FAMILY SOLUTIONS, LLC.
SONS AND DAUGHTERS OF THE MOST HIGH PUBLISHERS ®

Oh, Gracious Most High Heavenly father, Holy is your name,
Your Will Be Done Now and Forever!

"Therefore, it is no great thing if his ministers also be **transformed** μετασχηματίζω **Metaschēmatizō (Met-askh-ay-mat-id'-zo)** as the ministers of righteousness; whose end shall be according to their works. The KJV bible Greek Strong's Concordance "**#3345** μετασχηματίζω **Metaschēmatizō (Met-askh-ay-mat-id'-zo)** is the word for (**transforming**, and **transformed**). μετασχηματίζω **Metaschēmatizō** means: **to transfigure** or **disguise**; **to transfer**, **transform** (self); **to change the figure of**, **to transform**."

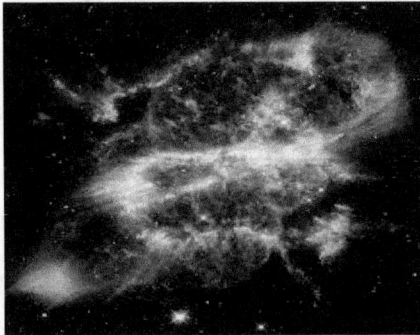

298

Yashu'a (Jesus) said: "Thou shalt love the Most High Heavenly Father, thy Sustainer with all thy heart, and with all thy soul, and with all thy mind. Thou shalt love thy neighbour as thyself."

Mind Gardening in the Creative Garden of Will (Your Mind) to Grow a Living Water Mentality!

Oh, Gracious Most High Heavenly father, Holy is your name, Your Will Be Done Now and Forever!

In the KJV bible book of John chapter 20 verses 11-18; it states: "But Mary stood without at the sepulchre weeping: and as she wept, she stooped down, and looked into the sepulchre, and seeth two angels in white sitting, the one at the head, and the other at the feet, where the body of Jesus had lain. And they say unto her, Woman, why weepest thou? She saith unto them, "Because, they have taken away my Lord, and I know not where they have laid him. And when she had thus said, **she turned herself back, and saw Jesus standing, and knew not that it was Jesus**. Jesus saith unto her, Woman, why weepest thou? whom seekest thou?"

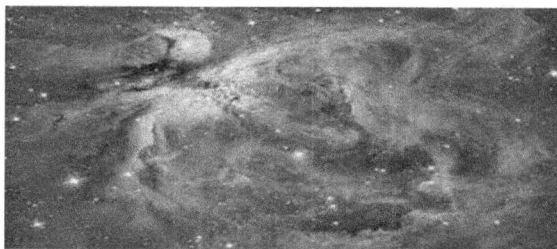

299

Yashu'a (Jesus) said: "Thou shalt love the Most High Heavenly Father, thy Sustainer with all thy heart, and with all thy soul, and with all thy mind. Thou shalt love thy neighbour as thyself."

Mind Gardening in the Creative Garden of Will (Your Mind) to Grow a Living Water Mentality!

CHILDREN OF THE MOST HIGH:
PRISTINE YOUTH AND FAMILY SOLUTIONS, LLC.
SONS AND DAUGHTERS OF THE MOST HIGH PUBLISHERS ®

*Oh, Gracious Most High Heavenly father, Holy is your name,
Your Will Be Done Now and Forever!*

"<u>She, supposing him to be the gardener</u>, saith unto him, Sir, if thou have borne him hence, tell me where thou hast laid him, and I will take him away. Jesus saith unto her, Mary. She turned herself, **and saith unto him**, **Rabboni**; (ῥαββουνί **Rhabbouni (Rab-bon-ee') - of Aramaic origin (meaning Master) <u>which is to say</u>, Master** (διδάσκαλος **Didaskalos (Did-as'-kal-os)** – meaning an instructor, doctor, master, teacher**.)" In the previous verses, the **True Vine (Yashu'a, Jesus)** is acknowledged as: "**Master**" and **thought** to be the "**Gardner**". **Thought** is defined as the **process of thinking**; or a **product of thinking** as **mental activity in the Mind**). Thus, **introducing the Creative Garden of Will (Your Mind) to thoughts of**: "Mind Gardner", "True Vine (Yashu'a, Jesus) Master Gardner", and "True Vine (Yashu'a, Jesus) Mind Master Gardner" **to give birth to the idea in your mind** that is essential to **Grow the Living Water Mentality**, through **the 9 True Vine (Yashu'a, Jesus) Mental Transformation Principles in action in your mind**!

300

Yashu'a (Jesus) said: "Thou shalt love the Most High Heavenly Father, thy Sustainer with all thy heart, and with all thy soul, and with all thy mind. Thou shalt love thy neighbour as thyself."

Mind Gardening in the Creative Garden of Will (Your Mind) to Grow a Living Water Mentality!

CHILDREN OF THE MOST HIGH:
PRISTINE YOUTH AND FAMILY SOLUTIONS, LLC.
SONS AND DAUGHTERS OF THE MOST HIGH PUBLISHERS ®

Oh, Gracious Most High Heavenly father, Holy is your name,
Your Will Be Done Now and Forever!

The **9 True Vine (Yashu'a, Jesus) Mental Transformation Principles** are:

1. **Love the Most High Heavenly Father with all of your heart, with all your spirit and soul, and with all your mind and entire being**. In the KJV bible book of Matthew chapter 22 verses 37-38; Yashu'a (Jesus) said: unto him, "Thou shalt love the Lord thy God with all thy heart, and with all thy soul, and with all thy mind. This is the first and great commandment." There is no knowledge higher than love. The Most High Heavenly Father is Love, and the Most High Heavenly Father loves us! Love replenishes everything without limitations. Truth and Love move, but are not ever moved! Always remember: you can't build your happiness on other peoples' sorrows without sowing your own seeds of sorrow that will only bring forth your own unhappiness!

Yashu'a (Jesus) said: "Thou shalt love the Most High Heavenly Father, thy Sustainer with all thy heart, and with all thy soul, and with all thy mind. Thou shalt love thy neighbour as thyself."

Mind Gardening in the Creative Garden of Will (Your Mind) to Grow a Living Water Mentality!

CHILDREN OF THE MOST HIGH:
PRISTINE YOUTH AND FAMILY SOLUTIONS, LLC.
SONS AND DAUGHTERS OF THE MOST HIGH PUBLISHERS ®

Oh, Gracious Most High Heavenly father, Holy is your name,
Your Will Be Done Now and Forever!

2. <u>**Be sincere about being obedient to the Most High while working to overcome the temptations of this world**</u>. In the KJV bible book of Revelation chapter 3 verse 10; the Messiah Yashu'a (Jesus) said: "Because thou hast kept the word of my patience, I also will keep thee from the hour of temptation, which shall come upon all the world, to try them that dwell upon the earth."

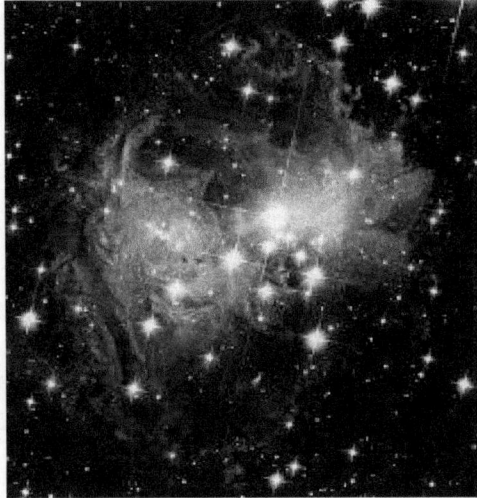

302

Yashu'a (Jesus) said: "Thou shalt love the Most High Heavenly Father, thy Sustainer with all thy heart, and with all thy soul, and with all thy mind. Thou shalt love thy neighbour as thyself."

Mind Gardening in the Creative Garden of Will (Your Mind) to Grow a Living Water Mentality!

CHILDREN OF THE MOST HIGH:
PRISTINE YOUTH AND FAMILY SOLUTIONS, LLC.
SONS AND DAUGHTERS OF THE MOST HIGH PUBLISHERS ®

*Oh, Gracious Most High Heavenly father, Holy is your name,
Your Will Be Done Now and Forever!*

3. <u>**Be non-judgmental of others while striving for perfection through peace, patience and truth**</u>. In the KJV bible book of Matthew chapter 7 verse 1; the Messiah Yashu'a (Jesus) said: "Judge not, that ye be not judged." In the KJV bible book of Matthew chapter 5 verse 48; the Messiah Yashu'a (Jesus) said: "Be ye therefore perfect, even as your Father which is in heaven is perfect." The KJV bible Greek Strong's Concordance word for "**perfect**" is τέλειος **teleios** and means complete (in various applications of labor, growth, mental and moral character, etc.); being balanced mentally, spiritually and emotionally; completeness: of full age, perfect. However, it does not mean the English perception of not ever making another mistake or physically being without defect or blemish.

Yashu'a (Jesus) said: "Thou shalt love the Most High Heavenly Father, thy Sustainer with all thy heart, and with all thy soul, and with all thy mind. Thou shalt love thy neighbour as thyself."

Mind Gardening in the Creative Garden of Will (Your Mind) to Grow a Living Water Mentality!

CHILDREN OF THE MOST HIGH:
PRISTINE YOUTH AND FAMILY SOLUTIONS, LLC.
SONS AND DAUGHTERS OF THE MOST HIGH PUBLISHERS ®

*Oh, Gracious Most High Heavenly father, Holy is your name,
Your Will Be Done Now and Forever!*

The True Vine "Yashu'a (Jesus) is the Perfect and Best Example of a Living Water Mentality in action! However, Yashu'a (Jesus) said to all children of the Most High: "Be ye therefore <u>perfect</u>, even as your Father which is in heaven is <u>perfect</u>." Now that we know how the KJV bible Greek Strong's Concordance defines "**perfect**" as τέλειος **teleios**, and that the Messiah Yashu'a (Jesus) told us to be perfect, why do many Ministers preach that it is impossible (**I'm-possible**) to become perfect while in human form? In the KJV bible book of 2nd Corinthians chapter 11 verses 13-15; it states: "For such are false apostles, deceitful workers, transforming themselves into the apostles of Christ. **And no marvel; for Satan himself is <u>transformed into an angel of light. Therefore, it is no great</u> <u>thing if his ministers also be transformed as the ministers of</u> <u>righteousness</u>**; whose end shall be according to their works."

304

*Yashu'a (Jesus) said: "Thou shalt love the Most High
Heavenly Father, thy Sustainer with all thy heart, and
with all thy soul, and with all thy mind. Thou shalt love
thy neighbour as thyself."*

Mind Gardening in the Creative Garden of Will (Your Mind) to Grow a Living Water Mentality!

CHILDREN OF THE MOST HIGH:
PRISTINE YOUTH AND FAMILY SOLUTIONS, LLC.
SONS AND DAUGHTERS OF THE MOST HIGH PUBLISHERS ®

Oh, Gracious Most High Heavenly father, Holy is your name,
Your Will Be Done Now and Forever!

In the KJV bible book of Mathew chapter 7 verse 15; the Messiah Yashu'a (Jesus) said: "Beware of false prophets, which come to you in sheep's clothing, but inwardly they are ravening wolves." Oh, children of the Most High; be aware of the children of the devil, and their **wolves in sheep clothing or ministers of satan** who preach and teach that you can't be **perfect** as Yashu'a (Jesus) told us to do.

305

Yashu'a (Jesus) said: "Thou shalt love the Most High Heavenly Father, thy Sustainer with all thy heart, and with all thy soul, and with all thy mind. Thou shalt love thy neighbour as thyself."

Mind Gardening in the Creative Garden of Will (Your Mind) to Grow a Living Water Mentality!

CHILDREN OF THE MOST HIGH:
PRISTINE YOUTH AND FAMILY SOLUTIONS, LLC.
SONS AND DAUGHTERS OF THE MOST HIGH PUBLISHERS ®

*Oh, Gracious Most High Heavenly father, Holy is your name,
Your Will Be Done Now and Forever!*

Also, as it relates the Messiah Yashu'a (Jesus) saying: "Be ye therefore perfect, even as your Father which is in heaven is perfect." Remember, the Messiah Yashu'a (Jesus) spoke the **Aramic/Hebrew language** and the **Galilaean/Syriac language** which are very close in dialect. At the day of Pentecost, in the KJV bible book of Acts chapter 2, **the devout men were all filled with the Holy Ghost**, and began to speak with other **tongues γλῶσσα glōssa (languages)**, **as the Spirit gave them utterance being able to understand one another in Yashu'a (Jesus) Galilaean language that he spoke**, which is why to the onlookers of this miraculous event asked: "are not all these which speak **Galilaeans**?" **Yashu'a (Jesus) did not speak the English and Greek languages**, therefore, it would be best for the children of the Most High to investigate the **Aramic/Hebrew** word for "**Perfect**" in Yashu'a (Jesus) own language or languages to overstand the meaning of the word from his perspective.

Yashu'a (Jesus) said: "Thou shalt love the Most High Heavenly Father, thy Sustainer with all thy heart, and with all thy soul, and with all thy mind. Thou shalt love thy neighbour as thyself."

Mind Gardening in the Creative Garden of Will (Your Mind) to Grow a Living Water Mentality!

CHILDREN OF THE MOST HIGH:
PRISTINE YOUTH AND FAMILY SOLUTIONS, LLC.
SONS AND DAUGHTERS OF THE MOST HIGH PUBLISHERS ®

Oh, Gracious Most High Heavenly father, Holy is your name,
Your Will Be Done Now and Forever!

What does the word **"perfect"** mean in **Aramic/Hebrew**? In the KJV bible book of Genesis chapter 6 verse 9; it states with Hebrew inserts: **6:9** אֵלֶּה תּוֹלְדֹת נֹחַ נֹחַ אִישׁ צַדִּיק תָּמִים הָיָה בְּדֹרֹתָיו אֶת־הָאֱלֹהִים הִתְהַלֶּךְ־נֹחַ: "These are the generations of Noah: Noah was a just man **and perfect** in his generations, and Noah walked with God." In the KJV bible Hebrew Strong's Concordance#8549, the word for the phrase **"and perfect"** is תָּמִים **tamiym** which means **moral integrity**, entire (literally, figuratively or morally); also (as noun) integrity, truth: — without blemish, complete, full, perfect, sincerely (-ity), sound, without spot, undefiled, upright(-ly), whole." So, it is essential that all aspiring children of the Most High character reflects **moral integrity**.

Yashu'a (Jesus) said: "Thou shalt love the Most High Heavenly Father, thy Sustainer with all thy heart, and with all thy soul, and with all thy mind. Thou shalt love thy neighbour as thyself."

Mind Gardening in the Creative Garden of Will (Your Mind) to Grow a Living Water Mentality!

Oh, Gracious Most High Heavenly father, Holy is your name,
Your Will Be Done Now and Forever!

The American Heritage Online Dictionary (2020) defines **moral** and **integrity** as teaching or exhibiting goodness or correctness of character and behavior: Steadfast adherence to a strict moral or ethical code: a leader of great integrity. The quality or condition of being whole or undivided; completeness." **Have selfless True-Faith in the Most High Heavenly Father**. In the KJV bible book of Hebrews chapter 10 verse 21; it states: **"Let us draw near with a true heart in full assurance of faith, having our hearts sprinkled from an evil conscience, and our bodies washed with pure water."**

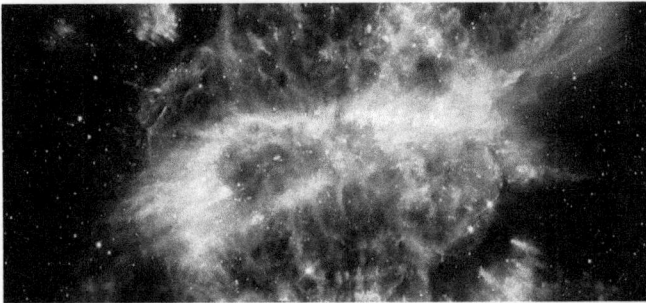

308

Yashu'a (Jesus) said: "Thou shalt love the Most High Heavenly Father, thy Sustainer with all thy heart, and with all thy soul, and with all thy mind. Thou shalt love thy neighbour as thyself."

Mind Gardening in the Creative Garden of Will (Your Mind) to Grow a Living Water Mentality!

CHILDREN OF THE MOST HIGH:
PRISTINE YOUTH AND FAMILY SOLUTIONS, LLC.
SONS AND DAUGHTERS OF THE MOST HIGH PUBLISHERS ®

Oh, Gracious Most High Heavenly father, Holy is your name,
Your Will Be Done Now and Forever!

4. <u>**Actively, generously, and selflessly further the progress of the well-being of others**</u>. In the KJV bible book of Proverbs chapter 14 verse 31; it states: "**He [or She] that oppresseth the poor reproacheth his Maker: but he [or she] that honoureth him hath mercy on the poor.**" In the KJV bible book of Proverbs chapter 29 verse 7; it states: "**The righteous considereth the cause of the poor: [but] the wicked regardeth not to know [it].**" In the KJV bible book of Isaiah chapter 25 verse 4; it states: Isaiah 25:4: "**For thou hast been a strength to the poor, a strength to the needy in his distress, a refuge from the storm, a shadow from the heat, when the blast of the terrible ones [is] as a storm [against] the wall.**"

Yashu'a (Jesus) said: "Thou shalt love the Most High Heavenly Father, thy Sustainer with all thy heart, and with all thy soul, and with all thy mind. Thou shalt love thy neighbour as thyself."

Mind Gardening in the Creative Garden of Will (Your Mind) to Grow a Living Water Mentality!

CHILDREN OF THE MOST HIGH:
PRISTINE YOUTH AND FAMILY SOLUTIONS, LLC.
SONS AND DAUGHTERS OF THE MOST HIGH PUBLISHERS ®

Oh, Gracious Most High Heavenly father, Holy is your name,
Your Will Be Done Now and Forever!

5. **Utilize will and faith to overcome material desires of the mind and heart**. In the KJV bible book of 1st John chapter 4 verse 4; it states: "Ye are of God, little children, and have overcome them: because greater is he that is in you, than he that is in the world." In the KJV bible book of 1st John chapter 5 verses 4-5; it states: **"Whatsoever is born of God overcometh the world: and this is the victory that overcometh the world, even our faith. Who is he that overcometh the world, but he that believeth that Jesus is the Son of God?"**

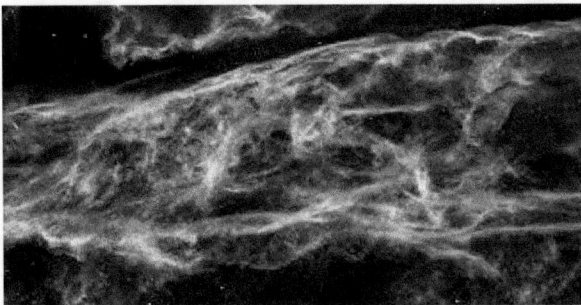

310

Yashu'a (Jesus) said: "Thou shalt love the Most High Heavenly Father, thy Sustainer with all thy heart, and with all thy soul, and with all thy mind. Thou shalt love thy neighbour as thyself."

Mind Gardening in the Creative Garden of Will (Your Mind) to Grow a Living Water Mentality!

CHILDREN OF THE MOST HIGH:
PRISTINE YOUTH AND FAMILY SOLUTIONS, LLC.
SONS AND DAUGHTERS OF THE MOST HIGH PUBLISHERS ®

Oh, Gracious Most High Heavenly father, Holy is your name, Your Will Be Done Now and Forever!

In the KJV bible book of Revelation chapter 3 verse 12; Yashu'a (Jesus) said: "Him **[or Her]** that overcometh will I make a pillar in the temple of my God, and he **[or she]** shall go no more out: and I will write upon him **[or her]** the name of my God, and the name of the city of my God, which is new Jerusalem, which cometh down out of heaven from my God: and I will write upon him **[or her]** my new name." In the KJV bible book of Revelation chapter 3 verse 21; Yashu'a (Jesus) said: "To him **[or her]** that overcometh will I grant to sit with me in my throne, even as I also overcame, and am set down with my Father in his throne."

311

Yashu'a (Jesus) said: "Thou shalt love the Most High Heavenly Father, thy Sustainer with all thy heart, and with all thy soul, and with all thy mind. Thou shalt love thy neighbour as thyself."

Mind Gardening in the Creative Garden of Will (Your Mind) to Grow a Living Water Mentality!

CHILDREN OF THE MOST HIGH: PRISTINE YOUTH AND FAMILY SOLUTIONS, LLC. SONS AND DAUGHTERS OF THE MOST HIGH PUBLISHERS ®

Oh, Gracious Most High Heavenly father, Holy is your name, Your Will Be Done Now and Forever!

6. **Allow Divine Love from the Most High and for the Most High through the Messiah Yashu'a (Jesus) to not be conquered by carnal love**. In the KJV bible book of John chapter 3 verse 16; Yashu'a (Jesus) said: "For God so loved the world, that he gave his only begotten Son, that whosoever believeth in him should not perish, but have everlasting life."

7. **Conquer grief, hope, fears and all human emotions that arise from human loves and desires through the Messiah Yashu'a (Jesus)**. In the KJV bible book of 1st John chapter 4 verse 18; it states: "**There is no fear in love; but perfect love casteth out fear: because fear hath torment. He [or She] that feareth is not made perfect in love.**"

312

Yashu'a (Jesus) said: "Thou shalt love the Most High Heavenly Father, thy Sustainer with all thy heart, and with all thy soul, and with all thy mind. Thou shalt love thy neighbour as thyself."

Mind Gardening in the Creative Garden of Will (Your Mind) to Grow a Living Water Mentality!

CHILDREN OF THE MOST HIGH:
PRISTINE YOUTH AND FAMILY SOLUTIONS, LLC.
SONS AND DAUGHTERS OF THE MOST HIGH PUBLISHERS ®

*Oh, Gracious Most High Heavenly father, Holy is your name,
Your Will Be Done Now and Forever!*

8. <u>**Exercise patience in all that you are allowed the ability to do**</u>. In the KJV bible book of Hebrews chapter 10 verse 36; it states: **"For ye have need of patience, that, after ye have done the will of God, ye might receive the promise."** In the KJV bible book of Hebrews chapter 6 verse 12; it states: **"That ye be not slothful, but followers of them who through faith and patience inherit the promises."** In the KJV bible book of Revelation chapter 14 verse 12; it states: **"Here is the patience of the saints: here are they that keep the commandments of God [the Most High Heavenly Father], and the faith of Jesus [Yashu'a]."**

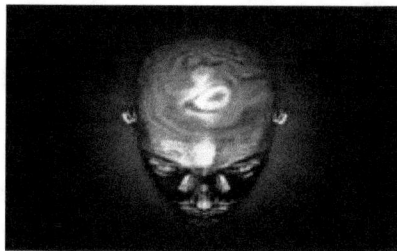

313

Yashu'a (Jesus) said: "Thou shalt love the Most High Heavenly Father, thy Sustainer with all thy heart, and with all thy soul, and with all thy mind. Thou shalt love thy neighbour as thyself."

Mind Gardening in the Creative Garden of Will (Your Mind) to Grow a Living Water Mentality!

CHILDREN OF THE MOST HIGH:
PRISTINE YOUTH AND FAMILY SOLUTIONS, LLC.
SONS AND DAUGHTERS OF THE MOST HIGH PUBLISHERS ®

Oh, Gracious Most High Heavenly father, Holy is your name,
Your Will Be Done Now and Forever!

Therefore; **Transfigure Your Thinking to Transform Your Mental Reality - True Vine (Yashu'a, Jesus) Master Gardener Mental Transformation Principles** are essential for **Mind Gardening in the Creative Garden of Will (Your Mind) to Grow a Living Water Mentality!**

314

Yashu'a (Jesus) said: "Thou shalt love the Most High Heavenly Father, thy Sustainer with all thy heart, and with all thy soul, and with all thy mind. Thou shalt love thy neighbour as thyself."

Mind Gardening in the Creative Garden of Will (Your Mind) to Grow a Living Water Mentality!

CHILDREN OF THE MOST HIGH:
PRISTINE YOUTH AND FAMILY SOLUTIONS, LLC.
SONS AND DAUGHTERS OF THE MOST HIGH PUBLISHERS ®

Oh, Gracious Most High Heavenly father, Holy is your name,
Your Will Be Done Now and Forever!

Chapter 19: True Vine (Yashu'a, Jesus) Master Mind Gardener – Living Water Mentality, Thinking on the Other Side of Hydrogen!

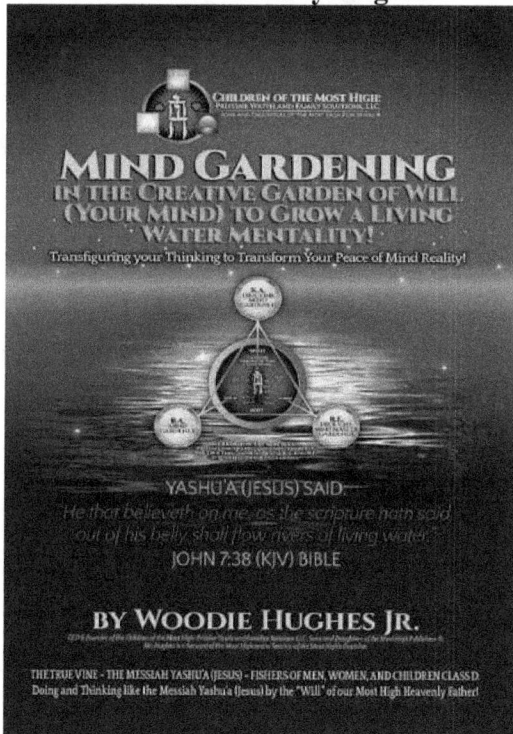

315

Yashu'a (Jesus) said: "Thou shalt love the Most High Heavenly Father, thy Sustainer with all thy heart, and with all thy soul, and with all thy mind. Thou shalt love thy neighbour as thyself."

Mind Gardening in the Creative Garden of Will (Your Mind) to Grow a Living Water Mentality!

CHILDREN OF THE MOST HIGH:
PRISTINE YOUTH AND FAMILY SOLUTIONS, LLC.
SONS AND DAUGHTERS OF THE MOST HIGH PUBLISHERS ®

Oh, Gracious Most High Heavenly father, Holy is your name,
Your Will Be Done Now and Forever!

In the KJV bible book of Proverbs chapter 23 verse 7; it states: "For as he [or she] **thinketh** (שָׁעַר **Sha`ar** (**Shaw-ar'**)– means: **reason out, think**) in his [or her] **heart** (נֶפֶשׁ **Nephesh** (**Neh'-fesh**) – means: **spirit, self, life**, creature, person, appetite, mind, **living being**, desire, emotion, passion, **that which breathes, the breathing substance or being,** soul, **the inner being of a person; seat of emotions and passions, activity of mind, activity of the will, activity of the character**) so is he: Eat and drink, saith he to thee; but his **heart** (לֵב **Leb** (**Labe**) is not with thee." The KJV bible Greek Strong's Concordance "#3820 לֵב **Leb** (**Labe**) for the word "heart". לֵב **Leb** means: **inner man [or woman], mind, will, heart, understanding, inner part, midst (of things), soul, mind, knowledge, thinking, reflection, memory, inclination, resolution, determination (of will), conscience, heart (of moral character), as seat of emotions and passions, as seat of courage."**

316

Yashu'a (Jesus) said: "Thou shalt love the Most High
Heavenly Father, thy Sustainer with all thy heart, and
with all thy soul, and with all thy mind. Thou shalt love
thy neighbour as thyself."

Mind Gardening in the Creative Garden of Will (Your Mind) to Grow a Living Water Mentality!

CHILDREN OF THE MOST HIGH:
PRISTINE YOUTH AND FAMILY SOLUTIONS, LLC.
SONS AND DAUGHTERS OF THE MOST HIGH PUBLISHERS ®

Oh, Gracious Most High Heavenly father, Holy is your name,
Your Will Be Done Now and Forever!

The Messiah Yashu'a (Jesus) said: "If ye love me, keep my commandments, KJV John 14:15." The children of the Most High **must only quench their thirst with the <u>Living Waters</u>** in order to successfully engage in **Mind Gardening in the Creative Garden of Will (Your Mind) to Grow a Living Water Mentality! According to the bible, what are the <u>Living Waters</u>?** In the KJV bible book of John chapter 7 verse 38; the Messiah Yashu'a (Jesus) said: "He that believeth on me, as the scripture hath said, out of his belly shall flow rivers of <u>living water</u>.

317

Yashu'a (Jesus) said: "Thou shalt love the Most High Heavenly Father, thy Sustainer with all thy heart, and with all thy soul, and with all thy mind. Thou shalt love thy neighbour as thyself."

Mind Gardening in the Creative Garden of Will (Your Mind) to Grow a Living Water Mentality!

CHILDREN OF THE MOST HIGH:
PRISTINE YOUTH AND FAMILY SOLUTIONS, LLC.
SONS AND DAUGHTERS OF THE MOST HIGH PUBLISHERS ®

Oh, Gracious Most High Heavenly father, Holy is your name,
Your Will Be Done Now and Forever!

"In the aforementioned verse, the word "**living**" is the KJV bible Greek Strong's Concordance#**2198** is the word: ζάω **Záō**, pronounced as: **dzah'-o**; and means: a primary verb; "**To live (literally or figuratively):—life(-time), (a-)live(-ly), quick; to live, breathe, be among the living (not lifeless, not dead); to enjoy real life, to have true life and worthy of the name, active, blessed, endless in the kingdom of God, to live i.e. pass life, in the manner of the living and acting of mortals or character, living water, having vital power in itself and exerting the same upon the soul, metaph. to be in full vigor, to be fresh, strong, efficient, as adj. active, powerful, efficacious.**"

Yashu'a (Jesus) said: "Thou shalt love the Most High Heavenly Father, thy Sustainer with all thy heart, and with all thy soul, and with all thy mind. Thou shalt love thy neighbour as thyself."

Mind Gardening in the Creative Garden of Will (Your Mind) to Grow a Living Water Mentality!

CHILDREN OF THE MOST HIGH:
PRISTINE YOUTH AND FAMILY SOLUTIONS, LLC.
SONS AND DAUGHTERS OF THE MOST HIGH PUBLISHERS ®

Oh, Gracious Most High Heavenly father, Holy is your name,
Your Will Be Done Now and Forever!

"In the aforementioned verse, the word "**water**" is the KJV bible Greek Strong's Concordance#**5204** is the word: ὕδωρ **Hydōr** and means: **water (as if rainy) literally or figuratively**: **of water in rivers, in pools, of the water of the deluge, of water in any of the earth's repositories, of water as the primary element, fig. used of many peoples.**" In the KJV bible book of Jeremiah chapter 2 verse 13: it states; "For my people have committed two evils; they have forsaken me the fountain of **living waters**, [and] hewed them out cisterns, broken cisterns, that can hold no water."

"In the aforementioned verse, the word "**living**" is the KJV bible Hebrew Strong's Concordance#**2416** is the word: **Khah-Ee** חי (**Khay** or **Chay**) and means **living**, **alive**. In the aforementioned verse, the word "**water**" is the KJV bible Greek Strong's Concordance#**4325** is the word: מים **Mayim** and means: **water, waters, watering**." The American Heritage Online Dictionary (2020) defines **Mentality** as: "**the sum of a person's intellectual capabilities or endowment.**"

Yashu'a (Jesus) said: "Thou shalt love the Most High Heavenly Father, thy Sustainer with all thy heart, and with all thy soul, and with all thy mind. Thou shalt love thy neighbour as thyself."

Mind Gardening in the Creative Garden of Will (Your Mind) to Grow a Living Water Mentality!

CHILDREN OF THE MOST HIGH:
PRISTINE YOUTH AND FAMILY SOLUTIONS, LLC.
SONS AND DAUGHTERS OF THE MOST HIGH PUBLISHERS ®

*Oh, Gracious Most High Heavenly father, Holy is your name,
Your Will Be Done Now and Forever!*

In the KJV bible book of Revelation chapter 1 verses 14-15; it states: "His head and his hairs were white like **wool**, as white as snow; and his eyes were as a flame of fire; And his **feet like unto fine brass, as if they burned in a furnace**; and <u>his voice as the sound of many waters (ὕδωρ Hydōr)</u>." So, the <u>"Living Water Mentality" is the sum of a person's intellectual capabilities of overstanding the Most High's Doctrine, and the active capacity to make calm, impartial decisions that reflects sound wisdom reasoning in action!</u> **How does a child of the Most High arrive at the point of growth that you speak of**? Only by the "**Will**" of the Most High Heavenly Father does a child of the Most High become aware with the inspirational thought of: "**there is more to know**!" This thought initiates the next thought: **A.S.K**: "**what do I need to know?**" <u>**NOW** is the **TIME**, and **CHANGE** is the **MOTIVE**!</u>

320

Yashu'a (Jesus) said: "Thou shalt love the Most High Heavenly Father, thy Sustainer with all thy heart, and with all thy soul, and with all thy mind. Thou shalt love thy neighbour as thyself."

Mind Gardening in the Creative Garden of Will (Your Mind) to Grow a Living Water Mentality!

CHILDREN OF THE MOST HIGH:
PRISTINE YOUTH AND FAMILY SOLUTIONS, LLC.
SONS AND DAUGHTERS OF THE MOST HIGH PUBLISHERS ®

Oh, Gracious Most High Heavenly father, Holy is your name, Your Will Be Done Now and Forever!

On the **earth's natural elements periodic table**, the element **Hydrogen** is the **first (1ˢᵗ)** physical element as **H1**. The second element **on the left side of hydrogen**, is **H2**, which is **Helium**. On the **earth's natural elements periodic table on the right side of hydrogen**, is **Nothing** (**No-Thing, No Physical Matter** that **Sum's up** to **Some-Thing**, or to the **Sum total of things**; or **Physical Matter** or a **physical element** or combination of **physical elements**). **Nothing (No-thing)** does not exist as physical matter or physical elements; yet it exists **by way of the Most High Heavenly Father**, **Who (HU-Creative Source and Creative Force of Will) created it! The Most High** is the speaker of the **word that became flesh as the Messiah Yashu'a (Jesus)**.

321

Yashu'a (Jesus) said: "Thou shalt love the Most High Heavenly Father, thy Sustainer with all thy heart, and with all thy soul, and with all thy mind. Thou shalt love thy neighbour as thyself."

Mind Gardening in the Creative Garden of Will (Your Mind) to Grow a Living Water Mentality!

CHILDREN OF THE MOST HIGH:
PRISTINE YOUTH AND FAMILY SOLUTIONS, LLC.
SONS AND DAUGHTERS OF THE MOST HIGH PUBLISHERS ®

Oh, Gracious Most High Heavenly father, Holy is your name,
Your Will Be Done Now and Forever!

"In the beginning was **the Word**, and **the Word was with God, and the Word was God**, KJV John 1:1." "And **the Word was made flesh, and dwelt among us, (and we beheld his glory, the glory as of the only begotten of the Father,) full of grace and truth**, KJV John 1:14." **The Word** that existed in the beginning where things began from hydrogen on through the elements on the periodic table or periodic chart. So, on one side of hydrogen is helium, **on the other side of hydrogen, God is a Spirit, and is the source of the Living Water Mentality!**

322

Yashu'a (Jesus) said: "Thou shalt love the Most High Heavenly Father, thy Sustainer with all thy heart, and with all thy soul, and with all thy mind. Thou shalt love thy neighbour as thyself."

Mind Gardening in the Creative Garden of Will (Your Mind) to Grow a Living Water Mentality!

CHILDREN OF THE MOST HIGH:
PRISTINE YOUTH AND FAMILY SOLUTIONS, LLC.
SONS AND DAUGHTERS OF THE MOST HIGH PUBLISHERS ®

Oh, Gracious Most High Heavenly father, Holy is your name,
Your Will Be Done Now and Forever!

In the KJV bible book of John chapter 4 verses 23-24; the Messiah Yashu'a (Jesus) said: "But the hour cometh, and <u>now is</u>, when the true worshippers shall worship the Father in spirit and in truth: for the Father seeketh such to worship him. God is a Spirit: and they that worship him must worship him in spirit and in truth." In the KJV bible book of John chapter 7 verse 38; the Messiah Yashu'a (Jesus) said: "He that believeth on me, as the scripture hath said, out of his belly shall flow rivers of <u>living water</u>. So, a child of the Most High **may** acquire the "**Living Water Mentality**" if he or she is obedient to the Most High, and if he or she has sincere divine love for the Most High Heavenly Father with all of their heart, all of their soul, all of their might, and all of their mind!

323

Yashu'a (Jesus) said: "Thou shalt love the Most High Heavenly Father, thy Sustainer with all thy heart, and with all thy soul, and with all thy mind. Thou shalt love thy neighbour as thyself."

Mind Gardening in the Creative Garden of Will (Your Mind) to Grow a Living Water Mentality!

CHILDREN OF THE MOST HIGH:
PRISTINE YOUTH AND FAMILY SOLUTIONS, LLC.
SONS AND DAUGHTERS OF THE MOST HIGH PUBLISHERS ®

*Oh, Gracious Most High Heavenly father, Holy is your name,
Your Will Be Done Now and Forever!*

According to (Hughes, 2019); "The **9th of the 9X9 True Vine (Yashu'a, Jesus) B.A.-K.A.-R.E. Sequential Order of Learning Habits of Success** are **the 9 True Vine (Yashu'a, Jesus) Values**" that may help a child of the Most High to **grow a Living Water Mentality**. The **9th of the 9X9 True Vine (Yashu'a, Jesus) Values** are:

1. **God is love**. In the KJV bible book of 1st John chapter 4 verse 8; it states: "He [or She] that loveth not knoweth not God; for God is love." In the KJV bible book of 1st John chapter 4 verse 16; it states: "And we have known and believed the love that God hath to us. God is love; and he [or she] that dwelleth in love dwelleth in God, and God in him [or her]."

324

Yashu'a (Jesus) said: "Thou shalt love the Most High Heavenly Father, thy Sustainer with all thy heart, and with all thy soul, and with all thy mind. Thou shalt love thy neighbour as thyself."

Mind Gardening in the Creative Garden of Will (Your Mind) to Grow a Living Water Mentality!

CHILDREN OF THE MOST HIGH:
PRISTINE YOUTH AND FAMILY SOLUTIONS, LLC.
SONS AND DAUGHTERS OF THE MOST HIGH PUBLISHERS ®

*Oh, Gracious Most High Heavenly father, Holy is your name,
Your Will Be Done Now and Forever!*

2. <u>**Love thy Neighbor**</u>. In the KJV bible book of Matthew chapter 22 verse 39; the Messiah Yashu'a (Jesus) said: "Thou shalt love thy neighbor as thyself."

3. <u>**Love One Another**</u>. In the KJV bible book of John chapter 13 verses 34-36; the Messiah Yashu'a (Jesus) said: "A new commandment I give unto you, that ye love one another; as I have loved you, that ye also love one another. By this shall all men [women and children] know that ye are my disciples, if ye have love one to another."

4. <u>**Love Your Enemies**</u>. In the KJV bible book of Matthew chapter 5 verse 44; the Messiah Yashu'a (Jesus) said: "But I say unto you, <u>love your enemies</u>, bless them that curse you, do good to them that hate you, and pray for them which despitefully use you, and persecute you."

Yashu'a (Jesus) said: "Thou shalt love the Most High Heavenly Father, thy Sustainer with all thy heart, and with all thy soul, and with all thy mind. Thou shalt love thy neighbour as thyself."

CHILDREN OF THE MOST HIGH:
PRISTINE YOUTH AND FAMILY SOLUTIONS, LLC.
SONS AND DAUGHTERS OF THE MOST HIGH PUBLISHERS ®

*Oh, Gracious Most High Heavenly father, Holy is your name,
Your Will Be Done Now and Forever!*

5. **Be ye therefore perfect**, even as your Father which is in heaven is perfect. In the KJV bible book of Matthew chapter 5 verse 48; the Messiah Yashu'a (Jesus) said: "Be ye therefore perfect, even as your Father which is in heaven is perfect."

6. **Glorify your Father which is in heaven**. In the KJV bible book of Matthew chapter 5 verse 16; the Messiah Yashu'a (Jesus) said: "Let your light so shine before men, that they may see your good works, and glorify your Father which is in heaven."

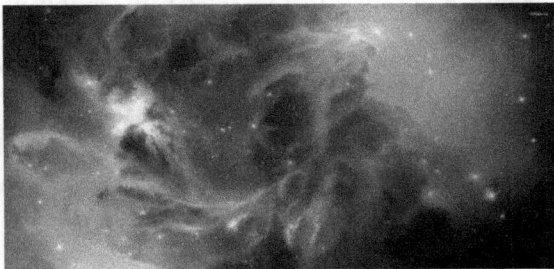

326

Yashu'a (Jesus) said: "Thou shalt love the Most High Heavenly Father, thy Sustainer with all thy heart, and with all thy soul, and with all thy mind. Thou shalt love thy neighbour as thyself."

Mind Gardening in the Creative Garden of Will (Your Mind) to Grow a Living Water Mentality!

*Oh, Gracious Most High Heavenly father, Holy is your name,
Your Will Be Done Now and Forever!*

7. **Bless them that curse you**. In the KJV bible book of Matthew chapter 5 verse 44; the Messiah Yashu'a (Jesus) said: "But I say unto you, love your enemies, bless them that curse you, do good to them that hate you, and pray for them which despitefully use you, and persecute you."

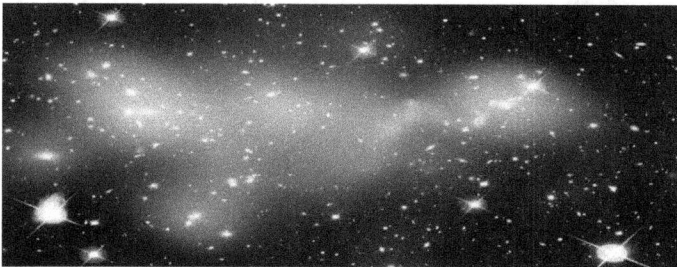

8. **Do good to them that hate you**. In the KJV bible book of Matthew chapter 5 verse 44; the Messiah Yashu'a (Jesus) said: "But I say unto you, love your enemies, bless them that curse you, do good to them that hate you, and pray for them which despitefully use you, and persecute you."

327

Yashu'a (Jesus) said: "Thou shalt love the Most High Heavenly Father, thy Sustainer with all thy heart, and with all thy soul, and with all thy mind. Thou shalt love thy neighbour as thyself."

Mind Gardening in the Creative Garden of Will (Your Mind) to Grow a Living Water Mentality!

CHILDREN OF THE MOST HIGH:
PRISTINE YOUTH AND FAMILY SOLUTIONS, LLC.
SONS AND DAUGHTERS OF THE MOST HIGH PUBLISHERS ®

*Oh, Gracious Most High Heavenly father, Holy is your name,
Your Will Be Done Now and Forever!*

9. **<u>Pray for them which despitefully use you, and persecute you</u>**. In the KJV bible book of Matthew chapter 5 verse 44; the Messiah Yashu'a (Jesus) said: "But I say unto you, love your enemies, bless them that curse you, do good to them that hate you, and <u>pray for them which despitefully use you, and persecute you</u>."

In conclusion, oh children of the Most High, consciously accept who you are by Nature and continue to work to improve in the ongoing process of becoming the best obedient child of the Most High that you were preordained to be! **Mine your mind for the jewels of your soul on your inner journey through the Messiah Yashu'a (Jesus), to our Most High Heavenly Father by Mind Gardening in the Creative Garden of Will (Your Mind) to Grow a Living Water Mentality M.I.N.D. (Making Intentional Noble Decisions)** in **A.C.T.I.O.N. (Activated, Conscious, Timely, Intentions, Obligated, Now)!**

Yashu'a (Jesus) said: "Thou shalt love the Most High Heavenly Father, thy Sustainer with all thy heart, and with all thy soul, and with all thy mind. Thou shalt love thy neighbour as thyself."

Mind Gardening in the Creative Garden of Will (Your Mind) to Grow a Living Water Mentality!

CHILDREN OF THE MOST HIGH:
PRISTINE YOUTH AND FAMILY SOLUTIONS, LLC.
SONS AND DAUGHTERS OF THE MOST HIGH PUBLISHERS ®

Oh, Gracious Most High Heavenly father, Holy is your name,
Your Will Be Done Now and Forever!

Appendix: What is the Children of the Most High: Pristine Youth and Family Solutions, LLC. Proclamation?

"We greet all in peace with a sincere heart. We are non-violent and agree with the Reverend Dr. Martin Luther King Jr. when he said: "At the center of non-violence stands the principle of love." We stay sober, we don't drink alcohol, we don't become intoxicated, we eat healthy, we exercise, and we don't smoke anything for the body is a temple where the spirit of the Most High dwells; so, our bodies and minds must be in a state of cleanliness! We respect nature, we respect the laws of nature, and the Most High Heavenly Father who is the source of it all. We don't hate any race, creed, religion, or sexual orientation. We advocate that humanity practice being just to the depressed, in mind or circumstances, the poor, and underserved underrepresented members of humanity. We advocate that humanity practice defending the poor, motherless and fatherless from all injustices. We seek to help deliver the poor and needy out of the hands of the wicked by teaching them how to activate the latent potential in them through their inborn gifts, by learning and applying the Most High's doctrine in all that they do, through repentance, and through the acceptance of the Messiah Yashu'a (Jesus), and through the eternal obedience to the Most High Heavenly Father's "Will" and commandments. We seek to help empower members of humanity to take that which is evil and to turn it into good. We seek to work with all members of humanity to help make the world a safer, peaceful, healthy, and poverty free environment for all youth and all adults to live in; and we obey Yashu'a (Jesus) commandment to love one another."

329

Yashu'a (Jesus) said: "Thou shalt love the Most High
Heavenly Father, thy Sustainer with all thy heart, and
with all thy soul, and with all thy mind. Thou shalt love
thy neighbour as thyself."

Mind Gardening in the Creative Garden of Will (Your Mind) to Grow a Living Water Mentality!

CHILDREN OF THE MOST HIGH:
PRISTINE YOUTH AND FAMILY SOLUTIONS, LLC.
SONS AND DAUGHTERS OF THE MOST HIGH PUBLISHERS ®

*Oh, Gracious Most High Heavenly father, Holy is your name,
Your Will Be Done Now and Forever!*

Below is a Prayer of Repentance:

In the KJV bible book of Psalms chapter 51 verses 1-19; it states: "**51** Have mercy upon me, O God, according to thy lovingkindness: according unto the multitude of thy tender mercies blot out my transgressions. [2] Wash me throughly from mine iniquity, and cleanse me from my sin. [3] For I acknowledge my transgressions: and my sin is ever before me. [4] Against thee, thee only, have I sinned, and done this evil in thy sight: that thou mightest be justified when thou speakest, and be clear when thou judgest. [5] Behold, I was shapen in iniquity; and in sin did my mother conceive me. [6] Behold, thou desirest truth in the inward parts: and in the hidden part thou shalt make me to know wisdom. [7] Purge me with hyssop, and I shall be clean: wash me, and I shall be whiter than snow.

Yashu'a (Jesus) said: "Thou shalt love the Most High Heavenly Father, thy Sustainer with all thy heart, and with all thy soul, and with all thy mind. Thou shalt love thy neighbour as thyself."

Mind Gardening in the Creative Garden of Will (Your Mind) to Grow a Living Water Mentality!

CHILDREN OF THE MOST HIGH:
PRISTINE YOUTH AND FAMILY SOLUTIONS, LLC.
SONS AND DAUGHTERS OF THE MOST HIGH PUBLISHERS ®

Oh, Gracious Most High Heavenly father, Holy is your name,
Your Will Be Done Now and Forever!

[8] Make me to hear joy and gladness; that the bones which thou hast broken may rejoice. [9] Hide thy face from my sins, and blot out all mine iniquities. [10] Create in me a clean heart, O God; and renew a right spirit within me. [11] Cast me not away from thy presence; and take not thy holy spirit from me. [12] Restore unto me the joy of thy salvation; and uphold me with thy free spirit. [13] Then will I teach transgressors thy ways; and sinners shall be converted unto thee. [14] Deliver me from bloodguiltiness, O God, thou God of my salvation: and my tongue shall sing aloud of thy righteousness. [15] O Lord, open thou my lips; and my mouth shall shew forth thy praise. [16] For thou desirest not sacrifice; else would I give it: thou delightest not in burnt offering. [17] The sacrifices of God are a broken spirit: a broken and a contrite heart, O God, thou wilt not despise."

Yashu'a (Jesus) said: "Thou shalt love the Most High Heavenly Father, thy Sustainer with all thy heart, and with all thy soul, and with all thy mind. Thou shalt love thy neighbour as thyself."

Mind Gardening in the Creative Garden of Will (Your Mind) to Grow a Living Water Mentality!

CHILDREN OF THE MOST HIGH:
PRISTINE YOUTH AND FAMILY SOLUTIONS, LLC.
SONS AND DAUGHTERS OF THE MOST HIGH PUBLISHERS ®

*Oh, Gracious Most High Heavenly father, Holy is your name,
Your Will Be Done Now and Forever!*

"¹⁸ Do good in thy good pleasure unto Zion: build thou the walls of Jerusalem. ¹⁹ Then shalt thou be pleased with the sacrifices of righteousness, with burnt offering and whole burnt offering: then shall they offer bullocks upon thine altar."

332

Yashu'a (Jesus) said: "Thou shalt love the Most High Heavenly Father, thy Sustainer with all thy heart, and with all thy soul, and with all thy mind. Thou shalt love thy neighbour as thyself."

Mind Gardening in the Creative Garden of Will (Your Mind) to Grow a Living Water Mentality!

*Oh, Gracious Most High Heavenly father, Holy is your name,
Your Will Be Done Now and Forever!*

In the KJV bible book of John chapter 14 verse 6; the Messiah Yashu'a (Jesus) said: "I am the way the truth, and the life: no man cometh unto the Father, but by me." However, according to the KJV bible book of John chapter 6 verse 44; only the Most High Heavenly Father can lead a person to the Messiah Yashu'a (Jesus). The Messiah Yashu'a (Jesus) said: "No man **[person]** can come to me, except the Father which hath sent me draw him: and I will raise him up at the last day." In the KJV bible book of John chapter 14 verse 21; the Messiah Yashu'a (Jesus) said: "He **[or she]** that hath my commandments, and keepeth them, he **[or she]** it is that loveth me: and he **[or she]** that loveth me shall be loved of my Father, and I will love him **[or her]**, and will manifest myself to him **[or her]**."

Yashu'a (Jesus) said: "Thou shalt love the Most High Heavenly Father, thy Sustainer with all thy heart, and with all thy soul, and with all thy mind. Thou shalt love thy neighbour as thyself."

Mind Gardening in the Creative Garden of Will (Your Mind) to Grow a Living Water Mentality!

CHILDREN OF THE MOST HIGH:
PRISTINE YOUTH AND FAMILY SOLUTIONS, LLC.
SONS AND DAUGHTERS OF THE MOST HIGH PUBLISHERS ®

Oh, Gracious Most High Heavenly father, Holy is your name, Your Will Be Done Now and Forever!

All obedient children of the Most High are seeking the Kingdom of God and the Messiah Yashu'a (the True Vine, Jesus), who will take those who have repented, accepted him as their personal savior, and received the holy spirit, to the Most High Heavenly Father. Once a person has accepted the Messiah Yashu'a (Jesus) as their personal savior, there is a Kingdom of God inside of them, but not there exclusively; and they are always being attacked by the children of the devil. "Love gives naught but itself and takes naught but from itself. Love possesses not nor would it be possessed; For love is sufficient unto love." (Gibran, 1968).

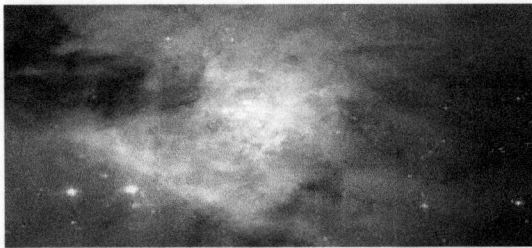

334

Yashu'a (Jesus) said: "Thou shalt love the Most High Heavenly Father, thy Sustainer with all thy heart, and with all thy soul, and with all thy mind. Thou shalt love thy neighbour as thyself."

Mind Gardening in the Creative Garden of Will (Your Mind) to Grow a Living Water Mentality!

CHILDREN OF THE MOST HIGH:
PRISTINE YOUTH AND FAMILY SOLUTIONS, LLC.
SONS AND DAUGHTERS OF THE MOST HIGH PUBLISHERS ®

Oh, Gracious Most High Heavenly father, Holy is your name, Your Will Be Done Now and Forever!

In the KJV bible book of Luke chapter 17 verse 21; Yashu'a (Jesus) said: "Neither shall they say, Lo here! or, lo there! for, behold, the kingdom of God is within you."

**"The kingdom of heaven is within you; whosoever shall know thyself shall find it."
Ancient Egyptian Proverb.**

In the KJV bible book of Revelation chapter 21 verse 24; it states: "And the nations of those **who are saved** shall walk in its light." So, as living souls, the children of the Most High are made aware that the Supreme Creator of the Boundless Universes, manifests through us as the breath of life!

Yashu'a (Jesus) said: "Thou shalt love the Most High Heavenly Father, thy Sustainer with all thy heart, and with all thy soul, and with all thy mind. Thou shalt love thy neighbour as thyself."

Mind Gardening in the Creative Garden of Will (Your Mind) to Grow a Living Water Mentality!

CHILDREN OF THE MOST HIGH:
PRISTINE YOUTH AND FAMILY SOLUTIONS, LLC.
SONS AND DAUGHTERS OF THE MOST HIGH PUBLISHERS ®

Oh, Gracious Most High Heavenly father, Holy is your name, Your Will Be Done Now and Forever!

What are the True Vine (Yashu'a, Jesus) Mind Gardening Daily Individual or Family Household Habits of Success? The True Vine (Yashu'a, Jesus) Mind Gardening Daily Individual or Family Household Habits of Success are:

1. Obey the Most High Heavenly Father's will and commandments now and forever!

2. Love the Most High Heavenly Father with all of your heart, all of your spirit, all of your soul, all of your mind, and all of your entire being!

3. Decrease so that the Spirit of the Messiah Yashu'a (Jesus) can increase in you!

4. Do unto others as you would want others to do unto you!

5. Always think positive!

6. Always be positive!

336

Yashu'a (Jesus) said: "Thou shalt love the Most High Heavenly Father, thy Sustainer with all thy heart, and with all thy soul, and with all thy mind. Thou shalt love thy neighbour as thyself."

Mind Gardening in the Creative Garden of Will (Your Mind) to Grow a Living Water Mentality!

CHILDREN OF THE MOST HIGH:
PRISTINE YOUTH AND FAMILY SOLUTIONS, LLC.
SONS AND DAUGHTERS OF THE MOST HIGH PUBLISHERS ®

Oh, Gracious Most High Heavenly father, Holy is your name,
Your Will Be Done Now and Forever!

7. Always have a positive attitude!

8. Open your heart before you open your mouth!

9. Remember, words should be soft, not hard!

10. It's nice to be important, but it is more important to be nice!

11. Mine your mind for the jewels of your soul!

12. Pray together daily!

13. Eat together in the same room a minimum of once a week!

14. Observe the Sabbath (Shu-Bat) weekly as a family!

15. Study and read the scriptures of the Most High as a family a minimum of once a week!

Yashu'a (Jesus) said: "Thou shalt love the Most High Heavenly Father, thy Sustainer with all thy heart, and with all thy soul, and with all thy mind. Thou shalt love thy neighbour as thyself."

Mind Gardening in the Creative Garden of Will (Your Mind) to Grow a Living Water Mentality!

CHILDREN OF THE MOST HIGH:
PRISTINE YOUTH AND FAMILY SOLUTIONS, LLC.
SONS AND DAUGHTERS OF THE MOST HIGH PUBLISHERS ®

Oh, Gracious Most High Heavenly father, Holy is your name,
Your Will Be Done Now and Forever!

16. Watch a TV show or movie at home a minimum of once a week!

17. Workout together as a family or ensure that all family members are working out on a weekly basis if their medical physicians have approved of them doing so.

18. Have family meetings once a week to discuss everyone's overall well-being, current events or anything else that is on any family member's mind, without the TV or any other electronic devices being on as a potential conversation distraction. One person speaks at a time, no arguing, no vulgarity, and all family members must respect each other!

19. Do some agreed upon, healthy, fun, and safe family event a minimum of once a month or weekly or bi-weekly together as a family.

Yashu'a (Jesus) said: "Thou shalt love the Most High Heavenly Father, thy Sustainer with all thy heart, and with all thy soul, and with all thy mind. Thou shalt love thy neighbour as thyself."

Mind Gardening in the Creative Garden of Will (Your Mind) to Grow a Living Water Mentality!

CHILDREN OF THE MOST HIGH:
PRISTINE YOUTH AND FAMILY SOLUTIONS, LLC.
SONS AND DAUGHTERS OF THE MOST HIGH PUBLISHERS

Oh, Gracious Most High Heavenly father, Holy is your name,
Your Will Be Done Now and Forever!

In the KJV bible book of Genesis, chapter 14 verse 18; it states: "And Melchizedek (Malkiy-Tsedeq, מַלְכִּי־צֶדֶק) king of Salem brought forth bread and wine: and he was the priest of the <u>Most High</u> (ELYOWN עֶלְיוֹן EL אֵל) God." In the KJV bible book of Psalms chapter 82 verse 6; states: "I have said, Ye are gods; and all of you are children <u>of the Most High</u> (is the KJV bible Hebrew Strong's Concordance#5945 which is the title: <u>ELYOWN</u> עֶלְיוֹן (the God) EL אֵל)." In the KJV bible book of Numbers chapter 23 verse 19; states: "<u>God (EL אֵל) is not a man</u>, that he should lie; neither the <u>son of man, that he should repent</u>: hath he said, and shall he not do it? or hath he spoken, and shall he not make it good?" However, for clarification it is critical that all children of the Most High know that in the KJV bible book of Genesis Chapter 1 verse 1; the original Aramic (Hebrew) word for "God" is "Elohiym" not the <u>Most High</u> (ELYOWN עֶלְיוֹן EL אֵל), the Sustainer, the Nourisher, the Provider of all Life, and the Omnipotent and the Omnipresent Creator of the boundless universes. So, the children of the Most High: Pristine Youth and Family Solutions, LLC. hopes that all children of the Most High acquire an overstanding of the differences between "God" ("אֱלֹהִים 'Elohiym") in the KJV bible book of Genesis chapter 1 verse 1, "the LORD, יְהֹוָה Yĕhovah, (Yahuwa, Yahweh, Jehovah, Yahayyu)" who <u>repented</u> to the <u>Most High</u> (ELYOWN עֶלְיוֹן EL אֵל) in the KJV bible book of Genesis chapter 6 verse 6; who is referred to as: "the LORD; and the יְהֹוָה Yĕhovah "God" "אֱלֹהִים 'Elohiym" who gets <u>jealous</u> in the KJV bible book of Exodus chapter 20 verse 5; ARE NOT TO BE CONFUSED AS BEING the <u>Most High</u> (ELYOWN עֶלְיוֹן EL אֵל), the Sustainer, the Nourisher, the Provider of all Life, and the Omnipotent and the Omnipresent Creator of the boundless universes who they all worship and do the 'Will" of!

339

Yashu'a (Jesus) said: "Thou shalt love the Most High Heavenly Father, thy Sustainer with all thy heart, and with all thy soul, and with all thy mind. Thou shalt love thy neighbour as thyself."

Mind Gardening in the Creative Garden of Will (Your Mind) to Grow a Living Water Mentality!

CHILDREN OF THE MOST HIGH:
PRISTINE YOUTH AND FAMILY SOLUTIONS, LLC.
SONS AND DAUGHTERS OF THE MOST HIGH PUBLISHERS ®

Oh, Gracious Most High Heavenly father, Holy is your name,
Your Will Be Done Now and Forever!

Nothing would exist if you Oh Gracious Most High Heavenly Father, The Creator didn't create it. You are alone in Your Greatness; you have no partners that share in your grace. To you all sovereignty is due and you are all powerful over everything. We seek refuge in you, the ever watchful Most High who hears and knows all things! Glory be to you as many times as the number of things you have created! All gratitude is due to you oh gracious Most High Heavenly Father, you are the Creator and Sustainer of all the boundless universes. You are the Yielder, and the most Merciful. The Ruler of the Day of Decision.

Yashu'a (Jesus) said: "Thou shalt love the Most High Heavenly Father, thy Sustainer with all thy heart, and with all thy soul, and with all thy mind. Thou shalt love thy neighbour as thyself."

Mind Gardening in the Creative Garden of Will (Your Mind) to Grow a Living Water Mentality!

CHILDREN OF THE MOST HIGH:
PRISTINE YOUTH AND FAMILY SOLUTIONS, LLC.
SONS AND DAUGHTERS OF THE MOST HIGH PUBLISHERS ®

Oh, Gracious Most High Heavenly father, Holy is your name,
Your Will Be Done Now and Forever!

It's you whom we worship and it is you alone whom we beseech for help, oh Guide, guide us to the narrow path (which reflects moral integrity and positive character traits in action) of the ones who stand straight, the narrow path of those who earned your grace not inclusive of those who brought an everlasting curse on themselves, those who conceal the facts of that which they know to be true in order to lead the sincere-hearted seekers of your truth astray. Amen

341

Yashu'a (Jesus) said: "Thou shalt love the Most High Heavenly Father, thy Sustainer with all thy heart, and with all thy soul, and with all thy mind. Thou shalt love thy neighbour as thyself."

Mind Gardening in the Creative Garden of Will (Your Mind) to Grow a Living Water Mentality!

CHILDREN OF THE MOST HIGH:
PRISTINE YOUTH AND FAMILY SOLUTIONS, LLC.
SONS AND DAUGHTERS OF THE MOST HIGH PUBLISHERS ®

Oh, Gracious Most High Heavenly father, Holy is your name,
Your Will Be Done Now and Forever!

About the Author

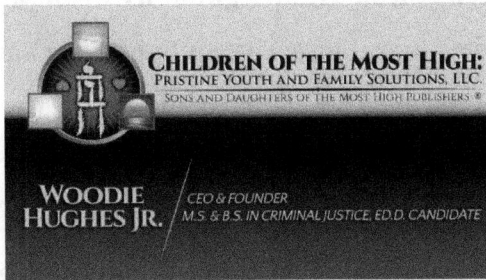

CHILDREN OF THE MOST HIGH:
PRISTINE YOUTH AND FAMILY SOLUTIONS, LLC.
SONS AND DAUGHTERS OF THE MOST HIGH PUBLISHERS ®

WOODIE HUGHES JR. / CEO & FOUNDER
M.S. & B.S. IN CRIMINAL JUSTICE, ED.D. CANDIDATE

Mr. Hughes is a Servant of the Most High, Teacher of the Most High's Doctrine, and a Youth and Adults Workshop and Presentation Consultant.

📞 478-538-1918
✉ INFO@CHILDRENOFTHEMOSTHIGH.COM
🌐 CHILDRENOFTHEMOSTHIGH.COM
🐦 @WOODIEHUGHESJR9
f CHILDRENOFTHEMOSTHIGHPRISTINEYOUTHANDFAMSOLUTIONS

342

Yashu'a (Jesus) said: "Thou shalt love the Most High Heavenly Father, thy Sustainer with all thy heart, and with all thy soul, and with all thy mind. Thou shalt love thy neighbour as thyself."

Mind Gardening in the Creative Garden of Will (Your Mind) to Grow a Living Water Mentality!

CHILDREN OF THE MOST HIGH:
PRISTINE YOUTH AND FAMILY SOLUTIONS, LLC.
SONS AND DAUGHTERS OF THE MOST HIGH PUBLISHERS ®

Oh, Gracious Most High Heavenly father, Holy is your name, Your Will Be Done Now and Forever!

Mr. Woodie Hughes Jr. is the CEO & Founder of the Children of the Most High: Pristine Youth and Families Solutions LLC., Sons and Daughters of the Most High Publishers. Mr. Hughes is a Servant of the Most High and a Teacher of the Most High's Doctrine. Mr. Hughes is an Author who writes books that are being put forth by the will of the Most High Heavenly Father to inspire all youth and all adults **who are children of the Most High** to acquire the **competitive edge** against the children of devil. Mr. Hughes is a career university educator. Mr. Woodie Hughes Jr. and Mrs. Tonya Hughes have been happily married for 20 years and have a son and a daughter. Mr. Hughes is a veteran who has received a United States Army honorable discharge for his 8 years of service with the Illinois Army National Guard.

Yashu'a (Jesus) said: "Thou shalt love the Most High Heavenly Father, thy Sustainer with all thy heart, and with all thy soul, and with all thy mind. Thou shalt love thy neighbour as thyself."

Mind Gardening in the Creative Garden of Will (Your Mind) to Grow a Living Water Mentality!

CHILDREN OF THE MOST HIGH:
PRISTINE YOUTH AND FAMILY SOLUTIONS, LLC.
SONS AND DAUGHTERS OF THE MOST HIGH PUBLISHERS ®

Oh, Gracious Most High Heavenly father, Holy is your name, Your Will Be Done Now and Forever!

Mr. Hughes is the son of Mrs. Annette Hughes and Mr. Woodie Hughes Sr. who have been happily married for 50 years (as of 2020)! For over 27 years, Mr. Woodie Hughes Jr. has continued to be a devout student and teacher of the Most High's doctrine who is guided by the will of the Heavenly Father, and the Messiah Yashua's (Jesus) spirit of knowledge, spirit of wisdom, and spirit of true-faith all working as the same spirits (KJV bible book of 1st Corinthians chapter 12 verses 8-9) of the Messiah Yashu'a (Jesus) which has graciously been bestowed upon him. Mr. Hughes has accepted the Messiah Yashu'a (Jesus) as his savior and is in the Body of Christ!

Yashu'a (Jesus) said: "Thou shalt love the Most High Heavenly Father, thy Sustainer with all thy heart, and with all thy soul, and with all thy mind. Thou shalt love thy neighbour as thyself."

Mind Gardening in the Creative Garden of Will (Your Mind) to Grow a Living Water Mentality!

CHILDREN OF THE MOST HIGH:
PRISTINE YOUTH AND FAMILY SOLUTIONS, LLC.
SONS AND DAUGHTERS OF THE MOST HIGH PUBLISHERS ®

Oh, Gracious Most High Heavenly father, Holy is your name,
Your Will Be Done Now and Forever!

The Children of the Most High: Pristine Youth and Family Solutions, LLC. Books are available on Amazon and are listed below:

SPIRITUAL TRILLIONAIRE

CHERISHING THE BEAUTY OF LIFE WHILE SIMULTANEOUSLY PREPARING FOR THE SHADOW OF DEATH

YASHU'A (JESUS) SAID: "Lay not up for yourselves treasures upon earth, where moth and rust doth corrupt, and where thieves break through and steal: But lay up for yourselves treasures in heaven, where neither moth nor rust doth corrupt, and where thieves do not break through nor steal. For where your treasure is, there will your heart be also."
MATTHEW 6:19-21 KING JAMES BIBLE

Positive Mental and Physical Health is Essential to Obtaining and Sustaining Positive Spiritual Health and Positive Spiritual Wealth.

BY WOODIE HUGHES JR.

CHD & Daughter of the Children of the Most High: Pristine Youth and Families Solutions LLC. Sons and Daughters of the Most High Publishers ®
Mr. Hughes Is a Servant of the Most High and is Teacher of the Most High Class A:

THE TRUE VINE - THE MESSIAH YASHU'A (JESUS) - FISHERS OF MEN, WOMEN, AND CHILDREN CLASS A:
Allowing the Most High to Divide the Disagreeable from Agreeable in Our Hearts. ®

345

Yashu'a (Jesus) said: "Thou shalt love the Most High Heavenly Father, thy Sustainer with all thy heart, and with all thy soul, and with all thy mind. Thou shalt love thy neighbour as thyself."

Mind Gardening in the Creative Garden of Will (Your Mind) to Grow a Living Water Mentality!

CHILDREN OF THE MOST HIGH:
PRISTINE YOUTH AND FAMILY SOLUTIONS, LLC.
SONS AND DAUGHTERS OF THE MOST HIGH PUBLISHERS ®

Oh, Gracious Most High Heavenly father, Holy is your name,
Your Will Be Done Now and Forever!

What is a **Spiritual Trillionaire?** Is it possible to become a Spiritual Trillionaire? If so, how can a person become a Spiritual Trillionaire? Why does becoming a Spiritual Trillionaire matter? How can becoming a Spiritual Trillionaire benefit youth and adults personally, professionally and globally? How can becoming a Spiritual Trillionaire improve the overall well-being of members of humanity? Can becoming a Spiritual Trillionaire increase a person's economic earning potential? What are the 9 Deadly Venoms of the Desires of the great dragon, that old serpent called the devil and satan which deceived the whole world? How can we create a world that is ruled by love and not ruled by negative emotions and greed, lust and love of money?

Spiritual Trillionaire: Cherishing the Breath of Life While Simultaneously Preparing for the Blow of Death, is being put forth by the will of the Most High Heavenly Father in an effort to inspire ALL youth and ALL adults who are children of the Most High to attain, maintain and sustain positive spiritual health and spiritual wealth on the path to becoming a Spiritual Trillionaire So, it is important to the Children of the Most High: Pristine Youth and Family Solutions, LLC that we, the true followers of the Real Messiah Yashu'a (Jesus Son of God) utilize this book as a 9X9 True Vine (Yashu'a, Jesus) Passionate Pathfinders of the Most High True Vine (Yashu'a, Jesus) B.A.-K.A.-R.E. Sequential Order of Learning that helps all youth and all adults to learn how to work together to create a world where all youth and all adults are happy, healthy, and balanced mentally, spiritually, physically, emotionally, financially, socially, personally, and professionally.

FOR MORE INFORMATION:
Please visit our website at: childrenofthemosthigh.com
Online ordering is available for all products at our Amazon Store Front.

ISBN 978-1-948355-01-8

346

Yashu'a (Jesus) said: "Thou shalt love the Most High
Heavenly Father, thy Sustainer with all thy heart, and
with all thy soul, and with all thy mind. Thou shalt love
thy neighbour as thyself."

Mind Gardening in the Creative Garden of Will (Your Mind) to Grow a Living Water Mentality!

CHILDREN OF THE MOST HIGH:
PRISTINE YOUTH AND FAMILY SOLUTIONS, LLC.
SONS AND DAUGHTERS OF THE MOST HIGH PUBLISHERS ®

Oh, Gracious Most High Heavenly father, Holy is your name,
Your Will Be Done Now and Forever!

CHILDREN OF THE MOST HIGH:
PRISTINE YOUTH AND FAMILY SOLUTIONS, LLC.
SONS AND DAUGHTERS OF THE MOST HIGH PUBLISHERS ®

THE DEVIL IS LUSTS, LIES, AND DELUSIONS;
— AND —
THE MOST HIGH IS LOVE AND TRUTH WITHOUT CONFUSION!

THE MESSIAH YASHU'A (JESUS) SAID:

REVELATION 3:20, MATHEW 24:4-5, AND REVELATION 2:9 (KJV) BIBLE

Is Your Heart Ruled by Lust or Ruled by the Love of God?

For, behold, the day cometh, that shall burn as an oven; and all the proud, yea, and all that do wickedly, shall be stubble: and the day that cometh shall burn them up, saith the Lord of hosts, that it shall leave them neither root nor branch. Behold, I will send you Elijah the prophet before the coming of the great and dreadful day of the Lord. And he shall turn the heart of the fathers to the children, and the heart of the children to their fathers, lest I come and smite the earth with a curse.
MALACHI 4:1,4-6 (KJV) BIBLE

BY WOODIE HUGHES JR.

CEO & Founder of the Children of the Most High: Pristine Youth and Family Solutions LLC. Sons and Daughters of the Most High Publishers ®
Mr. Hughes is a Servant of the Most High and a Teacher of the Most High's Doctrine.

THE TRUE VINE - THE MESSIAH YASHUA (JESUS) - FISHERS OF MEN, WOMEN, AND CHILDREN CLASS B:
"Be in the World but not of the World, Oh Children of the Most High; Become Aware and Accept How the Treasures of the Hearts of People Reflect what they Value the Most! In this the children of Most High, and the children of the devil are revealed!

347

Yashu'a (Jesus) said: "Thou shalt love the Most High Heavenly Father, thy Sustainer with all thy heart, and with all thy soul, and with all thy mind. Thou shalt love thy neighbour as thyself."

Mind Gardening in the Creative Garden of Will (Your Mind) to Grow a Living Water Mentality!

CHILDREN OF THE MOST HIGH:
PRISTINE YOUTH AND FAMILY SOLUTIONS, LLC.
SONS AND DAUGHTERS OF THE MOST HIGH PUBLISHERS ®

Oh, Gracious Most High Heavenly father, Holy is your name,
Your Will Be Done Now and Forever!

CHILDREN OF THE MOST HIGH
PRISTINE YOUTH AND FAMILY SOLUTIONS, LLC
SONS AND DAUGHTERS OF THE MOST HIGH PUBLISHERS ®

"For God so loved the world, that he gave his only begotten Son, that whosoever
believeth in him should not perish, but have everlasting life.
JOHN 3:16 (KJV)

"And their dead bodies shall lie in the street of the great city, which spiritually is called Sodom and Egypt, where also our Lord
was crucified. And they of the people and kindreds and tongues and nations shall see their dead bodies three days and a half,
and shall not suffer their dead bodies to be put in graves."
REVELATION 11:8-9(KJV)

For God sent not his Son into the world to condemn the world; but that the world
through him might be saved.
JOHN 3:17 (KJV)

This Dynamic Book: "The Devil is Lusts, Lies, and Delusions; and The Most High is Love and Truth Without Confusion", is being put forth by the will of the Most High Heavenly Father to inspire all youth and all adults who are children of the Most High to acquire the competitive edge against the children of devil. The Messiah Yashua (Jesus) said: "Enter ye in at the strait gate: for wide is the gate, and broad is the way, that leadeth to destruction, and many there be which go in thereat; Because strait is the gate, and narrow is the way, which leadeth unto life, and few there be that find it, Matthew 7:13-14 (KJV)." Therefore; it is imperative in this sacred moment in time that the children of the Most High are reminded that NOW is the TIME and Change is the Motive to ensure that our relationship with the Most High is in Order by throughly examining the content of our own character!

Mirror, Mirror on the Wall; Oh, Most High; Help us to become the best that we can Become in All! Is your heart ruled by lust and lies, or is your heart ruled by the love and truth in the Most High eyes? Are you predominately a peacemaker or a troublemaker? Does your heart and actions; reflect that you love the Most High like the Messiah Yashua (Jesus) with internal satisfaction? Do you want to avoid being deceived ever again by the son of perdition through sin? If so, this book will reveal the nature of the devil and the nature of children of the Most High in an effort for the children of the Most High to acquire the True Vine (Yashu'a, Jesus) the Messiah, adaptive leadership edge over the children of the devil by knowing how and why; The Devil is Lusts, Lies, and Delusions; and The Most High is Love and Truth Without Confusion!

FOR MORE INFORMATION CONTACT:
Please visit our website at: childrenofthemosthigh.com
Online ordering is available for all products at our Amazon Store Front.

9 781948 355025

Yashu'a (Jesus) said: "Thou shalt love the Most High
Heavenly Father, thy Sustainer with all thy heart, and
with all thy soul, and with all thy mind. Thou shalt love
thy neighbour as thyself."

Mind Gardening in the Creative Garden of Will (Your Mind) to Grow a Living Water Mentality!

CHILDREN OF THE MOST HIGH:
PRISTINE YOUTH AND FAMILY SOLUTIONS, LLC.
SONS AND DAUGHTERS OF THE MOST HIGH PUBLISHERS &

Oh, Gracious Most High Heavenly father, Holy is your name,
Your Will Be Done Now and Forever!

349

Yashu'a (Jesus) said: "Thou shalt love the Most High Heavenly Father, thy Sustainer with all thy heart, and with all thy soul, and with all thy mind. Thou shalt love thy neighbour as thyself."

Mind Gardening in the Creative Garden of Will (Your Mind) to Grow a Living Water Mentality!

CHILDREN OF THE MOST HIGH:
PRISTINE YOUTH AND FAMILY SOLUTIONS, LLC.
SONS AND DAUGHTERS OF THE MOST HIGH PUBLISHERS ®

Oh, Gracious Most High Heavenly father, Holy is your name, Your Will Be Done Now and Forever!

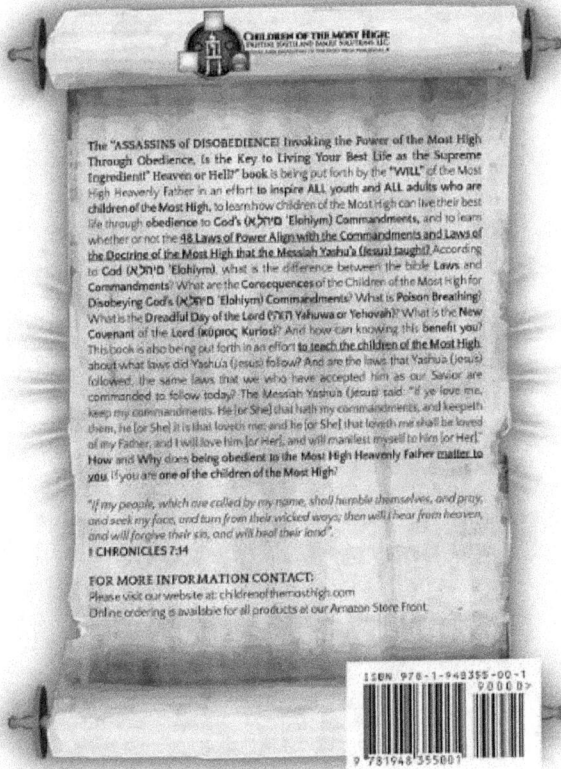

The "ASSASSINS of DISOBEDIENCE! Invoking the Power of the Most High Through Obedience, Is the Key to Living Your Best Life as the Supreme Ingredient!" Heaven or Hell?" book is being put forth by the "WILL" of the Most High Heavenly Father in an effort to inspire ALL youth and ALL adults who are children of the Most High, to learn how children of the Most High can live their best life through **obedience** to God's (אֱלֹהִים 'Elohiym) Commandments, and to learn whether or not the 48 Laws of Power Align with the Commandments and Laws of the Doctrine of the Most High that the Messiah Yashu'a (Jesus) taught? According to God (אֱלֹהִים 'Elohiym), what is the difference between the bible Laws and Commandments? What are the Consequences of the Children of the Most High for Disobeying God's (אֱלֹהִים 'Elohiym) Commandments? What is Poison Breathing? What is the Dreadful Day of the Lord (יְהוָה Yahuwa or Yehovah)? What is the New Covenant of the Lord (κύριος Kurios)? And how can knowing this benefit you? This book is also being put forth in an effort to teach the children of the Most High, about what laws did Yashu'a (Jesus) follow? And are the laws that Yashu'a (Jesus) followed, the same laws that we who have accepted him as our Savior are commanded to follow today? The Messiah Yashu'a (Jesus) said: "if ye love me, keep my commandments. He [or She] that hath my commandments, and keepeth them, he [or She] it is that loveth me: and he [or She] that loveth me shall be loved of my Father, and I will love him [or Her], and will manifest myself to him [or Her]." How and Why does being obedient to the Most High Heavenly Father matter to you, if you are one of the children of the Most High?

"If my people, which are called by my name, shall humble themselves, and pray, and seek my face, and turn from their wicked ways; then will I hear from heaven, and will forgive their sin, and will heal their land".
I CHRONICLES 7:14

FOR MORE INFORMATION CONTACT:
Please visit our website at: childrenofthemosthigh.com
Online ordering is available for all products at our Amazon Store Front.

ISBN 978-1-948355-00-1

350

Yashu'a (Jesus) said: "Thou shalt love the Most High Heavenly Father, thy Sustainer with all thy heart, and with all thy soul, and with all thy mind. Thou shalt love thy neighbour as thyself."

Mind Gardening in the Creative Garden of Will (Your Mind) to Grow a Living Water Mentality!

CHILDREN OF THE MOST HIGH:
PRISTINE YOUTH AND FAMILY SOLUTIONS, LLC.
SONS AND DAUGHTERS OF THE MOST HIGH PUBLISHERS ®

Oh, Gracious Most High Heavenly father, Holy is your name,
Your Will Be Done Now and Forever!

CHILDREN OF THE MOST HIGH
PRISTINE YOUTH AND FAMILY SOLUTIONS, LLC.
SONS and DAUGHTERS of THE MOST High Publishers ®

BEWARE OF THE PINK ASSASSIN
(YOUR TONGUE):

The True-Vine (Yashu'a, Jesus) Power of Life and Death is in the Tongue;
Speaking God's (סיהלא Elōhĭym) "Will" for Your Life into Existence!

- IF SOMEONE WERE TALKING BEHIND YOUR BACK, THEY WOULD BE IN FRONT OF YOUR FACE, BECAUSE YOUR FACE IS BEHIND YOUR BACK! -

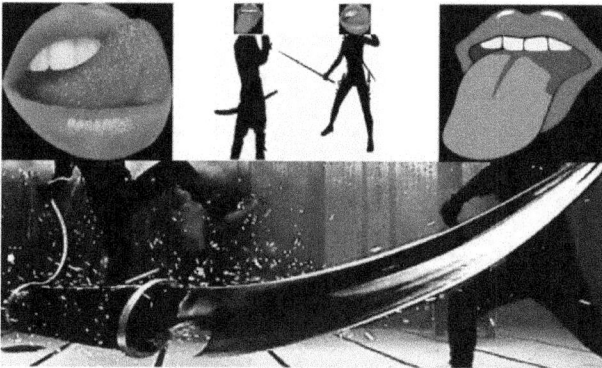

"Death and life are in the power of the tongue: and they that love it shall eat the fruit thereof,'"
PROVERBS 18:21 (KJV) BIBLE

"The Messiah Yashu'a (Jesus) said: 'Think not that I am come to send peace on earth: I came not to send peace, but a Sword!'"
MATTHEW 10:34 (KJV) BIBLE

"My Doctrine is not Mine, but him that sent me!,"
JOHN 7:16 (KJV) BIBLE

BY WOODIE HUGHES JR.

CFO & Founder of the Children of the Most High, Pristine Youth and Families Solutions LLC. Sons and Daughters of the Most High Publishers ®. Mr. Hughes is a Servant of the Most High and a Teacher of the Most High's Doctrine.

THE TRUE VINE - THE MESSIAH YASHU'A (JESUS) - FISHERS OF MEN, WOMEN, AND CHILDREN CLASS E:
Eliminating Poison Speaking, Poison Thinking, and Poison Words from Your Heart and Mind! ©

351

Yashu'a (Jesus) said: "Thou shalt love the Most High Heavenly Father, thy Sustainer with all thy heart, and with all thy soul, and with all thy mind. Thou shalt love thy neighbour as thyself."

Mind Gardening in the Creative Garden of Will (Your Mind) to Grow a Living Water Mentality!

CHILDREN OF THE MOST HIGH:
PRISTINE YOUTH AND FAMILY SOLUTIONS, LLC.
SONS AND DAUGHTERS OF THE MOST HIGH PUBLISHERS ®

Oh, Gracious Most High Heavenly father, Holy is your name,
Your Will Be Done Now and Forever!

CHILDREN OF THE MOST HIGH
PRISTINE YOUTH AND FAMILY SOLUTIONS, LLC
SONS AND DAUGHTERS OF THE MOST HIGH PUBLISHERS ®

This Dynamic Book: "Beware of the Pink Assassin (Your Tongue): The True-Vine (Yashu'a, Jesus) Power of Life and Death is in the Tongue; Speaking God's (סיהלא Elôhîym) "Will" for Your Life into Existence," is being put forth by the "Will" of the Most High Heavenly Father to inspire all youth and all adults <u>who are children of the Most High</u> to learn how to best listen and how to best communicate through Love, and how to <u>Only Speak through the portion of the Most High that exists in each of us</u>, like the True-Vine (Yashu'a, Jesus) did!

<u>Does the Power of your Tongue in the Name or Names you call on in Prayer, Eliminate Evil and Diseases in the Country that you live in</u>? If there was a way to speak "<u>The (לא 'EL) Most High (ןילע</u> Elyown) Heavenly Father's "Will" for your life into existence, would you want to learn about it? Are there **Love Words** that are **rooted** in the foundation of the **True Vine (Yashu'a, Jesus) Fruits of the Spirit of Positive Character-Building Essentials**? And are there **Hateful Words** that are rooted in the foundation of the **Deadly Venoms of the Desires of the great dragon, that old serpent, called the devil and satan that deceived the whole world** (KJV Revelation 12:7-9); that influences or determines whether or not we are in the habit of speaking **Life (Positivity)** or **Death (Negativity)** into existence through the **Power of our Tongues**?

So, this book affords the Children of the Most High the opportunity **to learn how** Wickedness utilizes the **Power of the Tongue** to deceive and influence what some people think and feel, and this book also affords an opportunity for the Children of the Most High **to learn how invaluable the words we think, speak, and internalize are to our overall health and wellbeing!** Consequently, our thoughts, words, and actions will tremendously continue **to influence the quality of our life experiences!** Therefore; it is **essential** that the children of the Most High: **Beware** (Be Aware) of the **Pink Assassin** (Your Tongue), because the **True-Vine (Yashu'a, Jesus) Power of Life and Death that is in the Tongue, <u>can give you the ability to Speak</u>** God's (סיהלא Elôhîym) "Will" <u>for Your Life into Existence</u>!

"And whatsoever we ask, we receive of him, because we keep his commandments, and do those things that are pleasing in his sight."
1 JOHN 3:22 (KJV) BIBLE

The Messiah Yashu'a (Jesus) said:
"But I say unto you, that every idle word that men (ἄνθρωπος, Anthrōpos—A human being) shall speak, they shall give account thereof in the day of judgment."
MATTHEW 12:36 (KJV) BIBLE

FOR MORE INFORMATION CONTACT:
Please visit our website at: childrenofthemosthigh.com
Online ordering is available for all products at our
Amazon Store Front.

ISBN 978-1-948355-04-9

9 781948 355049

352

Yashu'a (Jesus) said: "Thou shalt love the Most High Heavenly Father, thy Sustainer with all thy heart, and with all thy soul, and with all thy mind. Thou shalt love thy neighbour as thyself."

Mind Gardening in the Creative Garden of Will (Your Mind) to Grow a Living Water Mentality!

CHILDREN OF THE MOST HIGH:
PRISTINE YOUTH AND FAMILY SOLUTIONS, LLC.
SONS AND DAUGHTERS OF THE MOST HIGH PUBLISHERS ®

*Oh, Gracious Most High Heavenly father, Holy is your name,
Your Will Be Done Now and Forever!*

References

Bible, H. (2004). Holman Christian Standard Bible. Nashville: Holman Bible.

Carroll, R., & Prickett, S. (Eds.). (2008). The Bible: Authorized King James Version. OUP Oxford.

Fanon, Frantz (1970). *Black Skin, White Masks* (pp. 13-30). London: Paladin.

Gibran, K. (1968). Secrets of the Heart. Hallmark Cards Inc.

Gowan, D. E. (1988). From Eden to Babel: A Commentary on the Book of Genesis 1-11. Wm. B. Eerdmans Publishing.

Houghton Mifflin Company. (2020). Online American Heritage Dictionary. Fifth Edition.

Lane Arabic/English Lexicon (2003).

Lyubomirsky, S., King, L., & Diener, E. (2005). The benefits of frequent positive affect: Does happiness lead to success? Psychological bulletin, 131(6), 803.

Yashu'a (Jesus) said: "Thou shalt love the Most High Heavenly Father, thy Sustainer with all thy heart, and with all thy soul, and with all thy mind. Thou shalt love thy neighbour as thyself."

Mind Gardening in the Creative Garden of Will (Your Mind) to Grow a Living Water Mentality!

CHILDREN OF THE MOST HIGH:
PRISTINE YOUTH AND FAMILY SOLUTIONS, LLC.
SONS AND DAUGHTERS OF THE MOST HIGH PUBLISHERS ®

Oh, Gracious Most High Heavenly father, Holy is your name,
Your Will Be Done Now and Forever!

References

Mchie, Benjamin (2019). African American Registry® (the Registry).

National Institute of Health, (2020) Website.

Newberg, A., & Waldman, M. R. (2009). How God changes your brain: Breakthrough findings from a leading neuroscientist. Ballantine Books.

Online Britannica Encyclopedia, (2020).

Online checkers.com; (2020) Website.

Online Gesenius' Hebrew-Chaldee Lexicon, (2020).

Online Merriam-Webster Dictionary, (2020).

Zodhiates, S. (Ed.). (1991). The Hebrew-Greek Key Word Study Bible: King James Version, Zodhaites' Original and Complete System of Bible Study World Bible Publishers, Incorporated.

Yashu'a (Jesus) said: "Thou shalt love the Most High Heavenly Father, thy Sustainer with all thy heart, and with all thy soul, and with all thy mind. Thou shalt love thy neighbour as thyself."

www.ingramcontent.com/pod-product-compliance
Lightning Source LLC
LaVergne TN
LVHW051621080426
835511LV00016B/2098